SOCIAL WORK IN END-OF-LIFE AND PALLIATIVE CARE

Also Available from Lyceum Books, Inc.

Advisory Editor: Thomas M. Meenaghan, *New York University*

Modern Social Work Theory, 3rd Edition
Malcolm Payne

What Is Professional Social Work?
Malcolm Payne

Teamwork in Multiprofessional Care
Malcolm Payne

Teaching Resources for End-of-Life and Palliative Care Courses
Ellen L. Csikai and Barbara Jones

Ethics in End-of-Life Decisions in Social Work Practice
Ellen L. Csikai and Elizabeth Chaitin

Straight Talk about Professional Ethics
Kim Strom-Gottfried

Case Management: An Introduction to Concepts and Skills, 2nd Edition
Arthur J. Frankel and Sheldon R. Gelman

Essential Skills of Social Work Practice
Thomas O'Hare

Social Work Practice with Families: A Resiliency-Based Approach
Mary Patricia Van Hook

SOCIAL WORK IN END-OF-LIFE AND PALLIATIVE CARE

Margaret Reith
Princess Alice Hospice, Surrey

Malcolm Payne
St. Christopher's Hospice, London

LYCEUM
BOOKS, INC.
Chicago, Illinois

© Lyceum Books, Inc., 2009

Published by

LYCEUM BOOKS, INC.
5758 S. Blackstone Ave.
Chicago, Illinois 60637
773+643-1903 (Fax)
773+643-1902 (Phone)
lyceum@lyceumbooks.com
http://www.lyceumbooks.com

6 5 4 3 2 1   09 10 11 12

ISBN 978-1-933478-58-6

Library of Congress Cataloging-in-Publication Data

Reith, Margaret.
    Social work in end-of-life and palliative care / Margaret Reith, Malcolm
Payne.
        p. cm.
    Includes bibliographical references and index.
    ISBN 978-1-933478-58-6
    1. Social work with the terminally ill. I. Payne, Malcolm, 1947– . II. Title.
    HV3000.R45   2009
    362.17'5—dc22

                                                            2008045928

To Allison and Eleanor

CONTENTS

FIGURES AND TABLES

Figures

Tables

TABLE OF CASE EXAMPLES

Note: All case examples have been anonymized and identifying details removed or changed.

ABOUT THE AUTHORS

Margaret Reith is senior social worker at the Princess Alice Hospice, Surrey, U.K., where she was formerly the social work manager. During an extensive career in health-related social work, she was principal social worker/manager at a Marie Curie hospice, South Wales; social work team manager at South Wales Forensic Mental Health Service; senior social worker with the regional oncology and palliative care unit at Velindre Hospital, Cardiff; and a social worker in a mental health and learning disabilities team, and a pediatric multidisciplinary team. She is the author of research and professional papers in palliative care and forensic mental health, and of *Community Care Tragedies: A Practice Guide to Mental Health Inquiries*. She has presented papers in the United Kingdom, the United States, several European countries, and Japan.

Malcolm Payne is policy and development adviser at St. Christopher's Hospice, London, U.K., where he was formerly the director of psychosocial and spiritual care. After practice and management experience in the U.K. probation service and social services departments, he has moved between academic social work and practice and management posts, being chief executive of a community development agency in Liverpool, policy and development director of a national mental health charity, and professor and head of applied community studies at Manchester Metropolitan University. He is honorary professor in the faculty of health and social care sciences, Kingston University/St. George's University of London, visiting professor at Opole University, Poland, and docent in social work in the department of social policy, Helsinki University. He is the author of nearly three hundred publications in health and social work journals, and many books including the bestselling Lyceum Books titles *Modern Social Work Theory*, *What is Professional Social Work?*, and *Teamwork in Multiprofessional Care*. He has presented papers and keynote addresses throughout the world.

INTRODUCTION

Increasingly, end-of-life and palliative care are treated as the same thing, with palliative care regarded as a professional specialty that covers the whole field. However, there is a difference:

- Palliative care is a multiprofessional practice in which pain and symptom control is combined with concern for the psychological, social and spiritual issues that arise for someone who is dying and the family and community around them. It developed from services for people with cancer, and other serious diagnosed illnesses, and is a fairly short-term service with important medical and nursing input.
- End-of-life care is the provision of care services for people who are approaching the end of life. It has developed more recently, from a recognition that most people come to a phase of life in which they become increasingly frail, often with "multiple co-morbidities," the medical jargon for several illnesses affecting a person at the same time. In this situation, people may not need or receive extensive specialist medical and nursing help, but their families and people around them and nonspecialized health and social services in their community need to focus not only on the daily pressures of dealing with increasing frailty, but also the reality that this signals the approach of the end of life. This is sometimes known as nonspecialist, or general, palliative care.

In both end-of-life and palliative care, practitioners will be concerned also with people close to the dying person, or the person who is approaching the end of life, and the fact that they are beginning to experience significant emotions of grief and bereavement from the loss of someone important to them.

Most professional expertise in end-of-life and palliative care has developed in the specialist field of palliative care. People working in this field are increasingly diversifying their work into related fields. We argue throughout this book that all social workers will deal with the end of life of some of their clients, and can usefully build skills and knowledge from palliative care into their practice. Our aim is to introduce palliative care social work to practitioners who intend to specialize in this field and to describe and explore practice in palliative care in ways that will help other practitioners to deal with end-of-life situations that they occasionally encounter. In addition to referring to the literature, we have used some writing from patients and clients as well as experience and case studies from our own colleagues' and students' experience; these mainly call on the palliative care setting, but are chosen for their wide applicability. We have presented particular events within some of these narratives in some detail, because we find that people new to working in end-of-life and palliative care are anxious about dealing with the emotional intensity of the situations that sometimes arise. In these case studies, we have chosen models of responses that involve respect for clients' and families' emotional and cultural reactions and wishes alongside careful and methodical working through of the issues that have arisen in the situation. The poems were written during 2008 by patients at the St. Christopher's Hospice Creative Living Center.

The structure of the book is as follows:

Chapter 1 explores the nature and development of palliative care services, the role of social work in end-of-life and palliative care and how it developed in palliative care, in particular exploring the important concept of loss and explaining some problems with it as a basis for practice.

Chapter 2 explores information about the social and psychological processes that arise around death and dying; subsequent chapters about practice call on this.

Chapter 3 shifts the focus from a broad understanding about death and dying to understanding the importance of awareness of death and of communication about it in end-of-life situations. In most social life, people avoid talking about death, so this chapter focuses on what practitioners need to do to engage with people on the subject and plan to help them.

Chapter 4 focuses on how to engage with people in beginning to work with them on the end of their life.

Chapter 5 explores useful areas of intervention and interventions that have been found helpful in palliative care and that can be applied in end-of-life care.

Chapter 6 explores knowledge and practice relevant to dealing with a dying person's grief about his or her impending death and the bereavement of the people around that person.

Chapter 7 discusses how to develop multiprofessional work with colleagues in health-care services, who will always be playing an important role in end-of-life situations.

Chapter 8 discusses some important ethical questions that arise for practitioners and their clients in end-of-life situations.

Chapter 9 explores some macro interventions, including group work and community involvement in support and service development for dying and bereaved people. This is important because group work has been valued and found effective for mutual support, education, and as a therapeutic intervention with dying and bereaved people. Also, at a time when many populations in the West are aging, many dying and bereaved people experience a lack of social and community support, and it would be useful to develop resilience in communities to be able to respond more helpfully to death and bereavement.

Our aim in writing this book is to convey the experience and learning in end-of-life care that we have acquired during a working lifetime, as we come closer to the time of our own deaths, and we dedicate this book, therefore, to a future generation, our granddaughters, Allison and Eleanor, one of them American and the other British.

Margaret Reith
Malcolm Payne

Chapter 1

SOCIAL WORK, END-OF-LIFE AND PALLIATIVE CARE

CHAPTER AIMS

The main aim of this chapter is to introduce social work's role in end-of-life and palliative care.

After working through this chapter, readers should be able to:

- Understand why end-of-life issues are important in people's lives and in all social work;
- Evaluate concepts of loss in end-of-life and palliative care;
- Explain how end-of-life and palliative care developed;
- Describe the main features of palliative care services; and
- Understand the role of social work in end-of-life and palliative care services.

ALL SOCIAL WORKERS CARE FOR PEOPLE AT THE END OF LIFE

All social workers, whatever their specialty, help people with end-of-life issues. People need help as they experience or fear the end of life themselves, or as others important to them near the end of life. Also, people may have to deal with sudden or violent death, or face the risk or fear of death.

We all die; we will all be bereaved. Mostly we don't dwell on this. But death is always a possibility and always has to be dealt with at some time. This is as true for social workers in their personal lives as for their clients. Aiken (1994) classified deaths by how they occur. Corr and colleagues (Corr, Nabe, & Corr, 2006) classify human-induced deaths rather differently, drawing attention to how historic or world events can affect individuals' perceptions of death. Their examples include distinguishing between war and nuclear war. As you think about this distinction, depending on where you live in the world, you may feel that nuclear war might affect your death more directly because it is more generally devastating and that other wars are different, because they are more distant.

1

On the other hand, you may feel that non-nuclear wars are more likely to happen; indeed, although since the 1950s the number of wars has decreased, there is always war in some part of the world. We have regrouped both classifications as follows:

- Aging and disease
- Human-induced deaths;
  - accidents, of which road accidents are the most common
  - suicide
  - homicide (murder)
  - terrorism
  - genocide, including the Holocaust
  - war
  - nuclear war

Deaths are often in the news and affect public debate. For example, we debate the death penalty for serious crimes, or political decisions about whether soldiers or military pilots should risk death in war.

As well as this general involvement in death, social workers contribute to providing end-of-life and palliative care. End-of-life care is care and help given to people who are aware and accept that their death will take place soon, and are making preparations for it. Their awareness of approaching death may be because they have experienced a serious decline in health, or because they have become frail in old age. Palliative care is a multiprofessional service providing care for people who have a diagnosed illness that is "life-threatening," "life-limiting," or "advanced," that is, an illness that has gone beyond early symptoms to put the patients' life at risk. It aims to prevent and relieve suffering by identifying and managing pain and other serious symptoms and psychological, social, and spiritual issues for both patients and their families as people die or experience bereavement.

Services for dying and bereaved people originally developed through a concern to manage distressing aspects of the dying phase in cancer and other serious life-threatening illnesses; they were applied to AIDS when people became aware of that disease. Increasingly, however, people live for long periods with cancer, and diagnosis of cancer is often like learning to live with other chronic conditions rather than the death sentence it was a generation ago; the same is true of HIV/AIDS in Western countries. Moreover, in most countries people are living longer in each generation. Therefore, many people approach the end of their life through deterioration in a medical condition or disability that has been part of their life for some time, or through realizing that old age is inevitably bringing them closer to death. Some people experience end-of-life issues in their lives because of accidents, sudden events such as disasters and violent crimes, or suicide and self-harm. They may fear, plan for, or worry about such events befalling them, or they may experience bereavement because a friend or family member is affected. End-of-life care transfers and adapts learning and interventions from palliative care to apply them in broader end-of-life situations, such as care homes and nonspecialized care facilities for older people.

Pause and reflect—dying and bereavement in your work

If you are a social work practitioner, do a quick audit of your work at present or in a recent social work role; if you are a student, make a list of the kind of people and problems that you hope to work with. How might you expect to come across death and bereavement in your work?

Some suggestions

Both of the authors have come up against death, dying, and bereavement in their work outside of palliative care. When Malcolm worked with adult offenders, he had several clients who had committed murders and one who had caused the death of a child by dangerous driving. He has also worked with mentally ill people, and dealt with several people who had attempted suicide. In another job, he helped an elderly women who felt there was no value in her continuing life. She would say, particularly in very hot or very cold weather: "I'm so uncomfortable, I wish I could die."

Margaret has worked with families who had a profoundly handicapped child, often as a result of a severe genetic or chromosome disorder, many of whom died. She has also worked with mentally disordered offenders, many of whom had committed homicide; some subsequently took their own lives.

Most social workers' caseloads contain people who are coming up against death or the risk or possibility of death. Perhaps they fear or plot their own death. Social workers often work with people with health problems, who may fear a higher risk of early death and people with mental illnesses who may attempt suicide and self-harm. Kramer and colleagues (Kramer; Paroureke, & Harland-Scafe; 2003) identified a range of settings in which social workers dealt with end-of-life care. These include home heath care and domiciliary social care; palliative care teams or units in hospitals, hospices, emergency rooms, intensive care units, and hospital obstetric and neonatal intensive care units; neonatal and pediatric settings; pain clinics; community mental health and substance abuse agencies; and nursing and care homes. However, they also found that many social work texts did not include material on end-of-life care, even though it is relevant to all social workers and important to many different specialized social work roles. This book aims to respond to that need.

Pause and reflect—dying and bereavement in your own life

You have experienced death and bereavement in your own life. Do a quick review of your life. Who was the first person to die who was close to you? Make a few notes of how you felt, how you reacted, and then how you were involved in that person's death or funeral, and any experiences of bereavement afterwards. Who was the first person to die whom you had heard of? What did you feel, think, and do? Who was the most important person to you that has died? Perhaps there are several equally important people who died. What difference did their significance to you make on the way you were affected.

Some suggestions

The authors have reviewed their early experiences of death. Malcolm first experienced death in his teens, when a boy at his school that he did not know well was killed in a traffic accident. His first direct personal experience of death was his father collapsing at home with his second coronary thrombosis. This was before most homes in the United Kingdom had their own telephone, and Malcolm's mother sent him to a local shop to call for the doctor, who was at the time out visiting a patient. Malcolm then made a panicky call to the ambulance service, which located the doctor at a patient's house and sent him on to this new emergency. Malcolm's father was meanwhile talking to his mother in a way that showed that he expected to die. After the doctor arrived and examined his father, Malcolm took the doctor to the shop and listened as he arranged for a hospital admission, saying in Malcolm's hearing that it was very serious. Malcolm's father died in the hospital later that night. Forty years later, Malcolm still has nightmares in which he is unable to call for help in an emergency.

Margaret's first strong memory of death occurred as she walked to a piano lesson at the age of eight. She witnessed a traffic accident involving a truck and a car and saw both drivers pulled clear of the wreckage. She heard later that the truck driver had died at the scene of the accident. At the age of nineteen, she experienced the sudden death of her father in his forties, leaving her with no opportunity to say goodbye or to get to know her father as she became an adult.

We all remember vividly the occasions that we have been involved with death; the events stay with us. Clearly, what happened and our part in it are important to us, and so they are to most other people. Why is this?

Pause and reflect—Why is the end of life important to us?

Note down reasons why people may be concerned about the end of life, drawing on your own feelings and experience and things people have told you. If possible, try discussing reasons with colleagues.

Some suggestions

Among the reasons you list might be:

- We do not know what happens to our personality and identity after death. Our faith or beliefs may include some form of afterlife or other existence, but we cannot know; death is a mystery.
- We may fear illness, losing control of our bodies and loss of social relationships and individual identity.
- We may fear emotional discomfort or physical pain.
- Death is a fundamental transition in life for the dying person and those close to him or her.
- Death may break up a social group or family that is important to us.
- Death may signify the loss of valued friends and relationships.
- We may not be able to see children or grandchildren growing up.
- Other people may be distressed at losing us.
- We may fear not completing important tasks in life.
- We will no longer be able to defend or enhance our reputation or achievement.

We may sum up these points as fear or concern about loss when a significant change and transition occurs in our lives. However, while end-of-life care often raises issues about loss, there are problems with focusing solely on loss.

LOSS AND THE END OF LIFE

Pause and reflect—experiencing loss

Think about a recent occasion when you lost something—perhaps it was a book that you needed, or a case file that you left somewhere. Make a note of what happened and then note down how you felt.

Some suggestions

Perhaps you have lost your car keys. Did you go "hot and cold"? You were hot with embarrassment about your stupidity, perhaps people will think you are disorganized. The cold feeling was perhaps fear or anxiety. What's happening here: Have your keys been stolen so that someone can steal your car? Can you afford to pay for replacements? Perhaps you are angry with yourself or with someone else for not reminding you to pick up your keys.

Fairly minor events, like the one you remembered, illustrate that any loss, however small, leads to emotional reactions. There is that moment of panic, perhaps a desperate search, anger, depression, fear, or other reactions. The end of life is a major loss to others and to ourselves, so the emotional reactions are likely to be even more powerful. It is not surprising that sometimes people need help with it.

HELPING PEOPLE COPE WITH LOSS: THE SOCIAL WORK AGENDA

Loss at the end of life is nonfinite loss (Bruce & Schultz, 2001), that is, unlike losing car keys, it does not end. The dying person will lose his or her life and many things of importance connected to that life; the bereaved irrevocably lose the deceased person. Bruce and Schultz (2001) suggest some important principles for helping people with nonfinite loss:

- Help people gain control of their social situation and their life.
- Help people preserve their personal identity.
- Hone the significance of the loss that they experience.

These principles set the agenda for social work practice at the end of life. Loss takes place within a biography. People build their lives within a social context, a place, relationships, and social institutions that they are part of. They develop expectations of how their life will progress; death interrupts those expectations. An important social work aim is to help them get back in control.

Pause and reflect

Think about what expectations you have for your future life.

Some suggestions

Depending on the phase of life you are at, you may hope for marriage, children, career success, greater appreciation of art, music, or beauty, a relaxed and happy retirement, an opportunity to travel, or the chance to meet interesting people.

Social work in end-of-life care focuses on losses of identity and expectation. Our biography builds our personal identity through a succession of relationships from which we learn. Our identity defines us. It is continuous; we are recognizably today the person we were some years ago. But our identity also develops and varies, so we are also not the person we were. As the end of life approaches, we may fear losing our identity and the relationships that construct it. If we become ill, or frail, or have a long-term disability, all these things may change our identity or lead us to fear future loss of identity and life. We also lose our expectations.

Experiencing loss and bereavement leads to physical and psychological changes (Payne, Horn, & Relf, 1999). Among the physical reactions that people may experience are fatigue, insomnia or other changes in sleep patterns, aches and pains, loss of appetite, digestive changes, and an increased likelihood of minor infections. The psychological changes may include emotional, cognitive, and behavioral changes. Among the emotional changes may be depression, including sadness, anxiety, inability to relax, anger, guilt or self-blame, and loneliness. Cognitive changes may include poor attention and concentration, a preoccupation with the loss, helplessness and lack of hope in carrying on the tasks of daily living, and a feeling of detachment or disengagement from things that have previously been of interest. Behavior may change so that the person experiencing loss is more irritable, restless, and often distressed or withdrawn in social situations.

Payne and colleagues (1999) identify some important advantages and disadvantages of seeing end-of-life social work as a process of helping people cope with loss, set out in table 1.1. This suggests that we should avoid seeing loss as an individual "problem" and work with positive changes that people can make when experiencing a loss. Loss is always both personal and social, so the social work agenda needs to include family and social network responses to the end of life. In this book, therefore, we reflect the founding philosophy of social work, and its currently accepted international definition, and include social understandings of the end of life as well as individual psychological responses.

TABLE 1.1 Advantages and disadvantages of a loss and coping model of end-of-life social work

Advantages	Disadvantages
Explains physical and psychological impact of grief	Labels but does not explain responses to grief
Integrates biological and psychological factors in grief	Pathologizes grief, seeing it as a "bad" set of feelings
Explains some of the increased mortality in bereaved people	Individualizes grief, seeing it as a physical and psychological response, rather than responses to social expectations
Explains individual differences	Does not explain variable responses, which suggest cultural and social construction of grief; ethnocentric in its focus on individual responses
Offers suggestions for helpful ways of supporting people experiencing loss	Assumes grief and bereavement are a negative "threat" to stability, rather than a natural process

Source: Developed from Payne et al. (1999, 37–8).

The Argument of This Book

We argue in this book that the end of life is a process of social change for individuals, as they become aware that death is close to them; this change is part of a family's journey through community, society, and culture. The end of life involves adjustments by individuals together with their families and social networks, influenced by wider social understandings about death and the social processes of dying and bereavement.

End-of-life care relies, therefore, first, on knowledge and skill in providing individual care to those who need help in moving through this process. Second, it relies on practitioners to understand, influence, and react to how death is seen in the cultures of society and the policies that govern how services are provided.

Why is this? Many people avoid friends who are dying or bereaved because: "I don't know what to say." This leads to social isolation and exclusion from ordinary life for many dying and bereaved people. Another example of avoidance is the way people "protect" children and young people from knowing about deaths in their family and social networks. This is a two-way process. Dying and bereaved people do have psychological or social reactions that cut them off, at least for a while. But at the same time Western societies have adopted ways of dealing with death that prevent many people from responding to death, dying, and bereavement in a positive way. Yet we have seen already that we will all be affected by this natural, universal event; all children will eventually experience the deaths of others around them, and all social workers will have to deal with it as they practice their profession. Most Western societies have aging populations, people who are moving closer to death.

Unlike many other helping professions, social work seeks not only to help people with the problems in their lives but in doing so also to strengthen the fabric of our societies so that they can deal better with the issues that they face. This book, therefore, aims to have an impact on individual practice and practice that strengthens society to deal better with death and bereavement.

THE DEVELOPMENT OF SOCIAL WORK IN END-OF-LIFE CARE

End-of-life care has developed in the last half of the twentieth century, alongside the social changes that have made death a difficult issue in our lives. Small (2001a) suggests five stages in the development of ideas about grief and bereavement, which are more widely applicable; we have added another which has since gained relevance:

8

- 1940–60: The field opened up and initial studies developed.
- 1960–70: Services developed and alongside this, disciplines of hospice, palliative, and bereavement care emerged and began to develop, and informal networks began to build up.
- 1970–80: Formal networks and organizations developed in various countries; international links also developed.
- 1980–90: Many ideas continued to develop, such as stage and task models of bereavement, but concern grew about the failure of hospice, palliative, and bereavement care to have an impact on public and medical opinion.
- 1990–2000: A focus on understanding death processes, and in particular the idea of continuing bonds, developed to respond more appropriately than task and stage models to social perceptions of death and bereavement.
- 2001 onward: We would add to Small's analysis a developing concept of end-of-life care that moves the focus from diagnosed illnesses and bereavement as problems, toward concern for a much wider range of people approaching the end of their lives, and their families and caregivers successfully responding to that event in their family and community.

Four Important Pioneers

Four important pioneers inspired the development of thinking about how to deal with the psychological, social, and spiritual consequences of death during the 1960s and '70s. They are the foundation of social work in end-of-life care:

- Erich Lindemann (1944), a psychiatrist at Massachusetts General Hospital, together with his colleagues, worked with and researched the psychological and social aftermath of a nightclub fire in which 493 people died. He and his colleagues developed the idea that death was a transition in the lives of families affected. Families with successful experience of dealing with loss coped with a new loss better than those who had had unfortunate past experiences. Lindemann's colleagues the psychiatrist Caplin (1965) and the social worker Parad (Parad & Parad, 1990) developed a preventive technique, crisis intervention, which influenced social work theory and aimed to help people deal with crises in their lives effectively, strengthening their resilience in later crises.
- Cicely Saunders (2006), a British social worker, nurse, and doctor working with people suffering from cancer, created a new idea about hospices that developed into the medical specialty of palliative medicine and the broader concept of palliative care. Starting

9

as a social worker at the time that medicine became effective at cure, she felt that medicine was moving away from care of people who could not be cured. She researched pain relief and developed the idea that regular pain relief should be combined with a concern for "total pain," including psychological, social, and spiritual issues in cancer patients' lives. The idea of total pain is often helpful in reminding colleagues with a biomedical background about the importance of these factors in pain relief. Palliative care has extended this practice to other groups of people with advanced illness.

- Elizabeth Kübler-Ross (1970), an American psychologist, was the first to record and analyze the experiences of dying people, and develop the ideas that people moved through a recognizable series of emotional reactions as they adapted to the knowledge of impending death.
- Colin Murray Parkes (2001), a British psychiatrist who worked with colleagues on the Harvard Bereavement Study (see Chapter 6) of the experiences of widows, developed the idea that people also moved through emotional stages in bereavement and laid the foundation of services that provided counseling and personal help for bereaved people.

Parad's work led to a social work practice theory covering a wide range of services, particularly in mental health for dealing with crises in people's lives, which encouraged many social workers to think about loss, change, and transition. Saunders, as a former social worker, emphasized the importance of psychological and social factors in end-of-life care, and saw multiprofessional teams including social workers as essential to providing end-of-life care in a way that might not have occurred to a physician with only a medical background developing what became a medical specialty. Kübler-Ross and Parkes provided a range of practical ideas congenial to social work practice and spawned psychological and bereavement services across the world, using counseling skills as the basis for a blend of emotional, practical, and family help (Parkes, Relf, & Couldrick, 1996). These services employed many social workers to supervise volunteers providing the services and to do more complex work, as psychotherapeutic and counseling professions developed. End-of-life care and bereavement support were non stigmatizing areas of psychological care that helped to validate counseling and psychotherapeutic help as professions.

Palliative Care

Palliative care developed in North America by transferring Saunders's ideas to work in hospital teams, stimulated by the work of the Canadian doctor Balfour Mount, and Dean Florence Wald of the Yale School of

Nursing, who worked to open the first hospice in the United States, Connecticut, both of whom were influenced by Saunders. "Palliation" is reducing a patient's experience of the ill effects of an illness without curing it; and by extension reducing the problematic effects of anything without removing, and sometimes without being able to remove, the cause. These developments were the beginning of a worldwide hospice and palliative care movement.

From this grew an increasing commitment by governments and nongovernmental health care systems to provide palliative care. A significant international policy advance occurred with the report of the World Health Organization Expert Task Force (WHO, 1990), which called on governments to ensure that health care services made available trained staff for pain relief and related services and defined what those services should consist of. A similar recommendation came out of the Council of Europe (1999), concerned with the protection of the human rights and dignity of terminally ill and dying people.

Government activity responded to this in many countries. Seymour and colleagues (Seymour, Clark, & Marples, 2002), for example, show that since 1987 English health authorities have been required to make palliative care provision within their health-improvement plans, although this has been patchy. Matthew and colleagues (Matthew, Cowley, Billes, & Thistlewood, 2003) discussed an extensive range of U.K. government documents on palliative and end-of-life care, developing policy for service provision. Much of this development emerged from public and political perceptions of a demand for a good quality of care, particularly at the end of life, but responding to a perception of inadequate help and care for a growing population of older people. The development of medical and nursing specialties in palliative care also provided a professional impetus to developing services.

Much of this development continued to respond to anxiety about cancer. In the United Kingdom, the National Health Service (NHS) cancer plan (DH, 2000) led to attempts to coordinate cancer services and provide additional funding for palliative care services. The National Institute for Clinical Excellence (NICE, 2004) published authoritative recommendations about palliative care provision in cancer services, which have been considered the benchmark for palliative care services.

While end-of-life care emerged from a consumer movement and has increasingly become an essential element of health care services in Western countries, it also provided a crucial means of cost containment for increasingly expensive medical care facilities. U.S. studies show that palliative care in hospitals reduced overall patient costs, and home hospice care reduced hospitals stays, also producing savings (Fine, 2004). Hospice benefit under the Medicare state insurance system became available in the United States in 1983 (Luptak, 2004) followed by provision for palliative care in many private insurance schemes. These developments incorporate palliative care into a "vertically-integrated" (Luptak, 2004, p.10) range of services for older people, so that patients are shifted from expensive curative medicine to less-expensive care. This cost-containment imperative has had implications for social work, which may be seen as a dispensable provision in a health care environment. A survey of sixty-six American hospices showed, however, that social work involvement tended to reduce hospice costs partly because of more effective admissions decisions and discharge arrangements (Reese & Raymer, 2004). Palliative care's development is thus in some respects a cost-containment measure, since, while it is expensive compared with other forms of care for older people, it is less expensive than hospital care where there are significant symptoms requiring complex nursing and medical management.

END-OF-LIFE SERVICES TODAY

The financial, legal, and administrative structure of health and social provision in any state affects the way that a service concept such as hospice, palliative, or end-of-life care develops. The availability of Medicare, followed by private insurance financing, led to a rapid expansion of home hospice care, which became the most common mode of community palliative care in the United States. The Medicare benefit was also crucial in maintaining the original philosophy of palliative care and continuing to involve social work because it required a multiprofessional team of physician, nurse, and counselor or chaplain to be involved (Kovacs & Bronstein, 1999).

In the United Kingdom, in-patient hospice care is also widely available, having developed through charitable endeavor imitating and developing Saunders's original model at St. Christopher's, the first hospice. This not-for-profit provision is separated from the National Health Service (NHS), which provides most health care services, but is partially integrated through being commissioned to provide palliative and hospice care services for the NHS in localities where hospices exist. NHS hospitals increasingly have their own palliative care teams, and community home care is provided from hospices, if available, by outreach from hospital teams or as a specialist local provision. However, it always builds on a general health care service available free of charge to everyone through local general medical practitioners and their associated teams of community nurses. This leads to a pattern in which specialist palliative care is separated from end-of-life care, which is provided as part of generalist health care. Palliative care services interact with generalist care mainly through advice and consultation. The importance given to the range of provision in both palliative and end-of-life care is reflected in the recent Department of Health publication of an end-of-life care strategy, focused on integrating specialized and nonspecialized elements of care (DH, 2008). This also proposes wider training for nonspecialized social workers.

In many developing countries with some palliative care provision, the pattern is of much less extensive services, usually available through a visiting nurse and/or physician, without the panoply of services that may be typical of developed Western countries but are by no means universal.

Different Understandings of End-of-Life Care

This history has led to a number of terms being used for similar forms of care. Hospice care means a palliative care service based in a specialized building, the hospice, but is sometimes extended to mean all end-of-life care. This treats hospice as "a philosophy not a facility" (Corr, Nabe, & Corr, 2006, p. 184). Thus, hospice sometimes becomes a philosophy of care maintaining a special environment suited to the needs of people at the end of life within a busy hospital ward or community setting where an emphasis on treating illness and preventing death may be inappropriate to thoughtful caring for dying people (Seale & Kelly, 1997). Also, in the United States, it is helpful to distinguish hospice as a service available from state and private insurance often for people with diagnosed terminal illnesses, from palliative care as a more consultative service within hospitals and health care to a wide range of people with a similarly wide range of life-threatening conditions (Fine, 2004).

However, extending the term hospice to refer to all end-of-life care settings seems limiting for three main reasons. First, people come to the end of life in ways that do not require medical treatment for a life-limiting illness. Second, many people would prefer to die at home among their family rather than at a special place or mainly with help from professionals, and, third, hospice services need to be integrated with other health care provision. Therefore, calling end-of-life care services "hospice care" seems to stretch the term "hospice" too far.

"Palliative care" has therefore become the most widely used overall term. It is defined by the World Health Organization as:

> An approach to care that improves the quality of life of people and their families facing the problem associated with life-threatening illness, through the prevention and relief of suffering by means of early identification and impeccable assessment and treatment of pain and other problems, physical, psychosocial and spiritual. (WHO, 2007)

In the United Kingdom and some other countries, specialized palliative care is distinguished from general services. It is provided where an individual has a progressive, advanced disease with a limited prognosis and usually where there are complex or acute needs that require multiprofessional interventions from medical, nursing, social, pastoral, or therapy services (Matthew et al., 2003). Specialized palliative care has come to be associated particularly with palliative medicine, "the medical speciality concerned with the appropriate medical care of patients with progressive disease" (Matthew et al., 2003). The medical specialty, however, requires physicians to promote both physical and psychological well-being, so palliative medicine implies integrating responses to psychological and social needs within palliative medical care.

The idea of end-of-life care has become increasingly important to incorporate both palliative care and care for a wider range of people who are approaching the end of life. This wider focus identifies the need to be concerned with care services for everyone. One aim of doing so is to transfer practitioner skills from specialized palliative care and palliative medicine into end-of-life care services. Another aim is to develop the flexible and open style of communication and interpersonal multiprofessional care for all people who are dying as well as those with life-threatening illness.

Supportive care is an aspect of palliative care services that focuses particularly on providing psychological support to patients and their families. This may include work by social workers, but generally emphasizes psychological distress as a marker for the need for intervention and psychiatric factors, such as depression and anxiety as the focus of work. Again, it tends to take a problem-based and medicalized or psychologized approach to helping people at the end of life.

Palliative Care and Hospice Services

Palliative care and hospice services are important in end-of-life care because they form a nexus of expertise and commitment to end-of-life care provision. Palliative care may include any or all of the following, although there is no universal provision:

- In hospitals, palliative care consultation to other specialized teams. This service is usually provided by a team of doctors and nurses, sometimes incorporating other professionals, including social workers, counselors, and other therapists.
- Palliative care services in special beds in hospitals, which removes palliative care patients from the busy environment of curative services, also reducing costs. The team is sometimes multiprofessional, but nursing and medicine predominates.
- Palliative home care, including advice to generalist medical, nursing, and other practitioners and patients, and support for informal caregivers, usually by specialist nurses, who may be supported by specialist medical consultation.

- Hospice at-home services, offering nursing support in the home, particularly at night or in the last few days of life.
- Palliative outpatient services, including medical and nursing clinics, and multiprofessional services.
- Palliative in-patient care, either provided in a specialized setting in a local hospital, in a care home, or in a hospice, which might also provide respite care to relieve informal caregivers.
- Palliative care in care homes, provided either by a specialist palliative care community team or hospice team directly, or by their supporting the care home staff in providing appropriate end-of-life care.
- Palliative day care, to provide respite and support for informal caregivers, and to decrease patients' social isolation and provide activities to enable them to achieve self-fulfillment in positive activities in the life remaining to them.
- In-patient respite care to provide relief and support for informal caregivers (Ingleton, Payne, Nolan, & Carey, 2003).
- Complementary therapies such as acupuncture, aromatherapy, hypnotherapy, massage and reflexology are important aspects of the care available.
- Psychological therapies and social support provided by creative activities (Hartley & Payne, 2008) including creative writing (Robinson, 2004) and art and music therapy are also widely valued, although under-researched (Hilliard, 2005). O'Kelly (2002), for example, argues that music therapy encourages creative self-expression, decreasing stress and alleviating spiritual distress.

At its most comprehensive, a full range of this provision is available in many Western countries. The extent to which these services extend to more generalized end-of-life services depends on the infrastructure in any given country.

THE SOCIAL WORK ROLE IN END-OF-LIFE CARE

We have suggested in this chapter that social workers were involved from the beginning in the development of palliative and end-of-life care. In an extensive literature review on social work and palliative care, Small (2001b) suggests three reasons for social work's involvement in palliative care:

- Social work in many situations is concerned with loss, so death is a clear candidate for social work practice skills.

- Social work brings a whole system approach to dying, so it naturally incorporates family, community, and cultural perspectives into a health care service.
- Social work has a concern with ameliorating the practical and social impact of change.

Beder (2006) places hospice social work among a range of healthcare social work specialties and identifies its particular characteristics as making a contribution to integrated multiprofessional end-of-life care and ensuring that family caregivers are supported and involved in decisions about care. Luptak (2004) places the development of end-of-life care for older people in the broader context of medical or health-related social work, which has been one of the central specialized areas of social work for much of the twentieth century. She suggests that social work in the United States focused on experiences of death in the 1970s as medical science conquered many diseases that led to early death, making early death a less commonplace and more traumatic experience for many people.

Among important developments in achieving recognition for end-of-life social work was the adoption of the National Association of Social Workers' (NASW) guidelines on client self-determination at the end of life (NASW, 1994). This connects the development of an end-of-life role for social work to growing concerns in the United States about ensuring the autonomy of people to make decisions about their care at the end of life. A further professional development was the NASW (2003) *Standards for Social Work Practice in Palliative and End of Life Care*, which established guidelines on practice, education, and service development in this field. In the United Kingdom the foundation of what is now the Association of Palliative Care Social Workers provided an impetus for professional development in this field.

An important educational development in the United States validating social work in end-of-life care was the "Project on Death in America" of the Soros Foundation (OSI, 2004; Aulino & Foley, 2001). Among other developments, it promoted and funded leadership awards, a "summit" of leaders in this field at Duke University in 1992, and leadership education in end-of-life and palliative care, which in turn led to the development of an important advanced text (Berzoff & Silverman, 2004).

Meier and Beresford (2008) identify the training of U.S. social workers in counseling, understanding and working with family systems, understanding and use of community resources, and their role in undertaking patient and family psychosocial assessments in health care settings as the main assets of social workers in palliative care settings; this is probably similar to their role in most health care settings. They argue that while social workers make an important contribution to discharge planning, because of their skills in working across the boundary of a health care service with other community resources and engaging the support of family and community systems, emphasis on this role may mean that their other skills and training are not used effectively. Moreover, other professionals, particularly home care nurses, also compete for taking on responsibilities with families and psychosocial care generally.

Recent research in the United Kingdom (Clausen et al., 2005; Beresford, Adshead, & Croft, 2007) has suggested that patients and their families value the generalist focus of social work on a broad range of family problems, and the preparedness of social workers to being committed to the patient and family's own definition of their needs, as valuable contributions that social workers make to palliative care services.

YOU DON'T UNDERSTAND (LIVING WITH CANCER)

Within this book, we offer some examples of people's feedback about their lives as they approach death. This is a poem written by a dying man that conveys how advanced illness affects people's lives and the importance of social support.

> *Went to the doctor,*
> *Bad news I'm afraid,*
> *But not to worry.*
> *You don't understand.*
>
> *Operations, pain, sickness,*   5
> *You don't understand.*
>
> *Started my chemo at last*
> *Sickness,*
> *Bad tummy,*
> *Stomach cramps,*   10
> *Hair loss,*
> *Can't eat, won't eat.*
> *You don't understand.*
>
> *Feeling blue, end of my world,*
> *No more swimming,*   15
> *Cycling,*
> *Enjoying small pleasures in life.*
> *You don't understand.*
>
> *Three and a half years have passed,*
> *It's not gone away,*   20
> *"You look good" they say,*
> *I just reply "You don't understand."*
>
> *I look into my wife's eyes,*
> *A tear appears,*
> *We both cry;*   25
> *She understands.*

CONCLUSION: SOCIAL WORK IN END-OF-LIFE AND PALLIATIVE CARE

Our aim in this book is to identify, describe, and analyze the skills and practice of social work within end-of-life and palliative care and to stress the impact of end-of-life issues in all social work practice and services.

End-of-life care is different from palliative care. End-of-life care refers to care for anyone who is approaching the end of his or her life. Palliative care is a specialized, multiprofessional health and social care service provided for people with advanced illnesses that usually lead to death. Many people do not die of a specific illness; instead their life fades away over time.

People often need help, within their families and communities, in dealing with the knowledge that they are approaching the end of life; social work can make an important contribution to that help.

FURTHER READING

Small, N. (2001b). Social work and palliative care. *British Journal of Social Work, 31*(6): 961–71. This critical review of the literature provides a good introduction to the role of social work in palliative care.

du Boulay, S., & Rankin, M. (2007). *Cicely Saunders: The founder of the modern hospice movement.* London: SPCK.

Saunders, C. (2006). *Selected writings: 1958–2004* (ed. D. Clark), Oxford, England: Oxford University Press.

Clark, D. (Ed.). (2005). *Cicely Saunders—founder of the hospice movement: Selected Letters 1959–1999.* Oxford, England: Oxford University Press. Dame Cicely Saunders, the social worker/nurse/doctor, became something of a guru in palliative care. A biography, from a Christian press, concentrates on her spiritual concerns, and selections of her letters and articles are available. A professional biography by David Clark is expected shortly from Oxford University Press.

WEBSITES

Government websites on end-of-life and palliative care:

Canada: http://www.hc-sc.gc.ca/hcs-sss/palliat/index-eng.php (Health Canada)

UK: http://www.dh.gov.uk/en/Healthcare/IntegratedCare/Endoflifecare/index.htm (Department of Health); http://www.endoflifecareforadults.nhs.uk/eolc/ (national end-of-life care program—NHS)

USA: http://www.usa.gov/Topics/Seniors/EndofLife.shtml (citizens' website)

Chapter 2

DEATH AND DYING: AWARENESS AND UNCERTAINTY

CHAPTER AIMS

The main aim of this chapter is to help readers identify areas of knowledge about death and dying to inform their practice.

After working through this chapter, readers will be able to:

- Think through debates about the nature of death;
- Consider the role of awareness and uncertainty in dying processes;
- Understand different illness trajectories leading to death;
- Review evidence about common cultural, psychological, and social processes that occur around dying and death;
- Understand reactions to dying and death within families and social networks; and
- Consider the implications of the social processes of death and dying for social work practice.

WHAT IS DEATH?

When we die, something called "life" is extinguished. What does this mean?

Dying is a process that takes place over a period of time. When we say someone is dying, we may be thinking about a number of stages: people may be very old, or have an illness that usually leads to death, or not expected to recover after an accident, or be lying in bed taking a few fluttering breaths. This draws attention to the importance of practitioners being clear about precisely what the situation is of someone who we say is "dying."

When Is Someone Dead?

We only experience death once and when we have died, we cannot tell anyone about what happened to us. When people approach death, therefore, they confront a boundary between life and death that they cannot know about and that *is* hard to understand (Gillis, 2001). Some people think that "near-death experiences" might help with this. These are the experiences of people who have been close to death and recovered, or have died and been resuscitated. These experiences show that it is not painful or unpleasant to die, and people may have visions that reflect psychological or physical processes, or their state of mind at the time, but which sometimes become important to them (Fox, 2003; Bailey & Yates, 1996; Kellehear, 1996; Eadie, 1992; Morse, 1996; Fenimore 1991).

Is there any clear definition of that boundary, death? Traditionally, in the United States and most Western countries, death according to the common law occurred when blood ceased to flow and breathing stopped (President's Commission, 1981). Defining death presents increasing practical and ethical problems because technology has developed to the point that it enables circulation and respiration to be maintained artificially. Increasingly, organs from a dying person may be used for transplantation to other human beings to maintain healthy life; people's respiration and circulation may be maintained to keep the organs healthy until transplantation can be arranged, or the availability for transplantation may be affected by the point at which brain stem death is certified (Blank, 2001). In effect, some people argue, switching off artificial breathing, feeding, and circulation kills someone. Alternately, others see it as withdrawing human interference in a natural process of dying. These views often lead to political or spiritual debate.

An important set of ideas involve the connection between body, mind, and soul. Many spiritual ideas suggest that some aspect of the identity of a human being exists during life in the form of a soul or spirit and continues to exist after death. During life, the soul is part of the body, giving it energy, direction, and meaning. When the body dies, the spirit continues in some form, maintaining the existence of the human identity. Different religions see this differently; some Eastern religions accept reincarnation, in which the spirit moves to inhabit another body. How is the idea of the soul or spirit connected to the concept of the mind? At first sight, they seem rather similar, since the intellect and thinking processes may offer human beings stimulation and direction. Is a soul just an old-fashioned way of talking about the mind?

The conventional view about this issue is interactionalism. This view sees the body and mind as different aspects of a person, which interact and affect each other. Either the mind is produced by physical states, for example chemical changes in the body that create emotional or cognitive changes, or the mind is autonomous and influences behavior. The interaction may be both ways, with the mind being influenced by physical states and in turn influencing physical actions by its thinking. The soul, however, is usually seen as different from the mind, because it does not have this constant interaction with the body and is thought to have an existence outside the mind and body. However, we cannot scientifically observe or fully understand such an entity, if it exists. Flew (1964) provides an introduction to the complexity of these debates as they have swung back and forth across the centuries.

In everyday life, individuals may die if they have a serious accident, or if they have suffered a serious illness for some time, or if they are very old. If they are unmoving, cold to the touch, and look pale when we come upon them, we might check to see if they are dead by feeling for a pulse, or looking for breathing; we might hold a mirror to their mouth and nose to see if there is any condensation from slight breaths. Lack of a pulse tells us that the blood circulation has stopped, no sign of breathing tells us that respiration (breathing) has stopped. Lack of movement tells us that the brain is not functioning, particularly if automatic responses fail, for example, the pupil of the eye does not dilate when exposed to light. The context is important; we only accept these as signs of dying if there was an accident, illness, or frailty that made death likely.

However, for confirmation of death, we turn to the medical profession. Attempts were made in the United States during the 1970s to standardize determination of death. There has been controversy over whether death of the whole brain or brain stem death is a more appropriate marker than cessation of blood circulation and respiration. The brain stem is the area of the brain that controls the body's basic functions. Focusing on brain stem death is the convention in many Western countries, although it is less well accepted in other cultures, where lung and heart cessation is the preferred marker (Monaghan, 2002).

When Is Someone Dying?

If deciding whether someone is dead is controversial, it is even more complex to say when someone is dying. A physician might say that someone is dying when a major organ needed to sustain life has stopped functioning. This might include the heart, lungs, kidneys, and liver. Rather less clearly, we might consider that someone with an illness, such as cancer, that will in the future cause a major organ failure, is dying when the condition is worsening and no medical treatment can cure it or slow its progress. Doctors might also say someone is dying when they have a severe condition such as Amyotrophic Lateral Sclerosis (ALS) that has progressed to the point where many aspects of bodily functioning have stopped working properly. ALS, in the United Kingdom motor neurone disease, in France Maladie de Charcot, and in the United States known also as Lou Gehrig's disease, is a neurological condition that leads to progressive degeneration of body functioning. Less clearly, again, many long-term disabilities, such as Parkinson's disease or dementias such as Alzheimer's disease will eventually lead to death, and medical practice has identified an "end-stage" of these conditions, when the condition is severely affecting the patient and is likely to lead to death soon. However, this is complicated by the fact that many of these illnesses are long-lasting and coexist with other conditions that may lead to death before the disability reaches its end stage.

THE DYING PROCESS

If we see death as a process, people move from being alive, through a process called dying, to a point at which they die. They are then dead, and we can examine what happens afterward. However, looking at this process also raises the question of how we understand being alive: Is it the physical functioning of the body, or does it, as many people think, include awareness of the external world and ourselves, the capacity to engage in social relationships or pursue personal objectives or personal development? An example of a post-death process is that the deceased person may have donated his or her organs for transplant to help others, or permission may be sought from relatives for this. There may also be grief, mourning, and bereavement among people close to the deceased person (see Chapter 6). There are also processes and rituals through which the body is disposed of, and what happens as it decays and decomposes.

If we look more closely at this process, it becomes clear that we also have to question concepts that people might take for granted, such as the place of death in our society and accepted social rituals of dying such as funerals and bereavement. Although death is a physical process, how we behave when someone dies or is dying is affected by social expectations and is carried out through social institutions such as churches according to social conventions such as bereavement. We learn these expectations through our experience of life. Therefore, expectations about what we should do around death and dying will vary in different societies and among people with different ethnicities. So, a Latino man may behave differently from a Latina woman, because there are differences in gender expectations; both will behave differently from a man and woman of African background, because there are differences in cultural and ethnic expectations. These vary widely: a man and woman from the Indian subcontinent might behave differently according to whether they are Hindus (and so are most likely from India) or Muslims (and so are most likely from Pakistan); religious differences are also important. But the fact that they have migrated to the United States or the United Kingdom might cause those religious differences to be adapted to expectations in their new country, and it is likely that which of those countries they went to would also lead to differences because they are adapting to different cultures.

The Dying Process: What Happens as Someone Is Near Death?

After an accident, murder, or suicide, death may be sudden. However, if people are approaching the last few days of life because they are ill or aged, they go through a fairly predictable process. Furst and Doyle (2004) usefully summarize the main features in the terminal phase of dying as follows:

- People become tired, weak, and drowsy.
- People are less interested in things going on around them. They stop wanting to get out of bed or receive visitors, or do not have the energy to interact with visitors, though they may appreciate their presence.
- Sometimes they become confused, and may become agitated.

The main physical symptoms during this phase are pain, breathlessness or the feeling that one is becoming breathless, and vomiting. Most of these symptoms can be managed through medication.

During the terminal phase, the digestive system becomes less effective, and people may not want to drink or cannot tolerate liquids or food given by mouth. If they are likely to live for a long time, they would be given water using a "drip" through a needle in a vein in the arm. This stops them from becoming dehydrated, and so is called hydration. Within a few days of the end of life, hydration often leads to discomfort and the need to excrete urine, requiring catheterization, voiding the bladder through a tube. Therefore, in palliative care it is usual to remove drips, and concentrate on the patient's comfort by moistening the lips and mouth.

There are different views about this convention, at least partly because it connects in some people's minds with intensive life support designed to enable people to survive a medical crisis until they can recover their own capacity to breathe, drink, and eat. Some religious and other ethical views argue that food and water should always be given while someone is alive, because it offers the opportunity of recovery even if this is thought to be remote; they do not see artificial hydration or feeding as a medical intervention, but an extension of providing the necessities of life. People with such views may feel strongly that hydration and possibly artificial feeding should continue. Moreover, not every situation is as irretrievable as palliative care doctors may judge, and hydration can also be helpful in achieving a recovery. These arguments are reviewed in a book edited by Craig (2004) who has been a strong proponent of continuing hydration on both medical and ethical grounds.

Multiprofessional palliative care teams will take a general stance about such issues, but will also take account of the need to change general policies about hydration and artificial feeding in particular cases. Families and visitors need discussion and explanation about the practice followed in a particular setting. Similarly, it helps families to know in advance that when patients cannot take food, this is part of the natural movement toward death. They are not starving to death and experience no discomfort. Multiprofessional teams will sometimes have to reconsider their usual practice in withdrawing hydration if families have very strong ethical or other objections, or will need to consider and respect families' and patients' views by discussing fully reasons for their decision. Social workers may need to be involved both in explanation and also in advocacy for patient or family views.

Awareness of Death

An important factor in the lives of many people is their awareness that they are dying. Research on awareness of dying derives from the work of Glaser and Strauss (1965, 1968) in which they described patterns of awareness behavior:

- Closed awareness, where professionals and/or family members were aware but the patient was not
- Suspicion awareness, where patients suspected that they had a serious condition, but had not had this confirmed; this was very stressful
- Mutual pretence awareness, where there was awareness among those involved but it was not discussed
- Open awareness, where both patient and those involved knew that death was likely

Time is an important issue for people approaching death. Triparthy (2001) points out that cancer and similar illnesses are very heterogeneous conditions; it is impossible to generalize about them. People assume that medicine will be able to do more than in reality is possible. An added factor in this uncertainty is that medical science has not enabled doctors to make accurate prognoses about how long someone will live, because individual variations, variations in disease processes, care settings, and the environment in which patients have lived all interact in a complex way. There are a number of prognostic tools, which are not fully effective in the face of these variations (Lau et al., 2007). Other illnesses have a usual pathway, but people may be overly optimistic or pessimistic, and their view may be affected by their knowledge. For example, a person who has lived with HIV for many years and managed the illness well may feel that the development of full-blown AIDS signals the close approach of the end of their life, while another might feel that this is just another phase that they can handle. Good understanding of medical information, but also careful assessment and understanding of personal reactions to it, are crucial elements practitioners need to help appropriately.

Patients are vulnerable because they are ill, increasingly dependent, and fear death or the dying process, and may find difficulty taking in the reality of what treatment is possible. Therefore, people need to be aware of approaching death to give them time to carry out life tasks before they die or before their increasing illness restricts their energy or capacity to do what they want to do; we pick this up in later chapters. For all these reasons, social workers may have to help with tensions about awareness between dying people and their families, professionals, and members of their communities and social networks; they often disagree about whether the patient or particular people should be aware of the likelihood of death. Since, as we argued in Chapter 1, dying is a family journey, awareness is the key to making that journey in the company of family members.

In their later work, Glaser and Strauss (1968) focused on the "shape" of the dying phase in people's lives. Four likely courses through which expectations develop were:

- Certain death at a certain time, the position of the person condemned to death for a crime
- Certain death at an unknown time, the position of most of us
- Uncertain death but a known time when certainty will be known, for example waiting for medical test results
- Uncertain death and uncertain time for the issue to be resolved

Most hospital patients experience uncertainty in their knowledge about if, when, and where they are going to die. Pattison (1977) builds on this work by suggesting that for many people there are several phases:

- A period when people know they have an illness that might be fatal: "the potential death" phase
- An event when they are told or come to know that they are expected to die: "the crisis knowledge of death." People have vivid memories of being told that they are expected to die, so how this is done is very important for their adjustment within the dying process
- A subsequent period of anxiety as they come to accept the prognosis; this "the acute crisis phase" reaches a peak
- A subsequent period of declining anxiety during which they live with the knowledge of their impending death: "the chronic living-dying phase"

- The terminal phase, where physical and social factors are increasingly prohibiting people from achieving desired objectives within a good quality of life . . .
- . . . leading to the point of death

An important role of social work in end-of-life care, therefore, is to help people deal with the uncertainties that they face at the different times in the sequence of events they are involved in. Social workers need to think through the implications for each person and his or her family as they pass through these phases. We build on this in Chapter 3, which focuses on communicating the truth, so far as it is known, about someone's condition and managing that family's hope appropriately.

Illness Trajectories

Understanding illness trajectories can help practitioners manage issues of awareness and time. A "trajectory" in health care is how illnesses or conditions typically develop and change over time. If we apply this to social work, the trajectory is the progression of the combination of issues faced by a client.

Lynn and Adamson (2003) suggest that there are three main trajectories at the end of life, displayed schematically in figure 2.1. In the typical cancer trajectory, there is a slow decline in patients' ability to function over a few years, but a rapid decline over a few months leading to death. In the long-term conditions trajectory, typical of people with heart and

FIGURE 2.1   Trajectories of dying

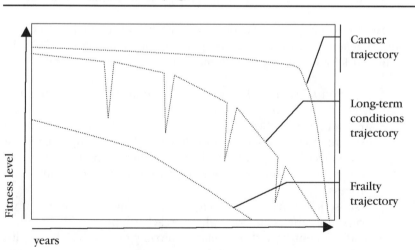

Source: based on Lynn and Adamson (2003)

lung failure, capacity to function is at a lower starting point and declines slowly over three to five years, with intermittent crises, followed by an apparently sudden death. In the frailty trajectory, again from a low starting point, patients mainly suffer from prolonged dwindling of function, usually because of dementia and general physical frailty. This continues over perhaps six to eight years with no sudden decline until death. Knowledge of these trajectories allows practitioners to adjust the pace of their interventions and judge how to discuss the progression of the client's condition. Practitioners need constant discussion with the physician or nurse providing health care to coordinate how they discuss the progression of the condition with clients and their family.

An important policy implication of these different trajectories is that palliative care services developed to meet the needs of patients in the cancer scenario, with curative services being cut off and replaced with palliative care. As we saw in Chapter 1, palliative care increasingly interacts with other aspects of end-of-life care with a more prolonged interaction between specialist palliative care and other care services. Robinson (2006) identifies three types of interactions: First, the usual position wherein people may receive only informal care and everyday care services up to the point of their death. People in this position mainly receive services from community and primary health and social care services, and nonspecialist human service professionals. Second, if they have a serious medical condition, people may receive curative health care until no further curative treatment is possible, and then, perhaps for a short period, transfer to palliative care or hospice services until death. This is a common position in the United States, since both insurance and public finance for care may depend on patients or physicians renouncing curative treatment, although there is usually some flexibility in this decision. Even so, treatment similar to that offered for the condition may be used to help manage symptoms and may be regarded as palliative treatment, as for example radiotherapy to reduce the size of tumors. In other countries, curative treatment for some aspects of the condition may continue alongside palliative care. This means that outside the United States, patients may keep their options open, without the psychological impact of giving up on a cure, although the social reality is usually that referral to a hospice or palliative care service signals to patients and families that the dying phase has arrived. Finally, Robinson's third position is a continuing interaction between informal and community health care palliative and curative treatment services, with the role of each rising and falling over time, depending on the patient's needs. Many hospitals or community health care services permit flexible interaction between curative and palliative care elements of their programs.

Ideally, preventive work with families and communities would help them respond more flexibly with better understanding of how long-term conditions may progress. Service policies have developed that aim to improve quality of life near end of life in the United States (Lynn, 2000) and promote good health and community support at end of life as part of health-promoting palliative care in Australia (Kellehear, 2005) (see Chapter 9).

DYING WELL

One of the aims of end-of-life and palliative care is that people should be helped to "die well" or experience a "respectful death" (Farber, Egnew, & Farber, 2004); older literature refers to a "good death." Dying well might be interpreted variously by different individuals and by different ethnic and faith groups, so research into people's views has tried to make clearer what we are trying to achieve. Dying well includes both medical and social ideas such as:

- Removing the impact of physical symptoms, such as pain
- Reducing psychological and social stress both for the dying person and for his or her family and social network
- More controversially, making available the freedom to end life at the choice of the dying person if that person cannot or does not want to continue to suffer unmanageable physical, psychological, and social stresses associated with the dying process (see Chapter 8)
- Byock's (1997) discussion of "dying well," which focuses on seeing this positively, being at peace and being able to take up the possibilities offered by moving toward the end of life

A qualitative study of 126 dialysis and HIV patients and patients in long-term care facilities for elders (Singer, Morting & Kelner, 1999) identified five domains that were considered to offer good-quality end-of-life care:

- Adequate pain and symptom management
- Avoiding inappropriate prolongation of dying
- Achieving a sense of control
- Relieving the burden of making decisions about care and arrangement for dying by sharing them with others
- Strengthening relationships with loved ones

Kellehear's (1990) important Australian study of a hundred people dying of cancer identified five aspects of dying well:

- Awareness of dying, usually derived from others' advice, particularly medical diagnosis and prognosis
- Social adjustments and personal preparation

- Public preparation, including legal, financial, religious, funeral, and medical arrangements
- Disengagement from work, which may be gradual or partial for some time
- Farewells

He also identified large variations in the ways in which people carry out these activities. In particular, the dying person and people around him or her may not want to make preparations. Dying may take place over a long period of time, months or years in societies where there is long life expectancy. Therefore, people may have had a "good inning" or conversely, if they are dying before seventy years, may be seen as unfortunately dying early. Older people were more likely to have made preparations for dying before they received a medical diagnosis of an illness likely to lead to death, whereas younger people may well not have thought about it until a diagnosis of a life-limiting illness brought them suddenly up against the prospect of death.

There are also studies of different minority ethnic groups. For example, Firth (1996) suggests that a dominant view of Hindu people is of death as a transition from one form of existence to another. A good experience of death for people committed to this faith and culture where it is dominant relies on the support and closeness of family members and local community rather than on medical, nursing, or hospice care.

THE DYING PROCESS: SOCIAL WORK ROLES

Corr et al. (2006, p. 143) identify four tasks that people often seek to carry out during the dying process:

- Physical tasks, satisfying bodily needs and minimizing physical distress
- Psychological tasks, achieving security, autonomy, and richness
- Social tasks, sustaining significant interpersonal attachments
- Spiritual tasks, identifying, developing, or affirming sources of energy and hope

Within each trajectory, several of Pattison's (1977) phases of the dying process, discussed above, might demand social work intervention. Parry (2001, ch. 2) identifies different models, but these may be integrated as follows:

- the diagnosis of a life-threatening condition, when social workers may need to help patients and their families react to the news, make decisions about treatment, and organize themselves to support the sick family member emotionally, financially, and practically

- the crisis of knowing about death, where again social work help may be needed to process the decision and decide on appropriate patient and family responses
- the point at which treatment ceases to prolong life, where again the patient and family must process the news and think about its consequences for the family's functioning
- the phase of living with dying, during which treatment aims to reduce the impact of symptoms and prolong active life, when social workers may need to help with prioritizing patients' and family members' completion of important life tasks. This may include preparatory grief, that is, grieving for a known future death, which the dying person may share with family members and caregivers (Mystakidou et al., 2007)
- the terminal phase, when social workers may need to help families with supporting each other and gaining confidence to deal with their experiences of the dying process
- death, when emotional support, practical planning, changed social status, and initial responses to grief are important

By identifying the likely scenario for a client, an appropriate combination of community services may be developed (Murray, Kendall, Boyd, & Sheikh, 2005). For example, it might be possible to prevent crisis admissions to hospital or care, or distressing incidents for families in the long-term conditions scenario, or to facilitate recognition of slowly increasing needs for support and care in the dwindling scenario. Practitioners may also be able to help patients plan for the likely progression of their condition. Many people see health care services as mainly about cure. With an identifiable condition such as heart or lung disease, they may have experienced periods of treatment that have left them "cured" of various obvious symptoms. However, they may only slowly become conscious that every treatment seems to leave them feeling or functioning less well overall. Patients and family members may become frustrated about lack of progress, when, with planning, they could learn to take advantage of periods when they feel reasonably well to meet some life objectives. Practitioners might help them identify attainable life aims, leading to an improved quality of life.

SOCIAL ASPECTS OF DYING AND DEATH

Death and Dying as a Social Event

Individuals die, but death is social. This is because:

- It usually takes place when others are present and involves them in social interactions as an individual dies.

- It affects the network of existing social relationships, because a dead or dying person's relationships with others are altered.
- It leads to social states and statuses such as being "at risk" of dying or suicide, or being bereaved.
- It involves social institutions that are specifically concerned with death, such as hospitals, clinics, social agencies, funeral homes, cemeteries, and crematoria.
- It involves social rituals, such as caring for and visiting dying people, dealing with dead bodies, certifying and investigating death, having funerals and making memorials of people who have died.
- It may also have an impact on a wide range of other social institutions and rituals through the social relationships involved; examples might be schools, community organizations, workplaces, and care homes for older people.

The range of social relationships, social institutions, and social experiences potentially affected by death, dying, and bereavement reminds us, first, that end-of-life issues will arise for social workers wherever they work. Second, health care agencies such as hospices, hospitals, clinics, and care homes require social interventions as part of their repertoire because they are social institutions dealing with people enmeshed in social relationships.

As with all social work, both psychological and social theories need to be incorporated into social work practice in end-of-life care. Death and dying are often metaphors for life issues that people face. For example, decay and decomposition of the body are a natural process that occurs after death, but may also be a metaphor of social and other forms of deterioration. Consequently, practitioners may need to help people to see that death does not mean that they are falling apart, but instead can be creative and make a contribution to their families and communities in this last period of their lives.

Sociological Perspectives in End-of-Life Care

Contemporary Issues in the Sociology of Death, Dying and Disposal (Howarthand & Jupp, 1996) identifies major sociological issues in death and dying:

- The place of death in social and political discourse, including Seale's (1998) issues of meaning—the importance given to heroism in combating illness and death, and its associations with nationalism, the role of violence as part of civilization, and the extent to which people in society are aware of and discuss issues about death and dying

31

- Social representations of death, in the media, in funeral and other rituals, in the way dead people are memorialized, and in attitudes about what constitutes a good death
- In the social roles and status of people who work with death (for example, doctors, nurses, or police officers)
- The social implications of medical and legal arrangements for death

Seale (1998) also raises issues about:

- The role and policy of social organizations in dealing with death
- Ideas about the importance of the body and changes in bodily appearance and how bodies are dealt with in media and in social organizations

Ritual is important not only in funerals and memorial services but also in religious and spiritual ways of helping dying people and their families. Social rituals exist around visiting dying people and, talking or avoiding talking about death, and in social institutions concerned with death, such as crematoria and cemeteries. Rituals often serve as a way of avoiding speaking about death; a ritual stands in place of "words about death" (Davies, 2002).

Patterns of Mortality

The pattern of dying in any community affects how people see death and dying, and the social processes that develop within societies to manage death and people's reactions to it. Mortality is the rate at which people die within a given population, usually expressed as the number of deaths per thousand people in the population being studied. Life expectancy is the average number of years that people of a given age may be expected to live. Worldwide, mortality declined very rapidly during the twentieth century. In 1950–55 life expectancy worldwide was forty-seven years, by 2000–05 it was more than sixty-five years, and by 2045–50 it is expected to be around seventy-five years. In developed Western economies, such as those of Australia, Europe, and North America, life expectancy was sixty-six years in 1950–55, seventy-six years in 2000–05 (less-developed economies: sixty-three years); and is likely to be eighty-two years in 2045–50 (less developed economies: seventy-four years). Mortality is a marker of health and social inequality: people live shorter lives in poorer, less-developed economies and poorer less-developed regions of rich economies. Life expectancy also varies with sex: worldwide, the female advantage is seven years in developed economies, three in less developed economies. For example, at the world level in 2000–50, women had a life expectancy of sixty-eight years and men sixty-three years. In the developed economies, men's life expectancy in the same period was about seventy-two years and women's over seventy-nine years, while in the less-developed economies the difference was between about sixty-two and sixty-five years. These statistics are drawn from a United Nations study (DESA, 2005). Most countries publish up-to-date statistics, which you can find on the internet using the UN listing at the end of this chapter. Most countries' statistics also include differences among ethnic groups and regions.

Currently, the major causes of death in the United States, and in most countries in the West, are chronic diseases, mainly cardiovascular disease and cancer; followed by chronic respiratory diseases; diseases common among older people, such as dementia and renal failure; infectious diseases; and injuries due to accidents. Deaths from cardiovascular diseases and cancer are falling. These trends vary somewhat among different ethnic groups (Sahyoun, Lentzner, Hoyert, & Robinson, 2005).

This pattern of death has changed in the last hundred years (Bern-Klug, Forbes, & Gessert, 2001). In 1900, most people died of acute infective conditions after only a few days or weeks of suffering from the illness. Death is also postponed. In the early twentieth century, 30 percent of deaths in the United States were of children under ten years of age; now it is 1 percent. At the other end of life, 30 percent of deaths in the United States in the early twentieth century occurred in adults age sixty years and older, while now it is 80 percent, and 40 percent of deaths in 1997 occurred in adults age eighty and older.

We read a recent newspaper report that talked about people being likely to die "unnecessarily" because they were obese. Of course, it is necessary for us all to die; the writer reflected a general acceptance that death before old age is unlikely and unexpected. Often, medical advances are presented as "preventing deaths," when they can only postpone them. Death being outside daily experience means that practitioners may have to help people with two social situations when they occur. The first is unusual distress and uncertainty when someone dies in middle age or younger and the second, a fear that old age may lead to a protracted, although often postponed, frailty. Bern-Klug (2004) usefully identifies the need to help people with the "ambiguous dying syndrome," where they can see their increasing frailty, and they may have emergencies in the long-term conditions trajectory, but are never really in a terminal phase of illness or a dying process. It may be useful for social workers to pick up conversations with clients that suggest they are thinking about these issues affecting them and offer the opportunity to discuss them. It may be helpful to spell out the need for more careful planning of family and service support either at the time or at a later stage, and start thinking through how the family will handle this.

Medical technology may prolong this period of frailty still longer, but this may be expensive in both money and stress for family members. Social workers may need to be prepared to talk over feelings about these issues, not only at the time they are raised by the possibility of a medical intervention but also beforehand. Many thoughtful older people want to express their views about decisions regarding their care, in case they cannot express them in an emergency or they lose their capacity to express or make decisions. This leads to advance care planning, deciding on and recording preferences about care and treatment well in advance of the need to do so (see Chapters 4 and 8). In particular, they may express a view about a "do not resuscitate" (DNR) decision. This is a judgment by their physician, usually agreed upon with the patient and family, that if patients have an infection or die from, for example, a heart attack, no attempt at aggressive treatment or to resuscitate will be made. This is a commonplace policy in palliative care, in part because most DNR techniques are ineffective in people with advanced illnesses.

People are therefore beginning to think about and debate whether they want to accept prolonged life in any circumstances. The philosopher Materstvedt (2007) argues that it does not make sense to most people to "accept" death, and that rage against it should be permissible. This connects to the discussion above about ending feeding, hydration, and unnecessary medication when someone is in the last few days of life. While, as we discussed above, relatives may support or disapprove of such actions as part of a process of not prolonging life, many people also feel that they do not want to accept aggressive medical interventions that will prolong an uncomfortable or unsatisfactory life. Others feel strongly that health care services should do everything possible to save life. This connects with people's strongly held personal, religious, and spiritual values and raises ethical issues for practitioners involved in these situations. There is also significant variation of attitude among different ethnic and cultural groups, and so practitioners should be careful to explore cultural perceptions, particularly when minorities are affected by such issues.

Death certificates developed as part of the increasing regulation and surveillance of life by the state in the nineteenth century. They have important social functions, since they mark the end of an individual's biography, express authoritative medical opinion about the cause of death, and are the first step in the process that leads to the funeral. Death and memorial notices and obituaries, often published in newspapers and magazines, report the event of a death and are important signifiers of the narrative of a life. So also are cairns by the roadside where an accident has taken place, or flowers left in memory of the deceased person where a murder has been committed.

The Medicalization of Death

Because death has become less commonplace in people's lives, and social perceptions of it have changed, many people have come to see dying as solely or mainly a medical matter. As a result, people see dying, death, and bereavement through a medical view of human and social phenomena. These stages of life are managed through medical and health care institutions and organizations. The sciences of anatomy and pathology have given medicine great understanding of the way bodies work (Howarth, 2007, p. 122), and, as we have seen, physicians are given the responsibility of determining and certifying death. Having knowledge about and ways of understanding activities or events gives individuals and groups—in this case an occupational group or profession—influence over how everyone understands death. Priests have been a major influence over understandings of death, in particular knowledge of preparation for death, funeral rituals, and bereavement, and organized religions were responsible for funerals and bereavement rituals. This influence has probably declined over time and the medical influence over determining death, and through medical treatment, has become more important. Public health actions delaying and preventing death, and health care institutions managing death have made medicine a more significant force in influencing conceptions of death and dying. Although hospice and palliative care initially sought to reduce the medical influence over the dying process, end-of-life care has steadily come to be influenced by palliative medicine as a health care specialty.

Small (2001a) points out that one of the consequences of medicalization led to a modernist approach to bereavement, including activities such as:

- Attempts to measure and compare bereavements in different people and different cultures
- A focus on therapeutic responses to problems of bereavement
- A focus on sequential time in the many stage theories of bereavement

These approaches are modernist because they assume that complex human experiences are structured and can be explained.

Medicine and health-care organizations have a particular conception of the social phenomena that they deal with. Their role is to identify conditions of the body and mind, illnesses, or disabilities, that through medical interventions may be cured or reduced in their impact. This is a service focused on individuals, based on biomedical science, and carried on in specific institutions, hospitals, clinics, and community health-care organizations. There are specific health-care institutions, hospices, that work particularly with death and dying. Medical care focuses therefore on the individuals and their bodies in special places for care, rather than wider social and family involvements in the process of dying, death, and bereavement. It tends to look for illnesses or problems to cure, with death as a criterion of failure. Edgley (2003) even suggests that dying may be considered a deviance in cure-oriented medical settings, and Singer (1994, p. 111) refers to the joke: "Life is a terminal disease sexually transmitted," according to the medical model of the world.

Medicine and other biomedical professions have introduced significant improvements in prolonging life and in managing care before death that is accompanied by illness. Pain and unpleasant symptoms therefore have less impact than previously. This is an integral part of end-of-life and particularly palliative care. However, concern has grown that medicine looks for deficits such as illness and disabilities rather than positive attributes in human beings and individualizes medical problems as inadequacies compared with an ideal human body to be investigated and treated through science and biomedical interventions. This neglects personal responsibility for making the best of life and treats people as though they were defined by the illness or disability rather than having alongside it capacities for human and social interaction and fulfillment. Thus, the medical literature on spirituality treats religious faith, investigated by surveys of the extent of people's commitment to religion, as a factor that may help people resist the progression of an illness, but to religious people it is a central part of their identity. Movements of people with disabilities criticize the "medical model" of disability as one that focuses on human deficits, while a social model identifies the failings in society and the environment that create disability by failing to provide a social environment in which people with disabilities might flourish despite physical or mental impairments. The social model may also be criticized, however: it neglects the distress caused by impairment and illness.

Accepting the validity of the critique of medicalization suggests that alternate models of professional practice and of conceptualizing death, dying, and bereavement need also to be represented in end-of-life care. Nursing, social work, and spiritual care professions make a contribution by making the conceptualization of dying, death, and bereavement more inclusive and holistic in our society. Social work, in particular, plays an important role in ensuring that social and family impacts of dying and bereavement processes are fully included in the services offered. It is important for social workers not to become seduced by the interest and involvement in the detail of care for particular conditions but to contribute the important broader perspective of the meaning of the condition for people surrounding the individual patient.

Is Death a Taboo?

Ariès (1974) and Gorer (1967) are both important writers who consider death a taboo in twentieth-century Western society; that is, while death may be significant in the way in which people think about their lives, people do not talk much about it and do not discuss it in the abstract. It is usually dealt with by professionals and depersonalized. Mourning rituals, in previous times, particularly Victorian times, were more powerfully established. Social workers may experience this, because they may deal with people who may not like to discuss the death of a relative with others, may not share information about death or bereavement with children or family members with intellectual disabilities, and may suppress public expression of grief.

Walter (1992), however, suggests that avoiding public grief and mourning is not unique to modern society, but commonplace in many societies. He argues that avoiding active discussion of death may be healthy because it allows people to continue with their life tasks. The period when death was a taboo subject was a specific one occurring in the mid-twentieth century after two major world wars and the Holocaust, at a time when medical progress seemed set to banish premature death. This has changed with better psychological understanding of death and bereavement and the development of the hospice movement.

Rather than being a forbidden topic, it is more appropriate to see death as hidden from ordinary life. This is because the death rate has been markedly reduced by medical advances, so that people do not experience death very often or very early in their lives. Also, the dying process is often hidden in care institutions rather than occurring in people's homes.

The medicalization of death means that health-care assumptions about confidentiality reduce the sharing of information. People avoid death because it most often occurs in health-care environments, and it is a conversational embarrassment to medical and nursing professionals, who focus on life and cure, rather than care in death. This contrasts with the period in which death was mainly a religious or spiritual matter, where concern for death as part of life is more acceptable. For example, Christians believe that Christ died to save his followers and was resurrected, and in Islam, faithful followers are assured of continuing life in a paradise.

People generally are less inclined to participate in formal rituals of bereavement and remembrance. However, this does not mean that they do not experience grief. Instead of formal rituals, less formal and populist rituals have developed. An often-cited example is the worldwide public reaction to the death of Princess Diana in 1997, when there was considerable public expression of grief, through signing memorial books and placing flowers in significant locations in her memory.

People have a range of frames for viewing death and bereavement: the practical, the spiritual, the biomedical, the lay, and the semi-psychiatric. In the practical frame, a funeral has to be arranged and money and property sorted out. In the spiritual frame, people reflect and meditate on the meaning of life. In the biomedical frame, reasonable standards of treatment and care are expected; families must visit the sick and support the family and caregivers. In the lay frame, people express their regrets, buy flowers, organize for people leaving work. In the semi-psychiatric frame, people recognize that there will be distress, stress, anxiety, and depression and allow for it. A public health frame covers many of the procedures for certifying death and disposing of bodies, a theological frame provides for some of the ritual, and a psychological frame provides for explanations and actions around grief and bereavement.

Spiritual Care in Social Work Practice

Rees (1997) comments on the importance given to death in people's imagination and thinking. In particular, religious and spiritual systems of thought give great significance to birth and death as important sources of meaning in people's lives. For example, people see their birth or existence as human beings as enabling them to make a contribution to the well-being of others through actions or social interactions; that contribution offers a meaning and value for their life. They also see death as a loss of social contribution, and a loss of the opportunity or capability to make a meaningful contribution to the world.

Spirituality is a complex aspect of human experience. It may include:

- Religious or other faith experiences
- Spirit as an energizing force. People are concerned with the spiritual to maximize this personal energy, through study, meditation, religion, and a variety of activities, which might include enjoying beautiful art, music, or nature
- Spirit as the nonmaterial, that is, not being concerned with achievement, money, or consumption of goods. The spiritual life is one than does not give priority to such things
- Focusing on meaning-making about nonmaterial and energizing issues in people's lives, that is, constructing a view about the personal implications of events in personal or social experience or in the wider world

Spiritual aspects of care often gain increased significance in social work practice in end-of-life care compared with other aspects of social work. This is because experiencing major life changes, such as approaching the end of life, often stimulates reflection on the meaning of the change in relation to life experience.

Social workers providing end-of-life care may come to deal with spiritual issues for several reasons:

- Spiritual issues are part of social and family issues faced by clients or informal caregivers that social workers often deal with. Clients may seek a holistic response from practitioners. For example, people may reassess their contribution to or assumptions about family relationships: "Have I done enough for my children?" "Did I really provide good care for my dying mother?"
- Specialist spiritual care advisers are not available.
- Specialist spiritual care advisers, particularly if their main focus is as pastor of a church, are not experienced in dealing with end-of-life issues in health and social care.
- Religious advisers are not acceptable to secularists or other faiths as advisers on spiritual care issues.
- Other professionals see spiritual care as part of the social work task, or it is integrated into or managed by a social work department.

Therefore, social workers may need to identify and address spiritual issues as part of their more general work, or substitute for specialist spiritual care advisers. Social workers without a religious faith or with a faith different from that of their client may view this possibility with anxiety because they cannot believe or empathize with the beliefs they are having to discuss. Our approach to this is to focus on spiritual issues, which are universal, rather than the expression of them in a particular religion.

An important principle of spiritual engagement is respect for the beliefs of the dying or bereaved person (Attig, 1995). This means that practitioners should avoid being intolerant of the particular beliefs of the people they are helping and of the ways they express them.

Case example: Henry

Henry was a Pentecostal Christian whose church believed that God would sometimes "save" the life of someone who had been diagnosed with a terminal illness. They believed that hope came through suffering, a common Christian belief. Henry was ambivalent about this belief, but found the support of church members helpful. The church organized a roster of church members to pray 24/7 for his deliverance from illness in his room at the Hospice. Staff in the hospice found this very stressful, and particularly found it difficult to ask church members to leave Henry's room when they were carrying out nursing and medical procedures. The group prayed in the hallway when this happened and upset other visitors and patients. Discussions with the church leaders about the noise of their praying was felt to be disrespectful, although staff tried to behave respectfully; however, a church member complained that he heard staff joking about the situation. As this death approached, the roster was increased, with five people eventually present praying for Henry to be saved, until the point at which the nurse said quietly to Henry's wife that he had died. Instantly, the prayer switched to prayer for the family to be healed in their suffering and for Henry's future existence in heaven.

An important intervention that helped staff in this situation was a spiritual care leader's comment that there was a difference between believing and knowing. The church members believed—they would have said "had faith"—that they were being helpful and that Henry would be saved, either in this life or the next, but they accepted that they could not know this; neither could staff. In other situations, it may be helpful to accept people's beliefs but to try to get them to understand that what happens after life or miracles of cure cannot be known. In this way, it is sometimes possible to get people to accept helpful interventions by caregivers, even though a miracle is expected.

Pause and reflect

It may be difficult to respond appropriately to direct comments about Allah, God, or Jesus Christ or other deities: "This illness is a punishment from God," "My pain is a test from Allah," or "Why has Jesus abandoned me?" particularly if practitioners are not familiar with the religion or denomination of clients or are not accustomed to talking about spiritual entities. What would you say, in response to statements or questions such as these?

Some suggestions

A useful approach is to see this as an important relationship in the client's consciousness, to address both sides of the relationship and both the relationship itself and its perceived content: "Why do you see your god as an abandoning, punishing, or testing god?" "Are there other aspects of your god's view of you?" "Why do you think you are someone that your god needs to abandon, punish, or test?" Assessment of what is important about the spiritual experience may also be valuable: "Are there any particular aspects of your illness or symptoms that make you feel abandoned?"

Another difficulty is that some denominations or religions may express views that are inconsistent with the trend of palliative care and end-of-life care practice. Members of Henry's church in their commitment to achieving hope through prayer, did not make it easy for hospice staff to discuss the prognosis of death explicitly with him. One approach to this kind of problem is to stimulate rational thinking about the issues. Practitioners might ask questions such as: "Do you feel weaker this week than last?" It can also be useful to help clients carry out important family tasks, without explicitly raising the issue of death. In one case, for example, the practitioner suggested to a son that he should spend time at the bedside reminiscing with his father about things they had done together when he was a child, and this would give him the opportunity to say how much he had appreciated all that his father had done for him. This enabled an important task of leave-taking to be completed; the son could let his father know how much he had valued what his father had done for him, without connecting this with impending death, which they both knew about, but did not want to discuss.

I AM HAPPY AND I AM SCARED

This poem, written by a man in a creative writing session at St. Christopher's Hospice Creative Living Center, reflects the uncertainty and ambivalence common among people who are dying.

> *I am happy and I am scared,*
> *I wonder why it has happened to me,*
> *I hear my wife laughing,*
> *I want to take her away somewhere nice.*
>
> *I am happy and I am scared,*   5
> *I pretend it's all going to be OK,*
> *I feel pain all the time,*
> *I touch my wife's hair,*
> *I worry who will look after her,*
> *I cry myself to sleep again.*   10
>
> *I am happy and I am scared,*
> *I understand it will work out alright,*
> *I say "don't worry darling",*
> *I dream of being well,*
> *I try to remember the good times,*   15
> *I hope they will return.*
>
> *I am happy and I am scared.*

CONCLUSION

In this chapter, we have emphasized that death, dying, and bereavement are social processes involving many different people. It is important for practitioners to understand the social processes involved and the social institutions and social structures through which people make sense of or deal with problems that arise for them in dying, death, and bereavement processes. This may include spiritual issues, which can become important to people at the end of life. Since dying and death processes are often medicalized in our society, and death is often hidden, we have argued that social workers have a particular role to play in ensuring that people can deal with the social issues involved in awareness and uncertainty of dying and death. They can bring an understanding and concern for the social as an important counterbalance to the individualized medical and health-care emphasis on physical care of the body of a patient. Social workers should seek to broaden the focus to an awareness of the impact of the client's death on his or her social networks and community life, and the influence of family, social, and community experiences on people's reactions to dying, death, and bereavement.

FURTHER READING

Good recent general introductions to the issues dealt with in this chapter are:

Auger, J. A. (2000). *Social perspectives on death and dying.* Halifax, Canada: Fernwood.

Corr, C. A., Nabe, C. M., & Corr, D. M. (2006). *Death and dying: Life and living* (6th ed.). Belmont, CA: Wadsworth.

Howarth, G. (2007). *Death and dying: A sociological introduction.* Cambridge, England: Polity.

Kellehear, A. (2006). *A Social History of Dying.* Cambridge, England: Cambridge University Press.

JOURNALS

A number of important journals are the main media for debate and analysis of issues concerning death and dying. These include:

- *Death Studies,* published by Taylor & Francis, Philadelphia.
- *Omega: The Journal of Death and Dying,* published by Baywood, Amityville, NY, in association with the Association for Death Education Counseling.
- *Mortality,* published by Routledge, London.

STATISTICS

A useful listing of websites providing countries' statistical information on the Internet may be found at http://unstats.un.org/unsd/methods/inter-natlinks/sd_natstat.asp

Chapter 3

TRUTH AND HOPE: COMMUNICATION AT THE END OF LIFE

CHAPTER AIMS

The main aim of this chapter is to lay the foundations of social work practice in end-of-life care by exploring communication in end-of-life situations.

After working through this chapter, readers will be able to:

- Empower people at the end of life to gain "hope" by increasing their autonomy and control of decisions and quality of life;
- Recognize when to discuss the "truth" of the end of life with people;
- Enhance the quality of communication with people about dying and death;
- Plan discussion with children about dying and death; and
- Consider requirements for communicating about death and dying with others who have special communication needs.

COMMUNICATION SKILLS IN END-OF-LIFE CARE

Communication

Communication involves a process in which a message is transmitted from a communicator to a receiver. A message may be expressed in words or through behavior; it may thus be unspoken.

Communication is important to working with people at the end of life, for a variety of reasons. As we saw in Chapters 1 and 2, the dying process is both individual and social, so individuals must communicate with others to engage them in the social dying process. And in Chapter 2, we saw that a common issue in the dying process is the different kinds of awareness that people have about it. Awareness develops through communication. We also saw in Chapter 2 that death and dying are often hidden in our society; we need to communicate to bring it out of hiding when we are trying to help people with the end of life.

So, communication is essential in end-of-life care to enable the social nature of dying and bereavement to develop; it is, therefore, also essential to professional practice in end-of-life care. How else can the nurse or doctor assess someone's physical pain? Buckman (2000, p. 146) argues that "effective symptom control is impossible without effective communication." For similar reasons, social workers need to discuss end-of-life issues with clients. And we argue in this chapter that, of the professions involved in end-of-life care, communication is central to social work. Therefore, we start from communication skills in end-of-life care and move on to social work engagement, assessment, and intervention processes in later chapters.

Both nonverbal and spoken communication may be unheard, misheard, or only partly heard, since the sender, receiver, and the medium of transmission may interfere with the communication. People's transmission and understanding of messages is influenced by language, class, and cultural factors as well as emotions and personality (del Rio, 2004, p. 454). Communication patterns are learned in relationships with the people around us, and this creates a shared social construction through which we agree with others about how we understand the world. Our understanding is also affected by the historical and social context in which communication and relationships take place. Therefore, people around us evaluate what we say or do or fail to say or do according to their expectations about what people say or do in those circumstances. So someone from an African background may misread someone of Asian ethnicity because their cultural expectations, developed in childhood, are different. People may choose not to talk about a grandmother's death to their daughter because they have learned that such things are not discussed.

The way people communicate also comes from the media. How people talk on television or the way newspapers deal with dying, death, or bereavement can inform how people talk about such issues in general. This might lead to over dramatization of feelings and attitudes, but at least it helps with the expression of feeling, since open expression is required in most drama and news programs.

Particular kinds of language may be helpful or unhelpful. For example, language that is seen as prejudicial, cold, dehumanizing, or discriminatory can heighten distress while language that emphasizes equality and similarities can make people feel more comfortable. Humor can relieve stress for people who share attitudes and experience but can increase conflict where there are differences. However, these different aspects of communicating can be in tension with one another, and practitioners need to think through the social expectations of the people involved.

Case example: The wrinkled patient

In a recent school project, a seven-year-old child asked a patient: "Why are you so wrinkled?" and everyone, including the patient, laughed, but it might have been different if a social worker or nurse had mentioned the wrinkles humorously. Since humor is so personal, it becomes sensitive, particularly where important emotions are also in play in end-of-life situations. Practitioners need to assess carefully the extent to which people might be receptive to a particular humorous intervention, whether it is culturally appropriate, and whether the timing and content of humorous comments are appropriate (Dean, 1997).

Communicating about Truth and Hope

Truth and hope are two important aspects of end-of-life situations and we need communication skills to work with them. Chapter 2 showed how uncertainty is a feature of end-of-life situations. Being hopeful, maintaining hope, and losing hope are all profound aspects of the experience of the end of life that social workers will have to deal with. However, to help with death and dying, practitioners need to be able to talk about it even though these topics are hidden in ordinary conversation. Therefore, social workers need to develop ways of introducing discussion of death and dying in socially appropriate ways.

Ideally, particularly with children, but also with adults, people should be involved in discussion about death and dying and practical issues before there is a crisis of knowledge, when they have to deal with the death of someone close to them. Family discussion about what people want in their funeral or how they want their property dealt with after death can be a valuable preparation to greater openness when there is a crisis. Social workers can encourage open discussion in their daily interaction with clients, picking up on an opportunity to talk about death and dying. However, we also have to deal with situations where the ideal has not been achieved and people are unsure what to say. We may have to deal as well with situations where cultural expectations are to avoid discussion of death, even with professionals, or where an individual prefers not to have this discussion, even though cultural expectations permit it; there is individual as well as cultural variation.

An important issue in bereavement is notification. Often a professional or the medical or caring team is the first to know that someone has died. When a death is confirmed, family members are usually informed before it is announced more widely. Often after disasters or accidents, for example, the police or media do not announce the identity of deceased people until the family is informed. When the family is told; there may be conflict over who should be told and who should be excluded. Family divisions and attitudes can be important aspects of communication at this time. This often happens when families have been re-formed after divorce; children of the earlier marriage may be excluded. Members of families who have been excluded from funerals or memorial events frequently seek help from social workers or spiritual care advisers.

Issues of notification: Michael

Michael had always shared a house with his brother, Tim, and they disliked a number of relatives who lived nearby. When Tim was diagnosed with cancer and went into the hospital, Michael tried to prevent the relatives from finding out. A relative discovered his hospitalization by telephoning the hospital and asking after him; the hospital confirmed his admission. Tim subsequently died, and Michael sought to avoid having other family members find out the time and place of the funeral, which he relocated to a nearby town. Some family members were very angry about this, and complained to the hospital that their relative's illness had been concealed from them, while the hospital felt that they had been complying with their patient's wishes. The relatives felt that they were unable to grieve properly, while Michael felt that he had attained a dignified funeral.

When neighbors and people in the community are aware of the family having been notified of a death, announcements may be made more widely. This is part of the social process of setting members of the bereaved family apart from normal social relationships, or requiring extra solicitousness toward them. Often, people gather together to support each other.

Social Work and End-of-Life Communication

Pause and reflect—Communication in end-of-life care

What reasons can you identify that would make communication more important for social workers than for health-care professionals? Can you also identify reasons why social work in end-of-life care might require stronger or different communication skills than other social work specialties?

Some suggestions

All health-care professionals have interpersonal interactions with people about difficult issues in their lives and may have to convey complex hard-to-understand information. The social work role presents three additional challenges. First, social work focuses on emotional responses about difficult issues in people's lives; many people find it difficult to talk about emotions. This may be because they are socialized from an early age not to express emotions to others, particularly strangers. Also, emotions are complex and people may not have the language or capacity for self-exploration to deal with emotional material effectively. Second, most health-care practice, including much counseling and psychotherapy, focuses on individual "patients" or "clients," whereas social work has a systems view, concentrating on communities, families and social networks. Therefore, social workers work with a wider range of people, who may already have difficulties in communication among them, before the social worker raises end-of-life issues. Third, social work helps people get services and support from other agencies, and takes a lead role in facilitating communications among agencies, where, again, staff may feel discomfort with end-of-life issues. Because social workers often carry messages from one participant in an end-of-life situation to others, clarity and appropriateness in communication is crucial to their practice.

Communication at the end of life might require stronger or different communication skills than other forms of social work because people experience strong emotions around the hope that they will not die, or the truth that they are dying. Social workers involved in end-of-life care may, therefore, have more frequent and more demanding involvement in situations where powerful emotions are circulating than many social workers. Their practice may also evoke strong reactions to their own death, and they will have to manage the boundaries around the disclosure of their own emotions and reactions to their clients' situation.

Case example: Claudette

Claudette was a hospice social worker in her late thirties who married but was unable to conceive a child. After medical assistance, in itself traumatic for her, she was able to conceive. Then, on two occasions, she experienced miscarriages in the early stages of pregnancy. Although she enjoyed working in a hospice, she found that talking with people about death every day in her work was emotionally stressful. She found it hard not to talk about her own feelings of loss. Eventually, she moved to an alternative social work job.

TRUTH AND HOPE:
CRUCIAL CONCEPTS IN END-OF-LIFE COMMUNICATION

Balancing truth and hope in people's lives helps to develop social work skills in end-of-life communication. In this section, we discuss each of these concepts and connect them with the ideas about loss and change discussed in Chapter 1.

Truth may be defined as a fact that has been verified, a statement that accords with observable reality. Such definitions raise questions about how and to what extent truths may be verified, and how and to what extent it is possible to observe and agree about what is reality. For example, we saw in Chapter 2 how with the advance of medical science it is sometimes hard to know when the dividing line between life and death has been crossed. Similarly, we saw that there are different religious and social views about what life and death consists of, and it is difficult to know the truth about how illnesses will progress. Medical prognoses cannot predict the time of death accurately, though many patients ask. However, we also saw that people expect medical science to be more exact than it is; they expect truth when there is uncertainty.

The reality of individual variation and the consequent uncertainty opens the door to hope, the desire or wish that a future expectation will be fulfilled. Hope is concerned with future events; it has two aspects. The first is a rational assessment of the probability that something will happen. The second is the emotional response that a person has to the future event.

Case example: Donald

Donald was home recovering from an operation for pro-state cancer, hoping for a long period of reasonable health. The rational part of his hope came from what hospital staff may have told him about the likely progress of treatment and of the illness. The emotional part came from what "getting well" and "home" meant to him. He had previously lived an independent life and had thought he would be able to return to that. After a lifetime of work, he found being at home boring and so had started driving a cab to earn extra money, to get out and feel that he was contributing. He later told his nurse that he felt too tired to carry on with this, and the cab company decided not to reemploy him for a period. Having a job, contributing to the household income, and not being around the house were aspects of his masculinity that he felt he had lost; he felt he had nothing to contribute to the family.

Donald had been told that there was a statistical risk of impotence and therefore he might lose the capacity to have an erection and achieve normal sexual intercourse after the operation.

The emotional element of his hope was affected by how important both his work and an active sex life was for him, he saw these as symbols of his masculinity. He valued the treatment that removed his cancer, but balanced extended life with loss of potency. His emotional response to "going home" was therefore more mixed than he had at first expected. The rational and emotional aspects of his response might be affected by a social worker's help in a variety of ways, for example, some advice in gaining sexual satisfaction in ways other than conventional sexual intercourse.

Since uncertainty is inherent in end-of-life care, hope and truth interact. People may have unrealistic hopes; the question for practitioners is how far they should disturb these hopes.

Pause and reflect—three case examples: Truth and professional trust

Generally, professionals, including social workers, are expected to be honest and truthful in their dealings with the people they serve. How would you respond in the following three common situations? If you feel that truthfulness is required, how would you present the truth? These are all end-of-life rather than palliative care scenarios, that is, they are everyday practice situations unconnected with a service that specializes in responding to death and dying issues:

Mr. Altmann has been becoming increasingly frail for a number of years, has had several falls while out shopping and now prefers to stay within his home, with neighbors doing his shopping. Then, he has a fall at home, and the social worker visits to assess his needs; the home has become disorganized and he is not feeding or washing himself adequately. Mr. Altmann says to the social worker: "I really feel I'm going downhill; I'm feeling very old just now. I don't know how long I can go on like this."

Mrs. Brant is admitted to a care home for elders. The caregiver works through the admission forms with her and she answers the questions willingly enough and is cheerful and positive about her move. The caregiver comes to the questions: "Have you made a will?" and "Do you have any preferences for your funeral arrangements?" She feels perhaps that Mrs. Brant is not at the stage of discussing such matters, so she thinks about leaving out these questions.

The social worker is visiting Mrs. Hooper, who has advanced breast cancer but has not yet told her thirteen-year-old daughter, Judy, that she has recently been told that no more curative treatment is possible. Judy asks the social worker, in her mother's presence: "We will be able to go on vacation this summer, won't we?"

Some suggestions

Mr. Altmann's comment is an opportunity to discuss his fears of increasing disability or death. In frailty or long-term illness trajectories, such comments are often an expression of fears of deterioration or death and people make them in the hope of stimulating a conversation. Therefore, it is appropriate to take them up. If Mr. Altmann did not intend to raise such issues, he can close off the conversation, and he is left knowing that the practitioner would be prepared to discuss such material in the future, which may give him the confidence to raise the issues when he needs or is able to deal with them. The practitioner might ask general questions about what he thinks about the future, refining these down to more specific points about his options. It is also useful to begin with clarifying precisely how Mr. Altmann sees the position. The practitioner could ask what particular events have led Mr. Altmann to feel that he is elderly or deteriorating. This might reveal specific concerns that need to be reported to a doctor or require intervention. If appropriate, it would also permit the practitioner to make a comment such as: "It seems as if you think that these changes are unstoppable," or "I wonder if you are thinking about whether we need to do more to help you."

Many residential care situations fail to ask the kind of standard question that Mrs. Brant should be asked. Practitioners use their discretion not to upset residents by asking unnecessarily. As a result, the information is not available when required or the questions need to be asked when it is even more upsetting or they cannot be asked because it is too late. Often, older people are comfortable with discussion about their death, having thought through their views, and are also practical about making appropriate arrangements for their affairs. It is helpful to preface the questions with the suggestion that it is useful for the care home to have information about a number of points in case of an emergency or to deal with any matters that come up later. Another point is that not all admission questions have to be asked at the same time or at inappropriate times. If Mrs. Brant is fussing over hanging her clothes, it might be more appropriate to say: "There are some additional points we need to go through, and I'll sit down with you later just to finish them off." With both Mr. Altmann and Mrs. Brant, you might think more about an organized system of advance care planning (see Chapter 8).

Judy's question raises issues of how far to go. We do not want to interfere with her mother's parental responsibilities but children benefit from openness, even if parents find it uncomfortable to start a discussion that they have difficulty in taking on board themselves; for many people, a comparable issue is when and how to raise sexual issues with their children. Judy may be expressing a need for truth, since she may have asked the question to push the adults into telling her what she wants to know. However, her question may also reflect unrealistic hope. Practitioners cannot know all that is going on in the relationship between mother and child, and other relationships may also be important, since the father or brothers and sisters may resist knowing or telling. A useful approach, therefore, may be to highlight for the mother the importance of the child's uncertainty and highlight for the child that there is uncertainty by saying something that acknowledges the child's concerns such as: "I realize that your mother's illness must make you feel worried about how things are going to turn out."

BAD NEWS

What Is "Bad News"?

Bad news is any information that adversely and seriously affects individuals' views of their life or future. Bad news is a message that has the potential, if people perceive it as truth, to shatter hopes for the future. People on the receiving end of bad news begin to reconsider their life and future, and this may involve both loss and change. A particular bad-news issue in end-of-life care is learning that you are going to die soon. Physicians are usually responsible for communicating this bad news to people at some point during treatment for an illness. Social expectations about how physicians should do this have changed over time, with greater openness now expected in Western cultures, although this is still unacceptable in many Eastern cultures. Research on how best to give bad news of this kind has led to some clear guidance about appropriate approaches. Other health-care professionals and social workers are affected because, after the initial communication from a physician, they are involved in confirming the assessment or aspects of it, helping people respond to it, and dealing with the consequences of it.

We saw in Chapter 2 that there is usually a series of phases as patients' awareness grows, rather than one clear moment of communication, when the diagnosis of a life-threatening illness is made. Along the illness trajectory, further bad news can occur at any point but is most likely associated with treatment options or the lack of them, disease progression, and deterioration. As we have seen in the case examples above, bad news may creep up on people as part of a frailty or long-term conditions trajectory, or as a result of a fall or other mishap. The bad news begins to dawn on the patient, who may ask questions of anybody. When this happens, it is important to make sure that the patient has a chance to talk to an appropriate physician for an authoritative medical view, since responsibility for diagnosis and prognosis is primarily medical. It is easy for a social worker in a long-term relationship with a client whose condition has worsened for some time, to slip into assumptions about frailty or progression of a disease. A careful medical assessment might point to possible preventive or treatment action.

Patients may not always understand fully what is said in a diagnostic interview or may want to discuss the implications further once the medical consultation has ended, perhaps after a period for the news to sink in and for family discussion. Therefore, other members of the multipro-fessional team must have the necessary communication skills to respond and support patients and their families appropriately. The social worker in the team is well placed to help because of the psychosocial conse-quences of bad news.

Emphasizing the bad-news status of a "short" prognosis, that is, a patient has only a short time to live, is an example of medicalization. It focuses on the assumption of cure and the medical diagnosis rather than the social consequences of the news: some people are pleased to know that their struggle will soon be ended. It also draws from palliative care an emphasis on prognosis for a definable disease, which is unhelpful for many people approaching the end of life. In a cancer trajectory, they may have received a diagnosis and prescription of drug, radiation, surgical, or other treatment at an early stage of an illness, and have lived with the ill-ness for many years, with relapses and remissions. The point at which their trajectory will soon lead to death is unclear. This may also be true for patients with HIV/AIDS. In a long-term-conditions trajectory, they may have experienced several crises and recovered quite well from them. For professionals it may be hard to know, and for patients and their families hard to accept, that the latest crisis may be the last. People in a frailty tra-jectory experience a slow, continuing diminution in their physical health and social functioning that often makes it impossible for a physician to give an end-of-life prognosis. Nevertheless, many people are aware of the likelihood of death at some point in the foreseeable future, and may need to discuss this to make suitable arrangements and complete important life tasks.

The social consequence of moving toward the end of life is that peo-ple often face a series of painful losses. They experience loss of social roles, employment, status, independence, body image, weight. They lose physical functions such as continence, and mobility. Perhaps most impor-tant, there may be loss of identity and dignity; then, there is loss of life. At each of these transitions, professionals communicate bad news in some way. For example, it might be the physical therapist who offers someone a wheelchair for the first time. Or it might be that the nurse decides that the time has come to hoist someone who has previously been able to transfer into her bath with assistance. As a patient becomes weaker, he or she may no longer be able to hold a ceramic cup and may therefore be given a plastic one. Such an apparently simple transition may be perceived as bad news because of what it symbolizes. A seemingly disproportionate emotional response needs investigation, because this particular change may be a symbol of loss of hope. Losses may be com-pounded by more losses, but the way these are communicated to patients affects how they feel about themselves. The experience of continued losses, especially significant losses, can lead us to question the meaning of life and can cause spiritual distress and pain (Moss, 2002). The personal account given at the end of this chapter is a good illustration of how this happens and particularly clearly expresses the nature of the spiritual issues that dying people face, since it expresses both negative and positive spirituality.

Helping People Deal with Bad News

The impact of being given bad news varies according to how the individual perceives the news and sees his or her future at the time. Therefore, it is important to gain a picture of how people see their progress, so that a fairly routine progression in treatment does not lead to serious upset. Practitioners need to be aware that change is a truth, and that it impacts on hope. You can say: "I wonder if you feel a bit unsafe getting into the bath like this. Perhaps we could try one of our hoists to see if that would be helpful for you?"

Assessment skills and sensitivity are, therefore, central to understanding where an individual is at on the information continuum and to meet his or her need for information appropriately. "Traditionally, healthcare professionals have determined the type, amount and format of the information given to patients in a health-care setting" (Drew & Fawcett, 2002, p. 443). Consequently, personalizing change means finding out, before any potentially bad-news communication, how patients and families understand and view the position, and what is concerning them about it. "Do you think your illness has gotten better or worse since we last met?" is a question that can lead on to: "How is that affecting you?" and then to: "Do you have any worries about that?" Also, people's information needs may change during the course of their illness, and they may need information repeated or highlighted. Such precise questions are also better than "How are you?" which invites a conventional positive response.

Usually, patients and family members raise issues that allow you to build a personal and direct statement of your assessment and the evidence for it. You can then give advice about further plans for treatment or care, involving them in making the arrangements. Then you can ask for questions, comments, and any other points. If it seems reasonable, you could ask the patient or family member to sum up, so that you can be sure of how much or how little they have understood.

When possible, written information can be useful in supporting information given verbally. Often patients can have a copy of a letter or report that will be written anyway. Offering a telephone number to call with any questions that arise later also helps. Patients will inevitably forget some information or need clarification after the interview; or they may become uncertain, and other family members may raise questions later too.

BALANCING TRUTH AND HOPE

Truth and hope have many positives, but they also have negatives. Truth may be confrontational; hope may be evasive. "The care provider may need to help family members balance their desire to avoid the reality of the terminal illness with their need to accept it" (Jeffreys, 2005, p. 198).

Pause and reflect—case example: The Jeranovic family

Mrs. Jeranovic was seriously ill with cervical cancer and needed to move to a care home. But when in the hospital for treatment, she expressed the wish to be able to go home and live independently. The social worker, asked to start the process for her move to a care home, felt that her hope was unrealistic. She talked through with Mrs. Jeranovic what she was currently able to do independently and how realistic it was for her to go home at present; she then discussed the benefits that a care home would offer. This led to a complaint from Mrs. Jeranovic's family that the social worker was ignoring their mother's wishes, not organizing the services she needed to progress, and being negative, upsetting their mother.

In this case, it seems that the practitioner has appropriately confronted Mrs. Jeranovic with the truth, which will allow decisions about her future care to be made with her consent and involvement. Yet neither she nor the family was ready for what this would mean. Can you think of ways in which you could have dealt with the situation that might have avoided the complaint and helped Mrs. Jeranovic to make progress?

Some suggestions

In this case, and in general, it is helpful to try to leave as many options as possible to permit flexibility for professionals and for clients and their families. The remainder of this section suggests a number of helpful strategies that are relevant to many situations. A more complex case, that of Colin and his family, which also uses many of these suggestions is described in Chapter 4.

Self-Assessment

Inviting the client and family members to say how they assess their present situation may, as with "bad news," make it possible to identify different views and clarify uncertainty.

"I Don't Know"

"I don't know" and "Nobody really knows" are important messages to be able to give. They help to maintain confidence and hope.

Plans A and B

It may therefore be useful to help people "plan for the worst while hoping for the best." Assumptions in the agency about the usual course of action may lead you to expect things that the client has not yet accepted. The practitioner could have worked through with Mrs. Jeranovic what would be involved in a return home. Then she could have suggested "plan B" in case the first plan did not work out. This approach acknowledges and values the client's view of the situation. Clarifying what would be needed to achieve plan A makes it easier for the client later to understand precisely why it could not be achieved, and helps the client accept the realities that require the use of plan B. Clarification also helps clients and family identify more helping resources in the family or community that might make their hopes realizable.

Choice and Control

For patients to have as much control as possible at the end of their life despite their terminal illness or deteriorating condition (remember, this is part of our social work agenda for end-of-life care—see Chapter 1) they need to know that they are dying, and must want to acknowledge this (Dunn & Forman, 2002, p. 123). This requires honesty and openness on the part of the practitioner, the patient, and often the patient's family. Ethically, people must be given information about their situation to enable them to make informed decisions. Having done this, it is important to help them come to the decisions they want to make, what to put off and what actions to take.

Even when people say that they want to know "everything," it is not always straightforward. "Everything" may include something unexpected that the person did not want to hear. People who want to know everything often expect that it will provide certainty, when everything usually includes uncertainty. Also, some people want to hear everything, but members of their family do not. Then, either communications are sent but not received and need to be repeated, or only some people can participate in making decisions.

People who "do not want to know" can also present complications. They often switch from facing the knowledge that they are dying one moment to planning their future the next. It is difficult to live with knowing that death is imminent twenty-four hours a day. As with grieving processes, therefore (see Chapter 7), people move in and out of knowing and appearing not to know.

Case example: Heather

Heather is someone whose hope became increasingly unbalanced between her emotional commitment to going home and a rational assessment that this was unrealistic. Age fifty, she had suffered from ALS for two years but remained positive and determined. She was admitted to a hospice for palliative rehabilitation, hoping that intensive physical therapy would improve her mobility and general strength. This achieved, she hoped to go home again with visiting paid caregivers. However, the hospice team looking after her found that she was gradually becoming weaker and more fatigued; also, her breathing was becoming shallower. As her physical condition deteriorated, the social worker worked to support her emotionally as she came to accept that her life was slipping away from her. This involved drawing out Heather's own perceptions about changes in her condition, enabling her to balance truth and hope.

The practitioner devised a new plan with Heather with achievable aims. Since her home was so important to her, continued connection with it helped maintain her emotional strength. She made plans to visit for a few hours to say goodbye to her home, her cat, and her garden. This made it unnecessary to discuss Heather's death. She accepted the practical arrangements, as a "plan B," while maintaining the emotional strength gained by hoping for another opportunity to live at home. Thinking through her priorities on her visit was motivating. Included in this was clarifying long-term arrangements for the care of her cat, building on the informal arrangements made for her period in the hospice. Taking responsibility in this way often helps people build their hope for the quality of life of those that they leave behind after they die.

COMMUNICATING ABOUT DEATH AND DYING WITH PEOPLE WHO HAVE INTELLECTUAL DISABILITIES (ID)

Exclusion of People with ID from Family Members' Deaths

People with ID present particular communication issues as they move toward the end of life. Those with complex needs are living longer than in the past. For example, in 1939, the mean age of death for people with Down syndrome was twelve years, whereas 80 percent of people with Down syndrome are now expected to live over fifty years (Brown, 2003, pp. 16–17); many survive into old age. Therefore, ID services may be based on an out-of-date assumption that people will die early; relatives may have been told this in early childhood and so may not be expecting to provide care for an aging person with ID.

Caregivers, both paid and informal, have in the past restricted communication with people with ID by withholding information and keeping secrets from them. Diagnosis of terminal illness is often late because people may communicate ill-health behaviorally, and ID may mask other symptoms.

As little as thirty years ago, people with ID were thought not to experience the emotions of grief following the death of someone close (Blackman, 2003, p. 38). It is still common not to inform or involve people with ID when a family member has a life-threatening illness, and this may lead to difficulties at the bereavement stage.

Case example: Mrs. Onukwe and Jeanette

Mrs. Onukwe was diagnosed with renal cancer with a prognosis of a few weeks. The social worker found that Jeanette, her daughter with ID, was cared for in supported housing by a mainly paraprofessional team, which had decided not to "upset" Jeanette by telling her about the likelihood that her mother would die soon; they thought that it would be best to inform Jeanette when this had happened. The social worker persuaded them to inform Jeanette, and reinforce the information by encouraging her to spend time with her mother. She argued that this would enable Jeanette and her mother to carry out important life tasks together. They created a memory box together (see Chapter 5) and talked about what her mother wanted to take place during her funeral, which Jeanette attended.

Assumptions

Similar assumptions may be made when the person with ID is dying, with damaging consequences. For example, it may be assumed that a person with ID may be unable to consent to treatment, and family members or social workers may have to ask for additional time to take a patient through a consent process. Professionals who are not accustomed to working with people with ID may fail to offer helpful treatments because they assume that patients will be unable to cope with the treatment. This may include positive experiences such as artistic work, which can offer fulfilling experiences (Hartley & Payne, 2008). Treatments may not be offered because professionals assume that a person with ID has a low quality of life and will not benefit from an expensive treatment. On the other hand, ID service specialists may have no experience of helping patients with more advanced treatments and may not be aware of the range of support that a palliative care service can offer.

Case example: Dorothy

Dorothy was a woman in her fifties, with ID, living alone supported by a visiting team of nurses and paraprofessional caregivers, having been discharged from a long-stay ID facility in her forties. She was a heavy smoker and developed throat cancer, which threatened to obstruct her esophagus. She had been in the habit of preparing and eating thick sandwiches using crusty bread for most meals, having learned the skills involved in preparing them in her discharge program. She also ate very quickly, a habit picked up in the institution. Caregivers now found it necessary to teach her how to prepare more suitable dishes, to eat in smaller bites, and to chew more effectively. As the esophagus became more blocked, the cancer surgeon offered an operation to insert a stent (a mesh tube) to enable Dorothy to take food normally. Paraprofessionals working with her were very upset by the idea of such an operation and how it would feel to have such a tube inserted in her throat; it was important that they felt confident and supportive in presenting the information to Dorothy. The social worker involved asked the palliative home care nurse to explain to the staff the benefits and problems of using this technique. The ID team then produced diagrams to explain repeatedly, over more than a week, to Dorothy what was being proposed, to facilitate gaining her informed consent to the operation. She had very little speech, but was upset by her inability to eat normally, and eventually decided that she would have the operation, which helped her for some while.

Practice Challenges

Telling a person with ID about a terminal diagnosis is likely to take time rather than being a once-only event (Blackman & Todd, 2005, p. 18). As with all patients, the amount of information given will depend on how much the person wants to know and his or her level of understanding (Blackman & Todd, 2005). The information given might increase in detail as the patient assimilates it. It may be helpful to give information as issues arise. The doctor who would usually give fairly comprehensive information in one consultation could be asked to provide guidance to paraprofessional caregivers.

Other challenges in working with people with ID who have a terminal illness or are approaching the end of life include supporting people to make their own decisions, enabling people to access services, and tackling problems of organizational culture and poor attitudes towards those with ID. ID practitioners may lack confidence to question and challenge providers of end-of-life care as advocates for their patients, partly because they may lack knowledge about available resources and services. Palliative care staff have expertise in pain assessment, for example, but because of communication difficulties may not be well placed to achieve good symptom control. Therefore, it is important that all staff work together to ensure that physical and emotional pain is appropriately assessed and treated (Tuffrey-Wijne, 2002).

Some Guidelines

Social workers need to consider the issues around consent to treatment, choice, control, and end-of-life decisions. People with ID are people first and have the right to information about their illness, treatment, and care presented in a way that they can understand and that will help them. "Close cooperation between all professionals, carers, family members and—most importantly—the client, together with the mutual sharing of expertise, is needed to ensure best possible care" (Tuffrey-Wijne, 2002, p. 231). Communication and spirituality are both important when supporting people through their own illness and helping those with ID understand the dying process. It is helpful to use simple language and go beyond words with visual aids and pictures, or use drawing and art to communicate, as in Dorothy's case.

Specialized books exist (Donaghey, 2002) to help people with ID who have cancer understand what is happening to them at the treatment stage, but it is more difficult to find material that helps with end-of-life care and dying. Increasingly, there are narrative accounts told by people with ID of their own journeys through terminal illness (see for example, Tuffrey-Wijne & Davies, 2007). It may be useful to use a communication board or memory book, and always use signs the person recognizes. As with all patients, it is usually helpful to get patients to explain what they understand about what is happening to them and try to make that meaningful. Improving access to information about terminal illness and dying is therefore crucial (Jones et al., 2006). Being open is fundamental to treating people with ID with respect and honesty.

Relationships are valuable, so it is useful to involve other family members and friends. Social workers can be alongside the person, supporting him or her through feelings of distress. An unfamiliar world of hospitals and medical staff can be very frightening and leave the person with ID feeling more isolated and disadvantaged. Being there in the role of advocate is, however, only one part of the social work role. Reaching out to the person on an emotional level and helping to make him or her feel more secure is equally important.

HOPE: A PERSONAL VIEW

This account of her experiences, written by a person with a diagnosis of advanced cancer, evokes the positive power of hope and the way in which the whole environment of care, including other patients and their families and conventional expressions of good wishes by friends sending cards and flowers, may contribute to hope. It also expresses the importance of emotions such as guilt and love in the process of dying.

When I was admitted to the hospice, my only wish was to die. The pain was so severe and my general feeling so distressing that hope or expectancy did not enter my conscious mind. My only thought was to get out of living, with the utmost expediency and the minimum of physical and mental awareness. Quality of life in the sense of meaning of life and purpose are all important to me. During that period my family and in particular my daughter [who had campaigned for hospice care] were very concerned and loving to me. After two to three weeks, I began to feel a little better and to realize I was not yet going to die. However, this realization brought with it thoughts about the emptiness of my future and the fear of being bedridden and a burden. I was not happy at being alive, and when my daughter visited me and I expressed these feelings quite thoughtlessly, I suddenly became aware of how deeply I had hurt her. [She had been fighting] for peace and dignity at the end of people's lives and seeing her own mother regretting being alive [raised questions about] her work. I felt terribly guilty and full of remorse. Fortunately, my dear son, levelheaded as his father was, resolved the situation and brought back peace. The emotional intensity during those few days was like a catharsis for me. I resolved that I had to do everything in my power to get better. From being unable to walk more than a few feet, with the help and encouragement of the [physical therapist], the nurses, and even total strangers who were witnessing my daily increasing walks up and down the corridor calling approvingly: "How many is it today?" or "Are you training for the marathon?" I tackled stairs, gradually washing myself alone and slowly regaining some independence.

At the same time too, going through the enormous amount of cards, flowers, messages, prayers, and other people's thinking of me, I realized that not only family but others too genuinely did not want me to die. It was a kind of telepathic communication where they had all congregated to increase the impact.

My efforts to regain my former sense of well-being and independence have continued since and are still persisting. I gradually got rid of my home caregivers, refused the offer of a stair-lift and various bathroom gadgets, first walked a few yards outside my house, gradually increasing the distances, pushing my wheelchair and only sitting back in it when too tired to proceed, until at present I manage what I call my constitutional walk of about one and a half miles taking about forty minutes. I am receiving friends, enjoy being taken out, shopping, an art exhibition; all partly in my wheelchair but sadly not driving anymore.

I admit sometimes it requires great effort to counteract my unwillingness or tiredness, but my fear of losing my mobility and being a burden spurs me on. I bought a pretty feminine walking stick decorated with colorful flowers, which for me epitomizes my acceptance and defiance.

My thanks [to the hospice and its staff] are far deeper than words can express. It is not only for the physical palliative care, but for its profound mental and in particular spiritual help. It has revived my interest in philosophy and religion [and] restored my faith in humanity in the sense that amidst all the exterior shallowness there is much goodness. I have become aware that if one is unhappy, one is selfish, thinking only of one's own desires; but if one feels at peace and contented, one's thoughts are for others, particularly those who love you. I do not want to die yet, I feel I am still of some use to others, and I hope my deterioration and end will not be too unbearable. (Downman, 2008, p. 429–430).

CONCLUSION

This chapter has emphasized the importance of communication skills in helping people approaching the end of life to understand that they are coming toward death and to balance the rational truth of their situation with their emotional hope for the future.

FURTHER READING

Sheldon, F. (1997). *Psychosocial palliative care: Good practice in the care of the dying and bereaved.* Cheltenham, England: Thornes. We consider this the best short general book about palliative care social work practice.

Read, S.(2007). *Bereavement counselling for people with learning disabilities: A handbook.* London: Quay. A useful, practical guideline, including many skills that can be used before death.

Tuffrey-Wijne, I, & Davies, J. (2007). This is my story: I've got cancer. "The Veronica Project": an ethnographic study of the experiences of people with learning disabilities who have cancer. *British Journal of Learning Disabilities, 35;* 7–11.

Tuffrey-Wijne, I., Hollins, S., and Curfs, L. (2005). End-of-life and palliative care for people with intellectual disabilities who have cancer or other life-limiting illness: A review of the literature and available resources. *Journal of Applied Research on Intellectual Disabilities, 20;* 331–44. These two papers give, respectively, a very good impression of the issues that people with intellectual or learning disabilities face at the end of life, and a general review of the research and literature.

JOURNALS

The major journals in palliative care are primarily medical and written by and for physicians, although they claim to be multiprofessional and occasionally carry papers about social matters, again written with a medical focus. These include:

- *American Journal of Hospice and Palliative Medicine,* Sage journals.
- *Palliative Medicine,* Sage journals.

Two general journals that have a more multiprofessional editorial policy and often carry excellent papers on social and spiritual issues are:

- *Journal of Palliative Care,* Centre for Bioethics, Clinical Research Institute of Montreal, 110 Pine Avenue West, Montreal, QC, Canada H2W 1R7
- *Progress in Palliative Care,* Maney publishing.

A major palliative nursing journal also often covers social and spiritual issues:

- *International Journal of Palliative Nursing,* MA Healthcare.
- The *Journal of Hospice and Palliative Nursing* (WoltersKluwer) is not in our view so useful for material on social issues, but may be useful to American readers in keeping in touch with palliative nursing issues in their country.

Chapter 4

ENGAGING AND ASSESSING IN END-OF-LIFE CARE

CHAPTER AIMS

The main aim of this chapter is to understand how to engage with clients approaching the end of life and how to assess their psychosocial needs.

After working through this chapter, readers should be able to:

- Identify counseling skills helpful in engaging in relationships with people at the end of life;
- Use a narrative approach to elicit clients' and family members' understandings of the end-of-life situation;
- Understand the value of exploring clients', families', and caregivers reactions to advanced illness and care needs;
- Manage a family meeting/conference;
- Identify and respond to difficulties in building relationships with clients, families, and caregivers; and
- Deal with their own personal difficulties in end-of-life situations and respond to clients' difficult emotions and behaviors.

SOCIAL WORK ENGAGEMENT AND ASSESSMENT IN END-OF-LIFE CARE

We argued in Chapter 3 that communication is fundamental to working with people in end-of-life care; allowing practitioners first to engage and then to assess and intervene with clients (Oliviere, Hargreaves, & Monroe, 1997). These processes, dealt with in this and the following chapter, build on communication skills and on understanding clients and their situation which are influenced by language and class, cultural factors, emotions, and the personalities involved (del Rio, 2004, p. 454).

Gelderd and Gelderd (2005) distinguish basic counseling skills for engaging people in a relationship and beginning to elicit their story from skills used in integrative counseling to help people change, which we cover in Chapter 5. Among the basic skills are:

- Greeting and observing clients and putting them at ease
- Inviting them to talk and tuning in to their attitudes and feelings
- Listening with interest, using minimal responses such as "uh-huh," "I see," "OK," and stronger invitations to continue, such as "and then . . ."
- Expressing support and interest through nonverbal behavior
- Speaking clearly at a suitable speed and volume and accepting silence appropriately
- Paraphrasing (not repeating) content to check and demonstrate understanding
- Experiencing and reflecting back your understanding of feelings that the client expresses
- Summarizing at appropriate points your overall understanding of what clients have said
- Closing the session comfortably

All these are commonplace social work counseling skills, directed here to people facing the end of their lives. This means that they will be dealing with a number of issues:

- Managing the practical and emotional consequences of increasing frailty, a progressive condition, or a life-threatening illness
- Responding to the "bad news" (see Chapter 3) of a short prognosis
- Living their life with their family and within a community
- Completing social and relationship tasks
- Preparing for death

End-of-life and palliative care present two different contexts for social work assessment. Social work engagement and assessment in palliative care start from medical and health-care assessments, but have a different focus. Physicians and nurses collect basic psychological, social, and spiritual data during their work. Collecting and organizing coherent information for psychological and social assessment may be left for social work colleagues; major pieces of information may be missing. For example, factual information about family relationships may be displayed in a genogram or family tree, but qualitative information about relationships or family difficulties may not be recorded. Also, such difficulties are likely to emerge later, as trust is built within the service.

In the end-of-life care context, social care services offering support in daily living may be separate from health-care services. For example, someone with long-term progressive conditions such as Parkinson's disease or cerebral palsy, serious injuries resulting from traumatic traffic accidents, or mental illness will often have social services that include social work support separately organized from medical or nursing care. Therefore, psychological and social assessments as such clients approach the end of life may be quite separated in time or service from important medical and nursing information. It may be hard to find out accurate information about changes in medical or nursing care decisions that have psychological and social consequences.

End-of-life concerns, therefore, will often be a specific aspect of a wider assessment system in a home care or other social agency, for example in health-related social work in a hospital or community health-care setting. The practitioner will identify within the established assessment system the particular end-of-life issues that emerge in wider work with the patient. Alternatively, social work assessment will be undertaken as a specialized activity within a palliative or hospice care setting, where the primary focus is on medical and nursing assessment. In both cases, social work end-of-life assessment relies less on end-of-life-specific or palliative-care-specific assessment tools and more on successful engagement with clients and their families to contribute a psychological, social, and spiritual element to a wider end-of-life assessment.

In this chapter, therefore, we build on Chapter 3 by focusing first on using narrative approaches to engage with clients and their families, as a basis for understanding relationships and needs that require social work intervention. Later in the chapter, we examine some basic assessment tools.

TAKING A NARRATIVE APPROACH

Our aim in end-of-life care is to intervene in a way that is right for an individual in his or her unique social context and to enable clients and their families to maintain their control of the situations and make informed choices and decisions about their care. What makes the interventions "right" is whether they are appropriate to meet the individuals' needs in the unique way that connects them more strongly with their emotions and cognitions. To do this, practitioners engage with the people involved to assess what is uniquely required in a particular situation.

A useful way to engage with clients' and families' needs and concerns is to take a narrative approach. This focuses on their primary concerns by asking them to tell a "story," which will include a sequence of events linked with the client's own explanations. Workers extract information required for intervention from the narrative, maintaining a connection between this agency-required information and the client's own focus. One way to explain the process to people is to say that finding ways of helping them is like doing a jigsaw puzzle. All the pieces are there and the story helps to organize them. Practitioners, clients, and families work together to fit the pieces together to give the right picture. Other functions of narrative assessment include building trust by listening to clients' perception of their experiences, reducing uncertainty by ensuring that everything is transparent, preventing unrealistic expectations by putting concerns into their developing context, allowing patients to adjust to and build a relationship with practitioners, and preventing a conspiracy of silence (Fisher & Barnett, 2002, p. 33).

The following case example about Colin and his wife illustrates several points:

- Why the practitioner needed to understand Colin's family and social background, his role within his marriage, and the vulnerabilities of his partner before being able to offer appropriate help; stimulating a narrative was important in achieving this
- Using plan A and plan B tactics (see Chapter 3) in which possibilities for intervention are constructed as alternate narratives
- How the balance of power and roles within a relationship alter as one of the partners becomes seriously ill; see also Chapter 5 on protecting vulnerable adults
- The importance of enabling people to complete unfinished life tasks so that they can die at peace. When time is short, completing personal business may become more important to clients than receiving further medical treatment that keeps them away from personal matters that they wish to address
- Using a family meeting or conference to find a way through apparently conflicting needs
- The value of enlisting support and help from other family members
- Why challenging denial is not always helpful
- Following on from the discussion in Chapter 3, offering hope even if the truth is that a long period of life is unlikely

Case example: Colin and Christa

Colin was admitted to a hospice because of a crisis at home. Both he and his wife, Christa, were in their eighties. Christa had a history of depression from early in their marriage following postnatal depression after the birth of two stillborn babies. Early in Colin's admission, he talked to the practitioner about his marriage, his wife's illness, his regrets and achievements. Colin felt that his support had kept Christa's depressive illness at bay. He had been his wife's caregiver and when his prostate cancer had made him too unwell to care for her, the situation at home had broken down. Local services provided paraprofessional caregivers to help at home, but Christa did not like people calling daily at their home to undertake tasks she saw as hers. This response is not unusual. Such help can be seen as threatening or intrusive to local, cultural, or social expectations of people's normal marital roles.

Christa became overwhelmed; she lost the confidence to drive and became unable to make decisions. She was neglecting her own self-care and was terrified of the responsibility of caring for her husband. When the social worker assessed Colin's wishes and needs, Colin was adamant that he wanted to go home, that he would somehow become stronger. He still had several financial and other family matters to resolve before he was ready to die, particularly Christa's financial security. Therefore, Colin and the practitioner explored the possibility of his going home. Initially, Colin was reluctant to consider making alterations to his home, but gradually he agreed it would be easier if he had a special bed downstairs. He also accepted that he would need visiting caregivers to help with personal care. But this still left several questions unanswered. Who would help him at night, how would the laundry, shopping, and cooking be done? How would he overcome Christa's reluctance to accept caregivers calling at the house several times a day?

Meanwhile, a physician talked to Colin about some disappointing test results that indicated his prognosis was very short. His deteriorating mobility and increasing fatigue were probably due to progressive disease and not the side-effects of pain-relief medication as Colin had hoped. The physical therapist confirmed that his weakness and difficulty with mobility were because of disease progression; she gently explained that he could not expect to get stronger. The multiprofessional team observed that Colin ignored this bad news and became angry with staff because they were not "making him stronger." Therefore, the social worker talked to Colin about having time at home to be able to sort his papers, see his financial adviser and lawyer, and put everything in order. Achieving these goals was essential to his psychological well-being; respecting their importance to him and understanding what was driving him was a prerequisite to meaningful planning with him. Colin's brother, Trevor, was key to resolving this situation in a way that would work for both Colin and Christa. He brought Christa each day to visit Colin at the hospice. Although he saw himself as primarily providing transportation, he also offered practical and emotional support to his brother and sister-in-law.

How a Family Meeting/Conference Helped

A family meeting/conference was held aimed at resolving these problems. Family meetings can be used as a structured form of family intervention, both in the community setting and, perhaps more commonly, in the hospice, palliative care unit, or care home. Held soon after admission, they allow information-sharing between practitioners, patients, and families. This can be useful to find out patients' and families' expectations of the admission and address misconceptions and fears that otherwise may remain unspoken. Family meetings may also be helpful to look at discharge plans and address the concerns and anxieties that the family may have.

For a family conference/meeting to be successful, a practitioner should be designated to chair the meeting or hold a key role for enabling the family to agree on the way forward. This practitioner then engages with significant family members and caregivers prior to the meeting to establish trust.

Neto and Trindade (2007, p. 106) suggest that as well as sharing information and feelings, a family conference/meeting "aims at changing and/or maximizing some of the patterns of interaction in the family." Difficult family meetings occur when there is family disagreement with the plan or some aspect of it. "It is not always possible to reach a consensus and there are sometimes very tense situations between families, patients and healthcare professionals" (Neto & Trindade, 2007, p. 108).

In Colin's family meeting, serious tensions between his wife and himself were resolved by recognizing Christa's unspoken difficulties and finding a different plan that took account of them. The social worker chaired Colin's meeting. Other people attending were Colin, Christa, Trevor, the primary nurse looking after Colin, the physician, physical therapist, occupational therapist, and the home-care nurse.

During the first part of the meeting, Colin explored his plan to use visiting services to enable him to stay at home. He insisted that the plan could work if Christa was not involved in any way in his care. However, Christa's body language was striking; she curled up in her chair, hiding her face under her arms. The social worker suggested to Colin that he ask Christa how she felt about his proposals, that Christa had to feel comfortable with his plans. With fear on her face, Christa was finally able to say that for her this discharge plan was impossible. It felt like dead-lock, but at least the reality of the difficulties was out in the open.

Following this, Colin was able to compromise a little, saying that he recognized that his plan could not work now, but that it would when he became stronger. It felt too destructive for Colin to challenge his denial in the meeting. However, the social worker took the opportunity to reframe the plans for discharge and to offer an alternate plan B. Knowing the resources in Colin and Christa's hometown, she suggested that Colin might move temporarily to a nursing home near their home; Christa could visit easily and he could get home for short periods to attend to his business.

Immediately, Colin agreed; knowing the nursing home, he saw this as a practical solution. But transportation was a problem because Christa worried about driving, and transferring Colin from wheelchair to car was difficult. The social worker suggested using wheelchair-friendly cabs for these journeys. Again, Colin was enthusiastic about this idea, seeing that he could do the things he wished. Christa also expressed a sense of relief from the burden of his care. The social worker asked Christa if the team could help her to look after herself, for example, by someone coming each day to help her get a meal. She resisted having outsiders in her home, so this was not the answer, but, through the discussion, she reached a solution herself: she could pay for a meal each day at the nursing home and eat with Colin. This is what happened.

Positive Responses to Denial

Despite the fact that the physician had given Colin the bad news about his prognosis, he was not ready to acknowledge it as a truth, and it was important to allow Colin the hope that he may be able to stay temporarily at the nursing home. Christa became used to visiting him at the nursing home, and having meals there. She got to know the staff. She came to have no interest in living in her own home. As Colin's disease advanced, he completed the tasks that would secure Christa's financial future. This enabled him to let go and die at peace with himself. Before he died, Christa decided to move into a room near Colin's in the home and to have all her care provided. Colin's brother arranged the practical details involved in the move, and Colin took care of the legal and financial issues.

Without understanding Colin's need to complete his life tasks, planning a discharge that was right both for Colin and for Christa was difficult. Christa's needs had to be assessed as well as Colin's to find a way forward. But it was only by the social work practitioner talking to Colin at the outset about his life, his fears for his wife, and his hopes that the team could really make progress at the later stage.

PERSONAL ENGAGEMENT

Careful listening is therefore key to engaging successfully with clients and moving forward toward assessment and intervention. Among the difficulties of listening are:

- Responding to silence. We have seen that end-of-life care involves dealing with important and powerful emotional responses. People may struggle to put into words what they need to say or may need to focus on and experience some of their reactions before they can express them. Social workers in end-of-life care need to see silence as an experience to share, rather than something to be hurried away.

- Resistance. Similarly, loss of expectations and identity may be so profound that people do not want to begin to express what is happening to them; it is important not to see this as resistance, but as a struggle to "come to terms" with change.

- Difference. To express and deal with difficult emotions, people need to trust their social worker. Therefore it is important to equalize status and social differences between practitioners and clients by engaging in a dialogue that is open to many influences, rather than being simply focused on what the worker wants to achieve.

- Body language and paralinguistics. People's tension and difficulty in communication, and much of their emotion, may be expressed in body language rather than in words; also, loss is often experienced physically (see Chapter 1). It is important for social workers to integrate into their understanding of the situation their awareness of physical reactions and experiences, and also to be aware of their own tension in dealing with difficult issues.

- Explanation. We saw in Chapter 2 that the end of life often occurs in a medicalized environment, where complex explanations, decisions, and consent processes are required. While death, dying, and bereavement are natural, personal, and social processes, people often have little experience of them. For both these reasons, people may need both explanation and repetition of explanation; moreover, they may need to explain their own story repeatedly as part of making sense of it.

This focus on mutual explanation is an unusual aspect of social work, which is often concerned with assessment for and provision of care services, or a structured form of problem solving, such as cognitive-behavioral, solution-focused, or task-centered therapy. Psychotherapeutic forms of practice, such as psychodynamic or person-centered therapy, can help to provide a focus on experiencing and making sense of feelings and thoughts, rather than mutual processes of explanation. An important aspect of skill in end-of-life social work practice, therefore, is sharing and testing out explanations with clients and their families. Our approach to this is to focus on making sense of alternative stories or narratives of the life biography within which people are experiencing loss, and of the events that the present practice is focusing on; you can see this process in Colin and Christa's case.

Before engaging with another person, social workers need self-awareness to know their own identity as a person, as a social worker, and as part of end-of-life care. Identity refers to those aspects of our personal life and experience that create the person we are, the people and ideas that we identify with, and the people and ideas that are now part of us (Payne, 2006b). This in turn helps us to know our own weaknesses and vulnerabilities and not to let our own needs get in the way of being alongside another person. Without a well-developed self-awareness we are at risk of projecting our own needs and judgments onto our client. Without self-awareness, our understanding of others will be colored by needs that impel us to work on issues in our own lives rather than those in the client's life.

For example, many clients live on their own or with frail family members and may find it difficult to call for help in an emergency. However, when people in this position come into a hospital or hospice, teams planning their discharge often worry about how patients returning home to die will be able to call for help if their condition suddenly deteriorates. Realistically, emergency medical help is inappropriate if the patient is dying, and it is better to accept dying peacefully at home in a loved one's presence rather than seeing the death as a medical emergency. Chapter 1 described Malcolm's experience as a teenager of having difficulty in calling for help for his dying father, and he is aware that accepting the possibility of a death without help often makes him unreasonably anxious; thus he often fails to question colleagues' avoidance of running risks when people return home. We need to be grounded in our own social and personal context to leave our own frailties behind so we are to be able truly to engage with our clients. We need to understand our motivation for becoming social workers, to avoid rescuing people or imposing our own solutions on people as we relive earlier experiences. Renzenbrink provides a useful overview of why self-awareness is crucial. She argues that without taking good care of ourselves we are at risk of falling into a variety of traps including burnout (Renzenbrink, 2004, p. 848–867). As she says: "Some people may be drawn to working with the dying and bereaved in order to resolve some of their own unconscious fears or past losses" (Renzenbrink, 2004, p. 852).

Two important skills derive from the research of Rogers (1961) and his colleagues (Carkhuff & Berenson, 1977): genuineness in our interest in our clients and empathy with their feelings about their experiences. Using narratives helps to show genuine interest in the person's unique story. Being nonjudgmental about people's lives also allows trust to develop and affirms to our clients that their lives are of value. Empathy is equally important, but what do we mean by it? Part of the skill of being able to help others is to have the capacity to tune into what is going on for other people, that is, what is important for them at this moment. We also need to be able to perceive where they are coming from, that is, the experiences and social context that have brought them to this point in their lives. To be empathic, a social worker needs to be able to understand the feelings of the other person and to communicate with that person in such a way that he or she feels understood. We need to try to see the world from our clients' perspectives, while recognizing that we can never really know what it feels to be the other person.

The communication micro-skills identified at the beginning of this chapter assist in conveying genuineness and empathy, for example, maintaining good eye contact, reflective listening, paraphrasing and clarifying, supporting and challenging. All of these communicate involvement and commitment to receiving and understanding the person's narrative as it unfolds. Helping your client to set goals and release unhelpful or painful emotions also improves the quality of communication between social worker and client. Buckman points out that research has shown that talking to someone who is ill about difficult things does not create new fears and anxieties. "In fact the opposite was true, *not* talking about a fear makes it bigger" (Buckman, 1994, p.10).

ASSESSMENT OF RELATIONSHIP ISSUES

There are four categories of difficulties in communication: practical difficulties, those that arise from our society and culture, those that relate to the individual client, and those that relate to ourselves. In this section, we examine each in turn and suggest appropriate responses in practice.

Practical Difficulties

Sometimes the places and settings where we are working are not ideal. It may be hard to achieve privacy. It is important to find the space and time among clients' personal routines, or hospital or institution timetables, to talk, and for the practitioner not to appear to be in a rush. It is all too easy to convey a sense of being too busy or being focused on tasks. Our body language will convey whether we really want to engage with the other person's narrative or not.

Society's Attitudes

The way birth and death are hidden and medicalized in Western society can hinder communication about death and dying. Many people find it hard to face their own mortality and wish to avoid talking about dying in our death-denying society. For some, the expectation that there must always be further treatment options available and an overdependence on the advances in modern medicine may give false hope.

Difficulties Relating to Patients

Fear of Dying and Protecting Others. People who fear dying or who anticipate that dying must automatically mean pain and discomfort may seek to avoid communicating about it. People often want to protect close family members from the reality of loss and grief, which may make openness difficult.

Physical Difficulties. The disease process itself may prevent open communication: some clients experience disease that affects their speech or hearing and thus makes talking difficult. The following case example is a practitioner's account illustrating her response to her client's physical difficulties in maintaining control and communication.

Case example: Rosa

Rosa, age eighty-five, asked to be referred to me because of previous contact we had had with each other. Some years previously I had worked with her brother, Stanley, who had been admitted to the hospice for terminal care; he later died there. Rosa and Stanley were both single and had shared the family home all their lives. Neither had any other surviving relatives. After Stanley died, I supported Rosa in her bereavement as she slowly came to terms with having no other family, during which time she sold the family home and relocated to a retirement apartment nearby.

At the point of this referral, Rosa had just been diagnosed with an aggressive glioma (brain tumor) and refused all treatment. She already had a right-sided weakness and her speech had become slurred and more difficult to understand. She was not afraid of her short prognosis, but was terrified of losing her speech, her mobility, her independence, and her dignity. She quickly set her affairs in order, and arranged to move into a nursing home rather than wait until she could no longer manage alone in her apartment. I suggested that while she had full mental capacity she complete an advance care plan giving clear details of her treatment wishes in case she later became unable to communicate, and worked through the form with her. Later, I continued to visit Rosa each week in the nursing home. She quickly lost all her speech, and was unable to write.

Acknowledging Rosa's frustration and sense of being trapped in a body that no longer worked properly was fundamental. Also it was important not to brush aside the reality that Rosa was losing control, by not dying "quickly enough," as she saw it. Asking closed questions that required yes/no answers lessened her communication difficulties, but I took care to think through what the most relevant closed questions might be that would help to reduce Rosa's feelings of frustration.

By using a communication card and pointing to a line that said: "Please tell me your news," Rosa made clear that she wanted me to bring something from the outside world to lessen her isolation. Self-disclosure is only rarely and carefully extracted from the social worker's tool-bag, but it felt right. I therefore included some news about my young children, showing a photograph of each of them. Rosa, a former teacher, was visibly delighted. So each week, part of our session together would be lighthearted news of the children's ups and downs at school and nursery. But the major part of each visit focused on Rosa's emotional and psychological distress, and she became adept at letting me know where the balance needed to lie between these two very different topics.

One day, I talked to Rosa about whether there was practical help I could offer. Rosa responded in the negative, so I suggested that perhaps what I could do was to keep visiting and be alongside Rosa, that my work was about "being" rather than "doing"; she vigorously agreed. I gave her a commitment that this was something I could do despite Rosa's increasing communication difficulties and frustration. Rosa squeezed my hand very tightly at this point, an indication that this was for her the most important aspect of the contact.

Cultural, Religious; and Language Difficulties. Cultural, religious, and language difficulties may also get in the way of open communication. Dein and Thomas (2002, p. 209) consider how "attitudes towards telling patients [about a fatal prognosis] vary enormously according to culture and religion" arguing that "approaches to truth-telling in the West are dependent on the Western understanding of individualism," whereas in other cultures the family may be considered more important than the individual. Individualism requires people to take personal responsibility for understanding and responding to their predicament. In Western societies we think people are weak, selfish, or "in denial" unless they accept this individual responsibility. Dein and Thomas illustrate the impact of culture by looking at Indian culture with its roots in Hindu religious philosophy, where the family is required to protect the individual members from information that might be so distressing that they are unable to cope mentally. The family then takes collective responsibility for the "bad news."

Also, language barriers can cause misunderstandings, misdiagnosis, and treatment difficulties such as not taking medication as prescribed (del Rio, 2004, p. 456). Agencies need to ensure that adequate translation services are available, and practitioners need to learn to use them well.

Our Own Difficulties: Blocking Behaviors

The fourth and final category is comprised of those communication difficulties that relate to ourselves. Many factors in our own lives and experiences can hinder good communication. For example, our own social and cultural background may have conditioned us to be uncomfortable with talking about death and dying. Similarly, our own fears of illness and death may get in the way. We might experience a tension between our motivation to be social workers to empower people to make positive changes in their lives and working in end-of-life care. We may lack the confidence or need additional training to open up potentially painful areas of discussion. We may fear saying "the wrong thing." We may fear being blamed for causing distress or upsetting patients. We may be afraid of other people's strong emotional responses. Also our own distress and discomfort at being alongside someone who is very sick or perhaps disfigured can prevent us from engaging openly.

This discussion of the ways in which our own issues may lead to communication difficulties that obstruct engagement with clients who are dying, leads us on to think about the ways in which we may obstruct engagement through blocking behaviors. Such behaviors hinder engagement with clients because we seem distant and not genuinely committed to their interests. As social workers, we need to be aware of difficulties we may have so that we can explore these in supervision, get help, or seek additional training. Some of the common distancing or blocking strategies that we need to be aware of include talking in a way that uses neutral material to avoid addressing real issues and, ignoring or missing cues or picking up selectively on cues.

Case example: John's Family

Several members of John's family were referred to the social worker. They were upset because a sudden deterioration in John's condition led to his sudden transfer from hospital to hospice for terminal care. The social worker saw them together, and responded to anger because of the medical decision to cease treatment, and they had a conversation about how to get information from a senior physician and to make a complaint. John's two sons had the most to say.

As part of this conversation, John's wife and daughter-in-law both said that it was important to discuss the sudden change in prognosis with John's grandchildren. However, in dealing with the sons' anger, the social worker failed to pick up on this other concern. The following day, the worker was asked to help the nurses deal with a situation in which two distressed children on the ward were refusing to visit their grandfather because they feared seeing someone who was dying. It appeared that angry exchanges at home about the complaint had frightened the children, who had not had careful preparation for visiting their grandfather.

One useful concept in understanding this event is the idea of emotional labor. James (1993) argues that any situation in which emotions have to be managed is hard work for the people involved, and different people in the situation take on different amounts of the work involved. Her research examined the emotional labor involved in disclosure of cancer; the labor is heightened by the potentially serious physical and social consequences, including the likelihood of death. Her research shows that a wide range of people, including both professionals and family members, are involved in managing the emotional consequences of disclosures. Divisions of emotional labor are affected by the depth of feelings generated, the public context in which feelings are expressed, and regulated and social distance brought about by hierarchies of those involved.

Thus, the social worker giving information to relatives, who has no close relationship with the people involved, operating in a public setting such as a meeting or case conference, will carry less of the emotional labor than, say, a nurse who provides daily intimate physical care to John in his private room. In turn, the nurse is likely to carry less of the labor than the wife of a patient dying of cancer, who has had a close personal relationship with the patient for many years, has been involved in the earlier stages of the illness, and has experienced the patient's physical deterioration.

Applying this to the situation of John's relatives, John's wife and daughter-in-law had to carry more emotional labor in talking to the children than the sons and the social worker. Similarly, the nurses on the ward carried the emotional labor of dealing with the children's distress, and the social worker needed to help by accepting some of this labor.

It is often useful to identify who will have to accept the emotional labor involved in dealing with a difficult situation, with the aim of focusing help on them, or relieving them of part of the effort. However, working through emotional issues contributes to future resilience, and avoiding this will not benefit someone who should be accepting part of the burden. The social work aim should often be to make the burden accepted by different people involved more equal; this is as true among colleagues in a multiprofessional team as it is among members of a family.

Pause and reflect—identifying emotional labor

Think about a situation in your private life or practice that generated a lot of emotion for the people involved. Who in the situation carried most of the emotional labor? Who carried less? Could they have helped? How could you have facilitated a fairer division of emotional labor?

Other blocking behaviors might be giving inappropriate encouragement, or premature or false reassurance—another issue in balancing truth and hope that requires practitioners to be careful in assessing appropriate responses. A social worker who feels discomfort may not allow silences or may change the subject. It can be easy to do this without seeming to diminish the patient, for example, by switching the focus from the patient's own story to talking to the patient about his or her family. Another common distancing tactic may be to hide behind bureaucracy or to pass the buck. "Staff may use endless meetings, case conferences, data collection, and report writing to avoid dealing with difficult situations" (Renzenbrink, 2004, p. 854). Rushing to engage in problem solving without hearing the full complexity of the problem is another trap we may fall into. If our own discomfort is too great, we may simply avoid the patient and distance ourselves from his or her distress.

If you are concerned about handling difficult questions to the extent that you avoid someone or you are concerned about upsetting the patient, it is important that you seek support from your supervisor or a colleague. You can jointly plan how to raise the difficult issue, or rehearse how to deal with distress appropriately. In a study of blocking behaviors used by nurses, Booth and colleagues (Booth, Maguire, Butterworth, &

Hillier, 1996) found blocking to be a major problem. However, when nurses felt their supervisors adequately supported them both practically and emotionally, they used blocking less. Similarly, Renzenbrink emphasizes the importance of both supervision and support so that we do not "distance ourselves from clients at a time when they are at their most vulnerable and in need of authentic, honest, and compassionate care" (Renzenbrink, 2004, p. 862).

Pause and reflect—Are you aware of blocking in your practice?

Write down a narrative about a situation in your home life or in your practice where people were presenting you with information that you found uncomfortable. Can you identify blocking behavior that you used, or that you had to avoid consciously? What was the outcome: Was it worse when matters finally came to a head, or was the issue never dealt with? What ways did you use to overcome your block? What other ways could you have used?

ASSESSMENT TOOLS

All health- and social-care agencies have their own assessment processes and documentation. Many of these are associated with funding mechanisms, such as managed care (U.K.: care management and NHS continuing health care), which often require extensive recording of information about clients and families. The process of assessment for services includes the following interpersonal processes, which the practitioner may be able to help with:

- Potential service users come to understand that a need exists and accept that receiving care services is a way of meeting it, partially or fully.
- A felt need is expressed and understood by practitioners, who enable users and caregivers to be secure in the knowledge that their felt need is understood.
- An understood need is expressed as an application for resource allocation.
- The commissioners and providers of services decide the extent to which and the ways in which the need will be met by their resources, for example, public services or insurance. (Payne, 2008a)

Specific forms of therapeutic intervention, such as cognitive behavior therapy (see Chapter 5) have their own assessment requirements. Our concern in this chapter is to emphasize the importance of examining the qualitative information about relationships that emerges from these assessment documents.

Commonly used assessment tools in palliative care for exploring relationships and then considering the emotional and practical importance of them may be helpful more widely in end-of-life care, so we introduce them here; they are particularly useful for people who prefer a diagrammatic rather than narrative or descriptive record.

Genograms or Family Trees

Genograms are diagrams that describe kinship relationships; usually we see them as family diagrams. They were originally used for identifying genetic conditions and may be simplified when used as social work assessment tools. An example of a fairly complex genogram that illustrates the range of symbols is displayed in figure 4.1. However, a wide variety of family relationships are acceptable in many Western societies. Morgan (1995, p. 11) helpfully builds flexibility when he describes families as "sets of practices which deal in chosen ways with ideas of parenthood, kinship and marriage—like the expectations and obligations which

FIGURE 4.1   Example of a genogram

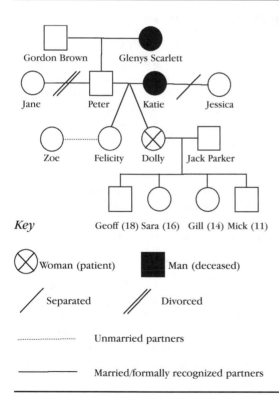

Explanation

Mr. Gordon Brown and Ms. Glenys Scarlett married and had a son, Peter. Glenys is now deceased.

Peter married Jane, then divorced, married Kate, was then widowed, then married Jessica, from whom he is now separated.

Peter and Kate had twins, Felicity and Dolly. Felicity has a relationship with Zoe, In some countries this might be a marriage, in the U.K. a civil partnership; so its lack of formalization might be significant in these countries. Dolly, the patient, is married to Jack, and they have four children.

Notes

Men are squares, women circles. A cross indicates the focal person or patient, blanked out squares and circles indicate someone who has died. Names and, if relevant, ages are written in. Each generation is on a separate line. Lines denote kinship and marriage relationships, dotted if it is not formally recognized. Sequences of relationships, such as marriages or partnerships, or a succession of children from a relationship, are read from left to right.

Key

⊗ Woman (patient)   ■ Man (deceased)

╱ Separated   ╱╱ Divorced

· · · · · · · · · · Unmarried partners

———— Married/formally recognized partners

are associated with those practices." This means that gay and lesbian part-nerships and families that have re-formed after divorce or separation may need to be noted. Also, a Western nuclear family of parents and children may not be the appropriate representation of how some minority ethnic groups would see the family, which might include extended family rela-tionships and members of the local community.

DeMaria and colleagues (DeMaria, Weeks, & Hof, 1999) emphasize how genograms may be seen as a way of analyzing intergenerational fac-tors in many different situations that individuals, couples, and families face. This includes the way attachments, culture, emotions, anger, and social reactions to gender, sexuality, and love are repeated across gener-ations, and family links are rejected and discontinued.

Other useful diagrams that may contribute to assessment are social network diagrams and ecomaps; these start from the client or another focus and draw lines to the various connections. Ecomaps include infor-mation about environmental factors in the links, such as physical distance between family members, transportation difficulties, and boundaries between agencies.

RELATIONSHIP ISSUES IN END-OF-LIFE CARE

One of the crucial aspects of engaging with people in end-of-life care is not excluding some family members from involvement. We suggested above that one of the important roles of social work assessment is to identify the quality of the relationships that are represented in assess-ment mechanisms such as the genogram. Unfortunately, an unbalanced truth and hope situation often leads to relationship patterns in which families exclude one or more family members from participation in deci-sion making. Emotions such as denial, anger, hopelessness, and depres-sion, challenge people's communication skills and existing relationships. They may become unable to accept or manage disclosure of painful infor-mation. Cultural and ethnic differences may also mean that family mem-bers react to painful situations in ways that are different from the expec-tations of other family members or professionals involved.

Collusion

Social workers often face situations where one family member asks us to share in some secret and not to tell someone else in the family. Col-lusion of this kind, apart from causing us to feel discomforted or dishon-est, often leads to further problems later. Perhaps more importantly, it can result in the person who is kept out of the information loop being disadvantaged in some way. This can lead to anger and distrust and is ulti-mately unhelpful.

Case example: Josie

Josie, who suffered from advanced cancer, was admitted to the hospital for terminal care and symptom management of an unpleasant fungating tumor, that is, one where the tumor had broken through the skin. For many years she had been married to Ted, who had suffered a serious traffic accident when he was younger that had left him paraplegic and in a wheelchair. For Ted to be able to visit Josie in the hospital, he needed assistance from one of their two adult children, Clare and Tom.

Josie, however, asked Clare and Tom not to bring their father to visit her because she did not want Ted to see her "like this," but only when she was "better." Clare and Tom visited their mother each day and felt unable to go against her wishes. They had always obeyed their mother, the more dominant of their parents. They both felt that they should not go against her wishes because she was suffering from a major illness and this would distress her even more; also, they were both afraid of her anger. Clare and Tom confided to the practitioner that they felt uneasy about colluding, but they did not seek help to address this since they had decided not to go against their mother's wishes.

The practitioner was concerned that Ted might not be given the opportunity to say goodbye to his wife or to see her again before she died and that this would cause him to have regrets and give rise to anger and distress in his bereavement. Also, his individual rights were compromised. While patients have the right to make their own decisions even where we disagree, practitioners must also look at the effects on others; see Chapter 8 for discussion about the ethical issues arising from social workers' responsibilities for families rather than their health-care responsibility for the patient only. The practitioner started by exploring with Clare and Tom how they thought Ted might feel if information were withheld from him that could have long-term consequences in his bereavement. They were particularly worried that he might blame them for not overriding their mother's wishes and that this might destroy his trust in them and possibly their relationship with their father. But still they were afraid to upset Josie.

Although they knew Josie would not get better, they both insisted that she should not be given this information. The practitioner asked what they thought would happen if she knew; they both expected that she would be unable to cope, would give up hope, and die in a very distressed state and that they would feel responsible for this.

The practitioner had already talked to Josie about her husband. Like the children, the worker found Josie still fixed on only seeing her husband again when she was better. Before the collusion could be challenged and communication could become more open the worker needed to build trust with Josie and her two children. The worker suggested that, while she did not wish to take away Josie's hope that she might get better, she might like to spend some time with Ted now as well as later. However, Josie remained adamant that Ted was not to see her like this.

Why did Josie need to maintain her defenses so rigidly by refusing to allow her husband to visit her? The unpleasant nature of the tumor and her own fears of losing her dignity might be part of the reason, but the practitioner needed to understand whether there were other factors in past relationships or the family's circumstances. She had only a few pieces of the jigsaw. So after a few short sessions with Josie, establishing trust, the practitioner spent a longer time with Josie listening to her story of her life, marriage, children, achievements, and disappointments. Through this she understood that Josie and Ted had a good marriage, that she had been her husband's caregiver and looked after him well until recently when she had been in great pain at home. Ted had tried to help more. However, his disability had made his role in the home limited, and he was quite slow and less skilled than Josie doing domestic tasks. Josie had become very irritable; she had snapped at him. Therefore, the time at home prior to hospital admission had become very tense. Josie was afraid to see Ted because she felt she had hurt him and that he may never forgive her. She had tried to hide this from her children. She was afraid that Ted would not want to see her and would be angry about her unkindness.

Having understood this, the practitioner suggested to Josie that she might feel relieved and helped if she could tell Ted she was sorry and that he would probably also feel better if he knew that she had not meant to hurt him. As she was still fearful that the meeting between them would not go well, the practitioner offered to facilitate their visit and stay if Josie wished. This gave her a sense of safety that angry feelings would not spiral out of control. Josie asked Clare to collect her father and bring him to visit and also managed to let Josie's children know something of what had happened at home before their mother came into the hospital. Ted visited Josie and they said sorry, cried together, and held each other. Following this visit, Clare and Tom brought their dad to visit each day, and he was with his wife when she died.

Pause and reflect—Bill

In another example, Bill was not told that he had incurable lung cancer. The physicians treating him said that he had not asked, and they felt that he did not want to know. He was no longer able to work and was increasingly depressed. Bill's wife, Barbara, had been told his diagnosis but felt unable to discuss this with him.

What might you say and how might you help?

Some suggestions

Here is the practitioner's account: I asked Barbara how she was coping with the knowledge of her husband's diagnosis that she could not share. How did Barbara respond to Bill when he was feeling gloomy about not getting better after what he thought was a respiratory illness? How had they approached difficult decisions in their marriage? Barbara and Bill had always shared important decisions, being honest with each other, and Barbara did not like how secrecy and dishonesty had displaced openness now that they were facing the biggest crisis in their lives. I asked her what she said to Bill when his mood was low; Barbara tried to distract him or made him a drink. When Bill felt brighter and talked about their next vacation or their garden, Barbara encouraged Bill to look at holiday brochures or gardening catalogs.

I therefore recognized, first, that Barbara was uneasy about the lack of openness. Second, she was unsure how to achieve greater honesty. I suggested that the next time Bill was despondent about his lack of progress, she could open up the subject of Bill's illness rather than keeping the lid on it. When I next saw them together, Bill said he had been afraid to ask if it might be cancer and kept thinking that the doctors would tell him if it was. His low mood lifted, saying that he had been depressed because he thought his employer would be thinking he was not making any effort to return to work. Also, he had felt he was letting his wife down by not helping more with the children. Once he knew that nobody was expecting him to return to work or to have enough energy for child care, he felt it was legitimate to rest. More importantly, knowing the truth enabled Bill to make plans with his wife for her future. He made a will and arranged financial provision for his family. Together Bill and Barbara were able to share decisions, make plans, and finally to say their goodbyes.

Excluding Children

It is not unusual to encounter situations where it is the children in the family who are excluded from openness about what is happening. Here again is the practitioner's account of the events.

Case example: Julie

Julie is a single mother who took her father in to live with her; he was dying from bowel cancer and had no one else to care for him. She had two small children, Jack (age four) and Sam (age six). Julie told a home care nurse that the boys were becoming naughtier, making a lot of noise in the house, and did not listen when she asked them to be quiet. Julie was more tired than usual and had less time for the children because of the demands of her father's care. The nurse asked me to try to reduce Julie's stress. I called her, but she would not see me, not wanting social workers interfering with her role as a mother. She was adamant that she did not want her children to know that Pop was dying, saying: "They would only be upset and I've got enough on my plate."

I felt stuck. Whatever I offered needed to be nonthreatening. So I asked Julie if she would let me mail her a leaflet that I had written; it was fine if she chose to trash it. The next time the nurse visited Julie the atmosphere in the home was much calmer. Julie explained that, having read the leaflet, she thought it best to explain to the boys that Pop was very ill with cancer and would not get better. The boys said that they knew this: they had overheard conversations. They had seen how ill he was becoming and the large number of calls from different healthcare professionals. Julie enlisted the boys' support, involving them in Pop's care. As a result, they were cooperative and motivated to make the last few weeks of his life as good as possible.

Anger

Anger is common at the end of life, a reaction to fear, uncertainty, and helplessness. It may be inappropriate or misdirected or it may be justified: professionals and services sometimes make mistakes. Anger can be targeted at something or someone specific or it may be generalized and unfocused. However, the principles of dealing with any anger, whatever its cause, are the same: anger must be acknowledged and allowed. To individuals, their situation is unique; by listening to their story, we can hear what is making them feel angry. Exploring the situation helps to diffuse the anger. It is often caregivers rather than patients who express anger, particularly if the demands of their role become unsustainable or continue over an extended period (Johnston Taylor, Baird, Malone, & McCorkle, 1993).

Case example: Annie and Jim

This is the practitioner's account of her work with Jim, the husband of Annie, who was admitted to the hospital with advanced breast cancer. Jim had been Annie's main caregiver for several years. He was reluctant to agree to her being hospitalized but was exhausted. At the hospital, Jim was very angry, accusing the nurses of neglecting Annie's care. He complained that she was not washed or given meals and that she had not been seen by a doctor. As I listened to Jim's anger, I knew that was not true: I had seen a nurse feeding Annie earlier; I had talked to the doctors about her condition after they had seen her. However, I did not want to be defensive or to challenge Jim. Instead, I listened carefully to Jim's distress and offered to see him each day. As I got to know him better, his anger subsided completely. He was afraid of losing Annie and had many regrets that he had not been as good a husband as he would have wished. Annie had a long history of schizophrenia. The couple had no children and Annie's mental health problems meant they had an isolated life. At times, he had reached breaking point and had hit Annie; he now bitterly regretted these occasions. It was almost more than he could bear to see the nurses caring so tenderly for Annie and providing the level of care she now required. Jim needed support to talk about his guilt and sadness, but also to talk about his need to hold on to her and not let her die.

Denial

Denial is an important defense if someone finds their reality intolerable. Therefore, as we saw in Colin and Christa's case above, it should only be challenged where it is obstructing intervention, and then with great care. It is only a problem if it gets in the way of someone getting the treatment they need or it prevents open communication to the detriment of someone else. "Unless there are issues about protecting the welfare of others, the principle of autonomy permits the dying person to choose to remain in ignorance or with a limited explanation" (Sheldon, 1997, p. 60). If someone is said to be in denial, it is always necessary to ask: Whose problem is it? And, Is what is being observed an adaptation to the situation rather than denial? It cannot be straightforward living with the knowledge that you are dying, so it is unsurprising that responses to coping with such an emotionally painful situation are varied and complex.

Often people seem able to move in and out of facing uncomfortable realities; an important skill for social workers is being able to tune into where someone is as their feelings vary.

Sometimes it is the family that finds it too painful to acknowledge that their loved one is dying; they sometimes literally cling to the person in the hope that they will live and not leave them (Jeffreys, 2005, p. 198). If families are not helped to face the reality of what is happening a mismatch between end-of-life care and unrealistic expectations can cause even greater distress. "The personal characteristics and emotional strain of family caregivers may create barriers to placement of patients in appropriate care settings, leading family inappropriately to insist on or reject care in the intensive care unit, long-term care setting, home, or institutional hospice" (Rabow, Hanser, & Adams, 2004, p. 489).

It is important that the social worker's wish to be open and honest does not override the wishes and needs of the client, responding to how they act, not what they say. Even people who have always claimed that they would want all the information and facts about their situation sometimes change their position when faced with their own illness. Therefore, it is essential not to prejudge or make any assumptions about how someone might respond to difficult and painful information.

Case example: My mother

The following is a social work practitioner's account of her mother's reaction to approaching death. My mother had previously said she would want to know everything if she was terminally ill, but she successfully blocked all attempts to communicate with her openly when she was faced with end-of-life decisions. Although she had extensive metastatic breast cancer, which had spread to her lungs, liver, and kidneys, and had recently undergone major surgery, when I suggested that hospice care might be appropriate she said she "could not go to a place like that." I asked why not; she said that the hospice would not accept people who "only had kidney problems." I knew that I must respect her wishes not to acknowledge her cancer or how ill she was, but was uncertain how to ensure that she received the care she required while maintaining this stance. Therefore, I suggested we do a deal: I understood that she did not want to talk about "it," being able to see that even using the word "cancer" would distress her, but that if this prevented her from receiving the services that could help her then, as her daughter, I could not go along with this. Therefore, the deal was that we would not talk about "it" (terminal cancer) but she would allow me to arrange the most appropriate help for her, in this case referral for hospice care. She was admitted to hospice, where she received excellent end-of-life care. During her hospice stay, the nearest that my mother came to acknowledging that she was dying was to say that she was becoming "weaker not stronger" and to agree when I suggested to her that she was in the "right place." This was her way of telling me that she was at peace with the fact that she was dying. She died a very peaceful death a week after hospice admission, with me, my sister, and my brother beside her.

Hopelessness and Depression

People are more likely to feel depressed in their illness at times when the news about treatment options is not good or is not what they want to hear. After a period of active treatment and improvement, it is understandable that patients will hope they are cured. When they find they are not, they are likely to feel let down, abandoned, and perhaps even more distressed than when they were originally diagnosed. This may be the case for both the patient and his or her family.

Because maintaining hope is one of the central concepts in working with people who are dying (Zilberfein & Hurwitz, 2004, p. 316), it is important to recognize when someone is overwhelmed with a sense of hopelessness and to consider how to intervene. There may be many possible causes of withdrawal and depression. Feelings of hopelessness may be transferred from the patient to those around him or her. Patients may leave friends and family feeling overwhelmed with this sense of hopelessness, who may seek social work help to find a way through. Counseling patients who are depressed or withdrawn can be emotionally demanding. How do you reach someone who has withdrawn from living?

Case example: Ricky

This is a practitioner's account of her work with Ricky, a twenty-five year old man suffering from poliomyelitis and end-stage non-Hodgkins lymphoma, a form of cancer affecting the blood. He had been transferred from hospital to hospice for end-of-life care. The nurses asked me to see him because I knew him as the hospital social worker from repeated admissions to the cancer hospital the previous year. When I visited him in the hospice, he literally turned his face to the wall. His eyes were closed and he was either not able or not wanting to communicate. Little was known about his family, who did not visit and with whom there had been some long-standing rift. I remembered that Ricky had previously talked about a girlfriend, Ellen, that she suffered from severe agoraphobia, and could only visit

Ricky when Doreen, her mother, was able to accompany her to the hospital. As a result, Ellen had only been able to visit Ricky on weekends and I had never met her. Although Ricky had always talked about her very fondly I didn't know how Ellen felt about him.

After spending some time trying unsuccessfully to engage with Ricky, I asked him if there was one thing that I could do that would improve his quality of life even a little. Ricky did not answer, but asking the question enabled me to suggest a possible answer; I wondered out loud if Ricky would like to see his girlfriend. I knew that Ellen would need help to come to the hospice and that perhaps I could arrange to bring her and take her home again. Ricky's face lit up, and with a smile he asked if I really meant it. We discussed arranging the visit. Ellen was so severely disabled by her agoraphobia that she would be unable to answer the telephone if I called her. I agreed to call Doreen to help. The following day, I collected Ellen from her home and brought her to visit.

The outcome of this particular intervention was striking. Ricky became animated and communicative. He talked to me about how he had always wanted to marry Ellen but now feared it was too late. I thought about this carefully before saying that if this was what they both wanted and right for them, it would be possible to arrange their wedding at very short notice in the hospice. Ellen might not know how short Ricky's prognosis was, and there was a lot of work to do to prepare Ellen emotionally for an uncertain future. Again, I enlisted Doreen's help: she supported the marriage and felt it would improve Ellen's self esteem. She felt this would help Ellen after Ricky died and give her a new status and sense of belonging in quite an impoverished town. I talked honestly with Ellen about how the doctor did not expect Ricky to live. In fact, Ricky's doctor was doubtful if Ricky had the strength to withstand the ceremony.

Within a week, Ricky and Ellen married in the hospice. Ellen stayed in the hospice with Ricky for a few weeks after the wedding. His health improved against all the odds, and I arranged for them to be re-housed together in a specially adapted apartment. Ellen grew in confidence, got to know her neighbors who all suffered from different disabilities, and became involved in the life of the complex. She was able to take Ricky out in his wheelchair. Together they were able to undertake activities of daily living that were too difficult for them individually. As a couple, they gave each other strength, and their love for each other sustained them. Ricky died eighteen months later. Ellen was able to stay on in the apartment in the community where she now belonged.

CONCLUSION

It is demanding to work with people at the end of life; in this chapter we have discussed engaging with people and their families over end-of-life issues, focusing on the importance of openness and equal dialogue between worker and client. A narrative approach allows practitioners to start from clients' own understanding of their situation and how they have arrived at this point, and to open up the factors in the family situation and the progression of the illness that have led to the issues that the clients, families, and caregivers face.

We have emphasized the workers' personal engagement and overcoming their own blocking behaviors that sometimes obstruct effective practice, and we have also explored how to work with a range of factors, especially the emotions that make it hard for clients and their families to achieve the life tasks that are important to them at the end of life.

In the next chapter, we move on to specific interventions to confront and change clients' and families' behaviors and social situations to strengthen their capacity and resilience both in the face of the death they face at the present time and for the future.

FURTHER READING

Monroe, B., & Sheldon, F. (2004). Psychosocial dimensions of care. In N. Sykes, P. Edmonds, & J. Wiles (Eds.), *Management of advanced disease* (pp. 405–437). London: Arnold. This extended discussion of social work in palliative care is an excellent introduction to many aspects of practice from two well-known and outstanding practitioners.

Monroe, B. (2004). Social work in palliative medicine. In D. Doyle, G. Hanks, N. Cherny, & K. Calman (Eds.), *Oxford textbook of palliative medicine* (3rd ed.) (pp. 1007–1017). Oxford, England: Oxford University Press. Another excellent account of social work in palliative care, giving good guidance.

JOURNALS

Two journals concerned with psychological palliative care may sometimes be helpful to social workers:

- *Psycho-Oncology*, Wiley Interscience.
- *Palliative and Supportive Care*, Cambridge Journals.

Chapter 5

INTERVENTION IN END-OF-LIFE SOCIAL WORK

CHAPTER AIMS

The main aim of this chapter is to explain useful social work interventions in end-of-life and palliative care.

After working through this chapter, readers should be able to:

- Identify appropriate end-of-life social work;
- Help clients' and family members' understandings about their end-of-life situation;
- Help clients and their families fulfill important life tasks and plan important life decisions, including care of children, during the dying period;
- Help clients and family members prepare life reviews and memorializations;
- Help clients and families with financial issues; and
- Help clients and families decide on ways to deal with presence at and the aftermath of the death.

PSYCHOSOCIAL CARE AND SOCIAL WORK IN END-OF-LIFE CARE

Because palliative care aims to provide "total" or holistic care, psychological, social, and spiritual care must be an integral part of it, and we saw in Chapter 1 how social work established a role as a contributor to palliative and end-of-life care; in this chapter, we expand on the details of that role and its application to end-of-life care. We start from patients' psychosocial care needs. All professionals involved with people who are dying and their informal caregivers and family members have to respond to psychological, social, and spiritual issues raised by patients. A broad literature review (Dix & Glickman, 1997) identifies psychosocial needs as follows:

Patients' needs:

- To maintain identity
- To maintain control and independence
- To receive psychological, emotional, and spiritual support

Family members and caregivers needs:

* To acknowledge individuality
* To recognize the part that they play
* To receive psychological, emotional, and spiritual support

Common needs of patients, caregivers, and family members:

* Recognition of ethnic, cultural, and spiritual needs
* Information about and access to state, private, and third-sector help, and self-help organizations and groups
* Advice and information on financial, housing, and other practical matters
* Access to specialized legal advice, e.g., on making a will
* Advice on post-bereavement practical problems

Two recent authoritative accounts of psychosocial care needs with cancer patients also provide an indication of issues that social workers, alongside their multiprofessional colleagues, might need to deal with. These are the formulations of the U.S. Institute of Medicine of the National Academies of Health (Adler & Page, 2008) and the U.K. National Institute for Clinical Excellence (NICE, 2004). Summaries of these evidence-based accounts are set alongside each other in table 5.1, and we can see that the formulation is similar.

The two reports include analysis of effectiveness of psychosocial interventions, both commenting that the lack of standardized terminology and classification of problems has made it difficult to establish good evidence of outcomes. Adler and Page's (2008) review of evidence suggests that tailoring information about the illness and likely effects on the patient and family is helpful, particularly if, as we suggested in Chapter 3, interpersonal information is supported by written reminders. There is evidence that help in coping with emotions is effective in reducing distress. peer support groups are useful in a wide range of illnesses (see Chapter 9), and counseling and psychotherapeutic interventions are also effective. Cognitive-behavioral work is effective with anxiety and depression, while supportive psychotherapies help deal with role changes and interpersonal conflicts and strains. Family and couple work help reduce illness-related family conflicts. People also benefit from help managing the illness and all the complex associated changes in life, and from help providing and organizing practical services such as transport, financial, legal, and educational assistance, and in managing disruptions in family, school, and work life.

The social work role in any specialty derives from the important purposes of social work as a profession, to achieve general social improvement through interpersonal help with problems affecting people because

TABLE 5.1   Psychosocial needs in cancer patients

Institute of Medicine of the National Academies of Health (U.S.)	National Institute for Clinical Excellence (U.K.)
Information about illness, treatments, health, and services	[NICE report treats information as a separate element of need]
Help in coping with emotions accompanying illness and treatment	Emotional support, which may be derived from engaging in social activities, companionship or befriending, and making contact with health and social care professionals
Help in managing illness	Help with personal care, such as bathing and dressing
Assistance in managing behaviors to minimize impact of disease	Help inside and outside the home, such as cleaning and shopping
Material and logistical resources, e.g., transportation	Practical aids, including wheelchairs and other equipment
Help in managing disruptions to work, school, and family life	Advice on work and employment issues; help to care for children and other dependants such as older relatives
Financial advice and/or assistance	Assistance to secure financial support through, for example, help in making a benefit claim

Sources: Developed from Adler & Page, 2008; NICE, 2004.

of the social consequences of life events (Payne, 2006c). Health care professions aim to cure patients of illness and help them manage for themselves the consequences of illness in their lives. While through the public health and health-promotion aspects of health care services they contribute to improving health generally in the community, social workers generally accept a stronger direct responsibility in daily practice for maintaining and improving cohesion and resilience in society. This is the special contribution of social work in the mix of professions concerned with psychosocial care.

Our emphasis on helping people achieve control of their lives as part of practice does not only derive from social work's value commitment to empowerment. Many people at the end of life feel that their health is out of their control, and they may focus on emotional help using social and spiritual support, making their lives bearable (Pacheco, Hershberger, Markert, & Kumar, 2003). Being able to die at home if you wish is an important factor in feeling in control. Karlsen and Addington-Hall's (1998) post-bereavement survey of 229 people who registered a death from cancer in an area of London found that to facilitate this practitioners needed to recognize that a home death was desired before crises arose. Then, it is possible to provide motivation to patients and caregivers to "stick with it" in adversity, providing practical community support to assist.

Powazki and Walsh (1999) studied the use of a psychosocial assessment in an American hospital palliative care team. Its greatest use was in discharge processes, and four major problems were the focus of social workers' activities:

- Problem solving
- Adjustment to and coping with the illness and prognosis
- The capacity to carry out the daily tasks of living
- Communicating concerns to others

Social Work Objectives

Working in biomedical settings emphasizes the way medical and nursing colleagues center their work on individual patient care. Hodgson (2005) suggests that consequently social workers in end-of-life care overemphasize working on psychological issues with patients or individual family members, rather than social needs in response to the dying person, because that fits with the individualized biomedical approach. She proposes Egan's (1992) concept of "best fit" as a way of working with the psychological within the social:

- Helping patients and others involved to "tell the story," rather than focusing first on issues that come from the practitioner's role or the service's objectives—the basis for the narrative approach to engagement that we suggested in Chapter 4
- Identifying and focusing on issues in which behavior and emotions are having an impact on families and social functioning
- Exploring alternative ways of seeing the situations and a range of possible solutions

We have also found this approach helpful in end-of-life settings, and much of the practice discussed in this chapter follows these precepts. The end of life is a time when people are particularly vulnerable because they face uncertainty, loss on an almost unimaginable scale, and a body that is failing them. They need help in dealing with facing the adjustment involved in a person's changed circumstances, the need for information, both practical and emotional, and the need for resources to make living more manageable. Monroe (2004, p. 1009), therefore, identifies the main objectives for intervention as being the need for information in order to solve problems, to help individuals and families communicate, and to enable people to act on issues they want to deal with if they do not have the resources they need to do so, including financial resources and social support.

Moving into Intervention

Previous chapters demonstrated the importance of a number of emotional experiences as the starting point of intervention in end-of-life care. These were:

- Loss
- Uncertainty
- Truth, hope, and denial

These issues never cease to be important in end-of-life care because, as we saw in Chapter 2, many people never "come to terms" with their own death and perhaps should not be asked to. That is, they never arrive at an awareness that they are approaching the end of life, and respond appropriately in their thoughts, feelings, and social relationships to this understanding. When someone attending a caregivers' group articulated her concerns that her husband had not come to terms with the fact that he was dying, the response from other group members was to question whether it is ever really possible to come to terms with such a situation.

Therefore, intervention in end-of-life care takes this continuing focus on in a new way. People have to deal with the practicalities of the change affecting them and their family, and as they are doing so they also have to manage continuing changes in their emotional reaction to these experiences. Gelderd and Gelderd (2005) see the skills involved aiming to help people manage change:

- Confronting clients respectfully when they are avoiding important issues
- Normalizing by helping clients understand where their behavior and reactions are appropriate to their situation
- Reframing stories or experiences so that clients can see them differently
- Challenging and changing destructive beliefs drawing on techniques from cognitive-behavioral therapy
- Helping clients to identify situations in which they hide important emotions or other aspects of their situations

- Helping clients identify and make use of their strengths
- Focusing on the here and now to see what we can change
- Exploring options for change
- Helping people take action through encouragement and influencing their environment

Approaching the end of life often raises for clients and their families the uncertainty and impermanence of their own lives, as well as the patient's life (Larkin, Dierckx de Casterlé, & Schotsmans, 2007). Therefore, a focus on emotions is an important starting point for caregivers as well as patients. Coffey's work with families facing catastrophic illness is informed by working through three questions: "What do I have to offer in this situation," "What does healing mean for this family," and "How might therapy, spirituality, and community interface be helpful?" (Coffey, 2004, p. 53). The answers change as the situation changes.

Case example: Heather

We mentioned Heather, age fifty, briefly in Chapter 3. She was diagnosed with ALS two years before the events described here. As she began to come to terms with her increasing weakness, she retained hope but kept revising what she was hoping for. Coffey describes the dilemma of this stage as "sustaining hope with continuing loss" (Coffey, 2004, p. 55). Heather stopped hoping to get home and instead began hoping that she would be kept comfortable and that she would not die choking. Following discussion, the team looking after her told Heather that if she wished she could continue to have hospice care for as long as she needed it; this gave her a sense of security and peace of mind. The social worker picks up the story:

My work involved exploring her adjustment following her diagnosis to the losses she experienced, including job, lifestyle, independence, mobility, role, interests, body image, confidence, and control. She and her husband, David, coped differently. Although they were close, they found it difficult talking about feelings and sharing their sadness and anxiety. This exacerbated Heather's feelings of isolation; she was convinced that David did not understand how ill she was. David's approach was to try always to "cheer Heather up"; he became visibly uncomfortable if difficult issues were raised in front of Heather. Yet he was aware of Heather's increasing difficulties and that her problems with swallowing, breathing, and feeding meant that she might not have long to live.

When Heather required ventilation at night, she became anxious and frightened. She feared she would suffocate from falling asleep with the ventilation mask over her face and die. She tried night sedation without using the ventilation machine, but the resulting deep sleep depressed her breathing. Her physician was afraid that she might stop breathing and die. She became exhausted, unhappy, and afraid of the coming of nighttime. David visited her each day and attempted, unsuccessfully, to lift her low mood by diversionary tactics. David also found it difficult to talk openly with their teenage children, age sixteen and thirteen.

My intervention consisted of several interviews with Heather on her own. Heather was clear that she wanted David to be able to acknowledge with her that she might not have much longer to live. She recognized that, earlier in her illness, she had been protecting him; her coping strategy had been to remain determined and positive. But as she realized she could not continue fighting the disease, she wanted more open communication with David but felt stuck. She asked if I would help her talk to David; we agreed on a plan.

David, however, wanted to talk to me on his own. He did not want her upset. He could see no point to being direct with his wife and felt I was pushing him to do something Heather did not want. Then we met together. I explained that Heather was concerned about him and was worried he may not fully understand the implications of the changes in her condition. He was indignant. I suggested that not talking about something that is worrying does not make it any less distressing, but can create a tension that becomes an additional burden. Heather articulated clearly why she wanted to share everything with her husband and how it was no longer helpful to keep secrets from each other. She stated that it was a huge relief to her to be having this conversation even if it was very painful for both of them. Eventually they were both able to hug each other, share their tears, and comfort each other. Heather became much calmer and died peacefully with her family around her a week later.

Anticipatory grief (grieving for a loss before it occurs) is thought to protect people in bereavement to some extent, but as Worden points out there are many other factors that make any simple correlation between grief and any one variable unreliable (Worden, 2003, p. 137). Nevertheless, it is usually helpful, as in this case, to facilitate difficult conversations when people have reached the point in their lives and illness where they want to have them.

PREPARING FOR DEATH

An important aspect of "coming to terms" with death is preparing for it, and this can involve more than individual work of the kind described with Heather. At St. Christopher's Hospice in London, the arts team works with people preparing for death in a range of ways:

- Enabling them to create a memorial by making craft, artistic, or other gifts to "give something back" for the care and support offered by caregivers and family members
- Enabling them to develop their skills and knowledge and achieve a fulfilling outcome
- Enabling them to express some of their feelings and responses to their end-of-life situations
- Enabling them to remember and memorialize important aspects of their lives and families (Hartley & Payne, 2008)

Another important way of preparing for death is putting financial and business affairs in order and dealing with outstanding relationship issues. The relationship issues are often characterized as follows, although we do not know the source of this palliative care practice wisdom:

- Saying "goodbye"; sometimes practitioners will need to find, inform, and reconcile long-estranged relatives.
- Saying "I love you"; this may be hard in particular for people from cultures and ethnicities where overt expression of love is unusual, for example between men, or fathers and sons.
- Saying "sorry"; Byock (1997) refers to this as a mutual process: "Please forgive me; I forgive you." Examples of this are apologies for anger during the illness, or care which has not been of the best; there are some examples of this in Chapter 4.
- Saying "thank you"; appreciation of care and valuation of the relationship and events shared may be important.

Life Reviews

Life review comes from the idea that people live through a series of stages in life. Transition from one stage to the next can be facilitated by rational processing of experience of previous phases (Haight & Bahr,

1984). Dying is seen as a social transition for the person, which is susceptible to the same kind of processing (Pickrel, 1989). This is connected to the practice of reminiscence, helping older people with memory problems (Lappe, 1987). Recent developments have included the use of narrative strategies to help people make connections between various events in their lives by "telling a story." The practitioner offers a questionnaire covering various phases or aspects of life a few days in advance of a meeting with the practitioner. This helps clients to plan their narrative. Commonly, the questionnaire covers:

- Childhood and family of origin
- Adulthood and work life
- The here and now—particularly focusing on the impact on the present phase of life of the illness and impending death (Lester, 2005)

RESPECTING AND WORKING WITH EXCLUDED GROUPS

We noted in Chapter 2 that many social groups may have difficulty in accessing end-of-life care services. As an important representative of a social science knowledge base that places issues of social justice centrally in its values, social work has a particular role in end-of-life care in ensuring that services understand, respect, and work with excluded groups.

Hearn (2005), referring particularly to bereavement, draws attention to a range of models of practice of social work, which identify likely circumstances in which we may exclude people and which apply more widely to end-of-life care:

- Social models of disability, which draw attention to the way in which societies create "disabling environments" that exclude people from participation
- Resilience models, which propose that we fail to identify people's varying vulnerability to different stresses in their lives, leading us to fail to identify and build on their strengths
- Disenfranchised grief, which suggests that some forms of grief are not socially or culturally acceptable
- Need, supply, and demand, which suggests that we often fail to meet needs because we have failed to develop appropriate services, but blame the person with the need for not demanding the services we have rather than the services they want (Smaje & Field, 1997)
- Dual process models of grief, which suggest that we fail to recognize the relevance of both practical and emotional concerns

Groups that may suffer from exclusion from end-of-life care services are:

- Older people, particularly those living in residential or nursing homes; it may be assumed that since they are receiving care, this will be enough to meet their needs for end-of-life care.
- Poor people may not be able to or fear that they cannot afford services; this may be because primary care services do not refer them to specialized palliative care. There is also evidence that people in poverty may not have access to informal social support (Bourjolly & Hirschman, 2001).
- People with dementia, intellectual disabilities or physical disability, where the focus may be on the condition rather than the likelihood of end of life occurring.
- Prisoners and residents in other institutions, since end-of-life care may not be available.
- People from minority ethnic groups, either because they take a cultural view that rejects end-of-life and palliative care in favor of curative treatment (research indicates that this may be true of African Americans, for example) or because discrimination excludes them from access, or they fear that this may be so (again, this has been shown in some American minority ethnic groups; Thomson, 2003), prefer discretion rather than truth-telling (this is often true of Chinese and other Asian cultures) (Boyle, 1998; Ng, Schumakher, & Goh, 2000). Another difficulty in poor areas (for example in the United States; Payne, 2004) has been the availability of or the ability to obtain palliative medicines, which are liable to be abused; and in some countries medicinal access to heroin derivatives such as morphine is restricted.

As examples of approaches to end-of-life care with such excluded groups, we discuss more extensively practice with minority ethnic groups and people with intellectual disabilities (see also Chapter 3).

Ethnic and Cultural Minorities

In the United States, the United Kingdom, and other Western countries, people from ethnic minority groups have been underrepresented in receiving end-of-life care; we therefore focus on working with the inequalities such groups face as an example of the need to work with other excluded groups. The many reasons for this seem to include:

- Hospices have often originated from charitable or political campaigns for service, which lead to their being sited where donations can be raised, or political and administrative support can be achieved for their foundation.

- Some religious or denominational affiliations may have beliefs that are inconsistent with palliative care principles. For example, Asian cultures may oppose acceptance that death is coming, and focus on prayer for a miracle, or may see the experience of illness as a test of religious commitment or death as a release to a better existence.
- Social conventions or expectations in a minority group may lead to a resistance to professional rather than family care, or demand specific provision that meets cultural or religious needs.
- Services may not provide for care needs, for example meals may not be appropriate to a particular minority group, or prayer facilities are not available.
- People from deprived minority ethnic groups may not be aware of the availability of specialized palliative care services.
- Some minority groups may focus strongly on maintaining efforts at cure, leading them to reject palliative care. This may be because they fear that discrimination may exclude them from opportunities to receive the best care and medical services, or because of a cultural preference to "keep on fighting."

Case example: Amelie

A practitioner was asked to help a black woman, Amelie, age thirty-nine, persuade her mother to accept her admission to a hospice for terminal care. Amelie felt that her mother's preparations for Amelie's care at home were inappropriate, while the mother wanted to maintain her hope that her daughter would improve, and practical preparations for care helped her to do this. The practitioner explored the disagreement jointly, and arrived at an agreement that they would not discuss their alternative perspectives. The multiprofessional team agreed not to discuss preparations for terminal care with the mother, but only with Amelie herself, until the progression of her illness helped her mother to accept the reality that death was close.

Added to these explanations, focusing on social systems, for the exclusion of people from minority ethnic groups from palliative care, people from minority ethnic groups may feel discomfort with the Western emphasis on openness about dying, preventing them from being sufficiently comfortable to access hospice care. Using the word hospice may itself be a barrier if openness is not an acceptable component of end-of-life care.

Pause and reflect: Case example—Santokh and Raveena

Santokh Singh and Raveena Kaur were married Sikhs. Raveena, age forty-eight, was dying of colon cancer. She lived at home with her husband, Santokh, and two sons, age eighteen and twenty-four. Raveena's husband was very protective of his wife and made it clear to health-care professionals visiting Raveena at home that he would not allow any discussion around issues of dying and prognosis. The palliative care nurse found it hard to assess the severity of Raveena's pain, because her husband would always answer on her behalf. The nurse thought he might be minimizing his wife's pain because he himself could not face how ill she was; however, the social work assessment was that it was more likely that the family's communication pattern was culturally driven.

The family were devout Sikhs and their religion was very important to them. Raveena's father, who lived in India, was not told his daughter was ill until after she had died because the family felt it would prolong his distress if he were to be aware of her illness in advance. Raveena and her husband retained traditional cultural roles within their family. Raveena's role was to provide for the family within the home. She managed all the domestic tasks and had sole responsibility for family and social matters. Only she knew when the family birthdays and celebrations were, for example. Mr. Singh's role was to work outside the home to provide financially for the family. Both were codependent and saw themselves as the perfect team. Any risk to the stability and continuity of this relationship was extremely threatening to the family's mechanism for survival. Understanding and respecting the family's beliefs and fears was essential to achieving a peaceful death for Raveena.

How might you approach this dilemma? What information might help? How could you address any learning needs you have?

Some suggestions

In the last few days of her life, Raveena was admitted to an in-patient hospice. Mr. Singh insisted that his wife not be told about the reason for admission and wanted her to believe that she was coming to a place that could provide nursing care for someone who was not ill enough to warrant hospital admission and that when her symptoms were controlled she would return home. For Mr. Singh, it became clear to the team treating his wife that maintaining hope of life was essential and absolutely fundamental to the family's belief system.

Responses to Ethnic Differences

Csikai and Chaitin (2006, p. 58) emphasize how "respectful care" depends on thinking through how race, culture, and gender affect an individual's personality and value structure. In some cultures, as Dein and

Thomas (2002, p. 209) report, it is the patient's family "which assumes the responsibility for health-seeking and decision-making and which shields the sick person from the truth about diagnosis and prognosis in terminal illness" and that "in many cultures . . . the Anglo-American practice of open disclosure is seen as shocking." Some efforts to deal with these issues involve offering general guidance about the typical expectations of different religions; for example, many Muslims like the bed of a dying person to be moved to face Mecca, and to pray facing Mecca, the holy city. However, as with Christian and Jewish people, there are strict and less strict adherents to the faith and there are many different cultural expressions of faiths; the only sensible approach, therefore, is to express your wish to make arrangements that are appropriate for the person you are dealing with and ask the client or family what they would prefer.

Another difficulty that sometimes arises is where families represent more than one culture or faith. It is often necessary to see different members of the family separately and negotiate arrangements for care, for the time of death, and for the funeral.

Case example: The Ferrari family

Mr. Ferrari was an Italian Roman Catholic living with a Muslim partner and their two young children after his separation from his wife. She and the two children of the marriage were Roman Catholic. His family did not observe their faith, but his wife's family, who traveled to the hospital in which he was dying, lived in Italy and were very strong believers. They had not been aware of the separation, and when they arrived difficult exchanges arose in the hospital. Discussing the situation with the social worker, a roster for visiting was arranged so that members of different branches of the family did not meet each other; in fact, over time, caring for and thinking about the children reduced the level of hostility. Then the matter of the funeral came up. The partner was prepared to relinquish the funeral arrangements to the family, and it was agreed that a nonreligious memorial event would be held in the hospital chapel after the death; the chapel was Christian, but this was acceptable to the partner. The Italian family had wanted to have the body returned to Italy, but had not realized how expensive this would be. In the end, they compromised with a Roman Catholic memorial Mass and a civil burial.

Werth and colleagues (Werth, Blevins, Tonssaint, & Durham, 2002) offer useful guidance for professionals dealing with these complexities, to which we have added some comments:

- Be openly prepared to negotiate, expressing the importance of respecting everyone's beliefs; in particular, it is important to be aware that in many cultures families take responsibility jointly for decision making and reject the Western convention of individualism that only the patient has the right to decide on treatment and care.
- Assess how the family communicates about illness, prognosis, death, and practical arrangements.
- Who makes decisions? It may be the patient, a leading member of the family (in many cultures the recognized head of the family), or some form of group decision making.
- Ask for the range of views about place and timing of death, who should be present, and what roles family members and professionals should take (in many cultures, a wife or family members should lay out the body in a prescribed form).
- Are the family fatalistic or active in wanting treatment, and what degree of control do they want over decisions? Their views may need to be negotiated with medical and legal conventions, which focus on the patient's decision.
- Consider gender and power relationships in the family; for example, cultural assumptions of traditional members of the family who may emerge to take charge in this important family event may lead to younger women being excluded even though they have adopted a more Western level of involvement in decisions.
- Consider religious, faith, or belief systems and the effect the family says they have on the meaning of death (e.g., belief in miracles or witchcraft).
- Establish what the family and patient want to be done with the body after death.
- Assess how hope is negotiated and assess how the family responds to prognostic decisions by health care providers.

So far, we have concentrated mainly on emotional issues, since these are so important in end-of-life care; in the remainder of the chapter we move on to work on wider end-of-life issues.

THE BUZZ

But before we move on, here is a poem, written by Clement Fuller, that expresses many of the emotions felt by dying people about the changes in their lives.

I miss getting up in the morning,
Going to work,
I miss taking someone's house apart
And putting it back together again.

It gives me a buzz   5
To see it all come together
And the client comes in
And sees the change.

I miss the challenge
Of doing things with my hands.   10
I wonder if I will ever be able
To do some of all of the things
That I love to do.

I went out to the park with my son.
I rode my bike   15
For the first time
With my son.
He was very happy
That we could ride our bikes together again.

I was very happy   20
To see the smile on his face.
It was as if his smile said:
"My Dad is back"
And it made me feel
That I was doing something normal.   25

I crave the buzz
Of doing something with my hands.

INDIVIDUAL WORK USING SPECIFIC THERAPEUTIC TECHNIQUES

Theoretical Perspectives in End-of-Life Social Work

All social work knowledge incorporates psychological and social knowledge. A wide range of social work theories exists (Payne, 2005), and all have something to contribute to end-of-life practice; practitioners transfer generic knowledge and conceptualizations into practice in specialized settings such as those for end-of-life care. However, we identify six major sets of theoretical ideas about social work practice that have particularly influenced end-of-life social work:

- Cognitive-behavioral theory. This and similar theories addressing behavior change provide widely used evidence-based techniques for devising and implementing behavior-change programs; we give some examples below.
- Narrative ideas. This relatively recently developed set of ideas focuses on facilitating clients and others to construct an account of events leading to and affecting the present situations, according

to the individual's perception. We use this approach in our discussion of communication, particularly in Chapters 3 and 4.

- Psychodynamic theories. Psychoanalysis and psychodynamic thinking has had an important theoretical influence on social work and on some forms of psychotherapy and counseling. While not central to much of his thinking, Freud's idea of the "death instinct," Thanatos, suggested that unconscious self-destructive impulses may be an important motivator of people's behavior. These developments were an important driver of ideas about reasons for suicide and for social disintegration, for example, of drug addicts or alcoholics. Psychodynamic ideas focus on the interaction of thinking processes, some of which may not be fully rational or fully within the individual's awareness, with social influences on people's development. A particularly important influence in end-of-life care is attachment theory, which suggests that people's early and continuing life experience of attachment affects how they react to losses in their lives such as death. We particularly use this theoretical framework in Chapter 6.
- Social construction theory. Social construction ideas examine how social expectations and beliefs influence how people think and behave in social situations.
- Systems ideas. These ideas suggest that everyone is influenced by individuals and social organizations that they interact with, and that to understand and influence how people react to events in their lives requires consideration of the social networks and social institutions that they are part of, often their family, community, work, and education networks.

Identifying appropriate social work interventions requires practitioners to build on assessment skills, discussed in Chapter 4, to develop an understanding of clients and their families to explore what might and might not be helpful.

We discussed narrative and systems approaches as integral to the contribution that social workers make in assessment in multiprofessional teamwork. Here, we discuss cognitive-behavioral work as an example of application of a specific social work theory, choosing this partly because its methods are well supported by evidence of effectiveness, at least for achieving short-term change. Using a cognitive approach to promote adjustment in end-of-life care is increasingly seen as a valid model to consider for palliative care interventions (Moorey & Greer, 2002). While open-minded use of integrative techniques is often the most sensible approach, some clients welcome a direct approach to problem solving because it gives back some control in a situation where the illness has sometimes taken over and loss has become the predominant focus.

Using Cognitive-Behavioral Therapy (CBT)

CBT is based on the premise that an individual's emotional and behavioral reactions to having a life-threatening illness are determined by the meaning this holds for the person and the interpretations he or she makes about the situation (Moorey & Greer, 2002, p. 51; Sage, Sowden, Chorlton, & Edeleanu, 2008). A person's thoughts, emotions, physical sensations, and behavior interact and can lead to patterns of negative thinking, which in turn lead to unhelpful responses and may be perpetuated by distorted thinking. The cognitive model proposes that by understanding these responses, an individual can control and thereby change unhelpful or intrusive thoughts. This is particularly helpful in end-of-life care, because regaining control of both emotional responses and social situations is an important objective for many clients.

Explaining the model in a way that makes sense to the client is usually a prerequisite so that the client can understand the rationale and fully participate in making changes that will alter his or her unhelpful or distressing thinking and behavior. Engaging with clients collaboratively to reach an assessment of the issue they are trying to tackle and what has contributed to it is the next task for a practitioner using this approach. It is also useful to examine the factors contributing to maintaining the behavior. Among important formulations are the "vicious cycle" and the "downward spiral." Having agreed upon a formulation with the client, the social worker can plan the intervention. What changes might be made that could help the client overcome the problem, perhaps by interrupting a vicious cycle or preventing a downward spiral? Creating cognitive behavioral formulations helps to identify effective interventions so that appropriate goals are set. Goals need to be achievable, relevant, and important to the client. They need to be clearly stated and specific so that progress and outcome can be measured. The example below highlights a very simple piece of work with an outcome that could have been achieved by a variety of social work interventions. However, in this case, adopting a cognitive approach enables the underlying problem to be identified quickly with the focus on the solution.

Case example: Andrea

Work with Andrea illustrates an example of CBT work; the practitioner's account follows:

As different problems emerged over the last year of her life, Andrea and I identified their triggers and set achievable goals, which gave her back a sense of control. I began by asking Andrea what she most wanted to change. Andrea had been forced to give up work a few weeks previously and now felt that her life lacked structure. As she put it: "Everything's fallen apart." She felt unable to do "anything," and she felt she had been "slung on the scrap heap." Andrea was able to recognize the mental traps she was falling into, to use CBT jargon, "all-or-nothing thinking": "If I can't work any more, I'm no good to anyone, everything's fallen apart." Another mental trap she identified was overgeneralization, feeling unable to do "anything."

The first challenge was to decide what could not be changed and needed accepting; the next challenge was to find goals that were right for Andrea. Accepting the limitations such as decreasing mobility caused by her cancer was necessary, but the negative thinking of "slung on the scrap heap" could be changed, and she could adjust more positively to the changes in her life. We agreed that the formulation that would help us understand her problem was a vicious cycle, set out in figure 5.1.

FIGURE 5.1 Vicious cycle in CBT: Andrea

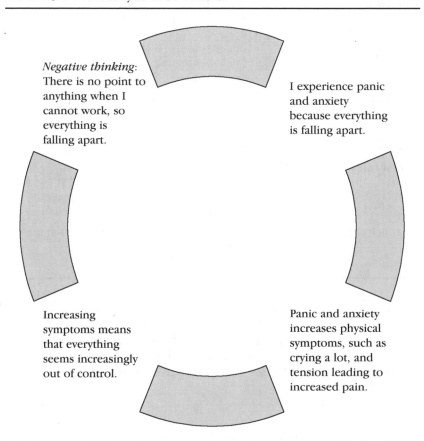

Negative thinking: There is no point to anything when I cannot work, so everything is falling apart.

I experience panic and anxiety because everything is falling apart.

Increasing symptoms means that everything seems increasingly out of control.

Panic and anxiety increases physical symptoms, such as crying a lot, and tension leading to increased pain.

Having used cognitive techniques to treat successfully the negative thinking and the panic attacks that followed, Andrea commented that her quality of life had improved considerably and she had some structure to her day. When, several months later, Andrea encountered a new problem she called to ask if I could see her again to work with her on this new problem, as set out in table 5.2.

TABLE 5.2   Example of CBT assessment: Andrea

Issue	*Andrea's analysis*
Specific definition of the problem:	Overwhelming periods of gloom which are very distressing and disabling and cause disturbing thoughts—they seem to come at any time and happen most days.
Thoughts:	• fear of future • worrying about what will happen • dread of hospitals • thoughts focus on all the things now unable to do such as walking, sport, being active • "losses" hit me
Feelings:	• anger at illness and its effects • feeling trapped in awful situation • loss of control
Behavior:	• crying
Mental traps:	• easy to get things out of proportion—over-generalization • all-or-nothing thinking—e.g., automatically associating pain with hospital admission
What helps?	• companionship—both family and good friends • good book • watching television

Andrea identified that she is more likely to experience the intrusive and distressing thoughts in table 5.2 when she is in pain. She worked out a plan to deal with these issues herself, as set out in Table 5.3. This proved effective as a basis for her to work on her own.

TABLE 5.3 Plan for tackling distressing thoughts using CBT

Action	Andrea's plans
Set precise goals	• Remind herself of good days rather than dwelling on bad days. • Ensure that activities are planned for each day, such as visits with friends, but make sure to pace herself so that there is always something to look forward to. Don't overdo things, to avoid making her pain worse. • See hospice nurse to review pain relief, but recognize that additional analgesia does not mean hospital admission is required. Hospice admission would be a better option if problems cannot be resolved at home. • Make a memory box for granddaughter. • Plan a trip to Australia to visit family.
Homework	Andrea will keep a record of when periods of despair occur, how long they last, what thoughts and feelings occur, and what alleviates them, using this to check that she is working on goals.

WORK WITH FAMILY MEMBERS AND CAREGIVERS

Enabling family members and informal caregivers to play their role in caring for a dying person and thereby strengthening the family in the long-term is one of the defining contributions of social work to end-of-life care. It is also an important political concern, since informal caregivers make a significant and irreplaceable contribution to meeting the needs of dying people; responding to their needs consequently has an important place in the U.K. end-of-life strategy (DH, 2008) and on the U.S. government website on end-of-life care (see Chapter 1 for the URL). In the United States, 50 million people at any given time provide care for family members, 60 percent of them women (NFCA, 2008). Family members of a dying person experience a range of emotions and cope in different ways. Losses from the deteriorating condition of the person dying, and changes in the balance within family relationships, affects the family system and leads to changes in role (Jeffreys, 2005, p. 201; Zilberfein & Hurwitz, 2004, p. 303). Spouse caregivers in a Canadian study (Jo, Brazil, Lohfeld, & Willison 2007) saw their care as a natural extension of family relationships, but experienced negative reactions such as fatigue, depression, anger, sadness, financial difficulties, and lack of time. Care recipients understood and acknowledged the stresses and were concerned for their spouses.

While preparing fully for someone dying is not possible, social work intervention to help people to let go may be timely and important. It can provide preparation such as addressing concerns about what happens to their body after death, negotiating legal issues, or discussing what sort of funeral they want; this allows negotiation about individual and family preferences to take place, as discussed above. For others, focusing on what to do after someone has died feels inappropriate and contributes to feelings of guilt. As always, social workers need the skills to assess what sort of intervention might be most appropriate. Timing is particularly important to avoid being insensitive.

Many dying people become increasingly dependent on family, friends, and other caregivers for practical and emotional help. For caregivers, whether a close family member or not, providing round-the-clock care and being frequently with a dying person interacts with their own feelings of loss. Enabling family members to combine their caring role with their own impending loss and grief at the same time is a fundamental task for health care, where social work skills and expertise in working with families is particularly valuable.

This emotional labor (see Chapter 4) connects powerfully with the burden of caring: "caring is hard work, becomes a full-time job and forces life changes of great magnitude to the extent that one's former life is lost" (Brown, 2003, p. 215). Following assessment, social workers can intervene by arranging practical supportive services as well as offering emotional and psychological support. Rabow and his associates state that: "adult day care, respite care, home care, social work services, and caregiver education and psychological support demonstrably improve caregiver satisfaction, quality of life, and burden" (Rabow et al., 2004, p. 489).

Jo and colleagues (2007) point out that although the unit of care in any palliative care service should be the patient's family in addition to the patient, research in this area only rarely includes studying the family experiences of both the caregiver and the care-receiver. Hence, they set out in their study to "examine the perspectives of both the spousal caregiver and care recipient on the end-of-life caregiving experience in home-based palliative care" (Jo et al., 2007, p. 12). Their findings reinforce the view that caregiver needs and concerns (as well as those of care-receivers) must be understood and addressed by health and social care professionals for successful outcomes to end-of-life intervention.

Sustaining families has the secondary gain of also helping the patient. Rabow and colleagues highlights this fact: "Family caregiving is typically at the core of what sustains patients at the end of life" (Rabow, Hauser, & Adams, 2004, p. 483). They also identify "five burdens of family caregiving (time and logistics, physical tasks, financial costs, emotional burdens and mental health risks, and physical health risks)" (Rabow et al., 2004).

Similarly, Harding and colleagues state that, "the needs of informal carers of patients attending specialist palliative care are multi-dimensional, including psychological support, information, fatigue, financial support and respite. Indeed in the final days of life the needs of the family may exceed those of the patient" (Harding & Leam, 2005, p. 639).

While social work interventions with caregivers and family members may be offered on a one-to-one basis, their extreme stress may be more effectively counteracted by meeting with others in similar situations (NICE, 2004). Because the task of caring is so complex, mixed emotions are common. Maintaining hope in the face of despair or feeling a sense of relief at the prospect of the caring role coming to an end can lead to feelings of despair and guilt. When "caregivers find themselves in support groups with other 'like' members, these barriers are removed, and members are able to share their feelings openly and honestly" (Sutton & Liechty, 2004, p. 510). While such help can be provided individually, research shows that some of these "important processes occur only, or occur best, in a group setting" (Sutton & Liechty, 2004). We therefore examine individual help in this chapter, and examine group work with caregivers in Chapter 9.

ABUSE OF PATIENTS AND ADULT AND CHILD PROTECTION

The negative side of family relationships also arises in end-of-life and palliative care: people approaching the end of their lives may be abused by the people around them. All palliative care patients are vulnerable people and their families are going through a stressful and difficult period in their lives, when emotions run high. Moreover, many families will not previously have had serious involvement with health care and social work professionals visiting their homes. Most palliative care patients are elderly, and prevalence studies internationally demonstrate that a small proportion of older people are liable to be abused, often by people who care for them, both professionals and family caregivers. The recently published study of prevalence of abuse of older people in the United Kingdom provides the first authoritative estimate of the extent of abuse of older people in their own homes: between 2.6 and 4 percent of the population over sixty years of age. The most common forms of abuse found were neglect and financial abuse (O'Keeffe et al., 2007). Pillemer and Finkelhor's (1988) U.S. study in Boston came up with similar results. Visiting professionals also need to be alert to the possibility of child abuse or neglect in families and of domestic violence. Though they may not themselves be working with these children, any professional should take action to protect abused children. Changes in the dynamics of the family during the dying and bereavement processes may increase the risk of abuse.

111

Abuse is any situation where the human rights of people are compromised by those who have power over them acting in ways that may hurt them physically or emotionally. The watchwords for professionals are ALERT, AWARE, and ACTIVE, that is, being alert to the possibility that abuse may be taking place, aware of the local procedures for responding to such situations, and active in doing something about it—and communicating with professional colleagues.

Examples of neglect or abuse encountered in palliative care are as follows (Payne, 2008c):

- A former paraprofessional caregiver spending a patient's disability pension inappropriately. The caregiver claimed that the patient and the caregiver intended to get married. The patient was dying and had a history of mental illness.
- A patient with intellectual disabilities fell into rent arrears. Asked about rent-payment methods, the patient revealed that a neighbor who was a drug user had been forcing him go to the ATM and hand over his weekly income.
- A patient receiving oral morphine said she was frightened of her fourteen-year-old daughter's friends coming into her house because the friends used drugs recreationally and were aggressive.
- A patient with a history of mental illness, who was being cared for at home by her son, claimed that he hit her.
- A man caring for his dying wife in a chaotic apartment was neglecting her care and medication.

When concerns about abuse arise, the patient's welfare takes priority. However, in certain situations there will be concern for the welfare of the caregiver as well as the patient. For example, the son of the mentally ill woman acknowledged his mother was verbally aggressive toward him and that his frustration caused him to hit her. He was frustrated and exhausted looking after his mother at home rather than going out to work. In this case, both parties were vulnerable. People are often ambivalent about their lives. The son wanted to care for his mother, but he also wanted freedom and to be able to work. When she was aggressive, he became frustrated and regretful about the life-decisions he had made. The mother wanted the son to care for her. She appreciated what he did. However, that appreciation did not prevent her mental illness causing aggressive behavior.

People are also afraid to reveal the abuse that they are suffering. They fear that the "authorities" will disturb the only close relationships and the only care that they have. Patients often recognize why their abuser is finding it difficult to provide appropriate care, or respond to a new development in their relationship. Most patients want to be protected (Payne, 2005) and may also want help for their caregiver, who may also be their abuser.

Abuse is often a continuation of a previously existing pattern of behavior that becomes inappropriate and abusive because of increased vulnerability of the patient (Payne, 2005); as we discussed in Chapter 4, power relationships in families often change as someone becomes frail or ill. For example, some families have "robust" arguments, shouting and threatening each other in a way that seems very aggressive to outsiders. If the behavior is established and is not causing the client to feel unusually upset, then we should think very carefully about whether it is necessary to intervene. A private talk between the patient and the practitioner to find out the patient's feelings would be key to deciding what to do. However, when a patient becomes ill, he or she may be less able to cope with behavior that was previously acceptable. Other members of the family may need help in understanding how a change in the patient's health makes their behavior now inappropriate.

Assessing abuse is often not about blame. It is more about examining what is going wrong in family relationships. Patients' increasing frailty makes them more dependent on and vulnerable to others' behavior. The practice of safeguarding adults does not require practitioners to judge people's behavior. Instead, they should focus on:

- How can a vulnerable person be protected?
- How can the situation be improved for everyone involved?

The assessment process must examine and make clear people's vulnerabilities. At the end of life, vulnerability may be physical, psychological, or social. Physical vulnerability may mean that patients are more likely to bruise, fall, or break their skin and bones than previously. People may not be conscious of, or accept, their increased vulnerability. Their hope for cure, or misunderstanding of their condition or treatment may place a suddenly frail person more at risk than someone whose frailty has developed slowly. The reverse may also be the case. When people know they are at the end of life, they may be more psychologically at risk. They may be unaccustomed to, or not recognize, high levels of depression and anxiety. They may not realize that treatment is available for psychological distress.

Approaching the end of life may render patients socially vulnerable. They may be anxious to mend a relationship with a family member, maintain social contacts, or organize care for their dependents in the future. Thus, they may be more open to manipulation. They may accept misuse of their money or being insulted to "keep the peace" when most people would think that the person they are dependent on is behaving unreasonably. For example, a man accepted that his caregiver would not spend money to replace a broken hearing aid and spectacles because he was going to die soon and it was a waste of money, when the social worker felt that this unreasonably cut the patient off from social contacts and leisure activities.

Possible interventions for the protection of a vulnerable adult might include:

- Interventions to help people care more appropriately for a patient, e.g., relatives may receive training in techniques of moving and handling frail patients that reduce distress.
- Interventions to improve relationships in the family or social network around the family, e.g., stressed family members might be given help in managing anger.
- Providing additional support to informal caregivers, such as respite care, or "night sitters" combined with additional nursing or care support in the home.
- Coordinating contacts with the patient among professionals so that the patient's condition is regularly checked.
- Making alternative arrangements for the management of finances and warning banks and financial regulators to look out for unexpected transactions.
- Warning or setting boundaries for caregivers or others in the patient's social network about appropriate relationships.
- Helping family members to plan their contact with a patient and think about the future. For example, anxious family members may need to understand that they are putting too much pressure on the patient to meet their own emotional and physical needs.

Pause and reflect—Joan and Kim

During the final phase of her bowel cancer, Joan moved in with Kim, the eldest of her three daughters. When Kim ran out of money after paying some rent arrears, she took some money from her mother's purse to pay the milkman. A sister mentioned this to the home care nurse that she thought this was wrong. Another sister visited the hospice social worker to blame Kim for not feeding their mother: Joan had been losing weight and all the members of this family were overweight; eating well was an important family issue.

The question for the team was: "Is Kim exploiting or neglecting her mother?" What would you do?

Some suggestions

The situation required sensitive communication with all family members to find out what was happening. While the home-care nurse took Kim aside for a discussion, the doctor discussed with Joan how she felt about her care. She wanted to stay with Kim, but she agreed that she had been treated roughly. Following the local procedure for dealing with allegations of abuse, the social worker called a "strategy meeting" of the professionals involved, working with the lead agency for adult protection.

Ideally, the family should have planned transparent financial arrangements when Joan moved in with Kim, carefully accounting for expenditure and bringing fears to the surface. However, families coping with a serious illness do not always plan their caring roles carefully and rationally, and a history of poor relationships may get in the way. Picking up the concerns expressed to the doctor, the team arranged for a physical therapist to give Kim training in lifting and moving her mother. The allegations of financial abuse and poor care were brought out sensitively with family members by the home care and adult protection workers. The strategy meeting arranged for professionals to plan family visits so that someone saw them almost every day as a protection against things going wrong before they developed into a family dispute.

PLANNING FOR IMPORTANT LIFE DECISIONS

Children

Parents who are dying while their children are still dependent have many issues to consider and social workers are likely to be involved. Social work training and expertise equips social workers more than other health professionals on the multiprofessional team to address the complex dilemmas and concerns facing the patient and family.

Assessment is an essential requirement, but, as we saw in Chapter 4, the initial task is to develop a relationship of trust and understanding with the person who is ill and other key family members. Social workers need to find out what help patients and their families want. The initial reaction on the part of a parent who is ill, especially if it is the mother, can be fear and reluctance to engage with social work. Part of the reason may be a belief that social work involvement might mean that professionals consider the mother to be too ill to care adequately for her children, resulting in compulsory care. Parents are often affected by social myths that the role of social work is about child protection. Positive intervention cannot take place without first engaging to build a strong base from which to support and assist.

The practitioner will need to build a picture, including knowledge of the family's support networks, who is looking after the children at present, and whether the children's schools are aware of the situation. Other factors to think about include the ages of the children, what they have already been told, and how they have reacted. Asking parents what worries them most, or what they would like help with most, may provide an initial way into a very complex and emotionally painful situation. Engaging with other family members with the patient's permission will usually provide a way forward. The pain of other family members, the patient's partner and siblings, and the children's grandparents must first be acknowledged and support offered. The family's trauma of losing a young adult with dependents is particularly harrowing and distressing.

It may become important that care arrangements are made to ensure the future care of the children. This will involve great sensitivity on the part of the social worker, who must hold and balance the emotional needs of the dying parent, the children, and other family members. Finding appropriate ways of supporting parents to face their own pain and being able to talk to their children about what is happening can feel daunting to the inexperienced social worker. Having the skills that enable social workers to feel more confident is very empowering.

Case example: Alice, Molly, and Jonathan

The practitioner's account follows. Alice was married with one daughter, Molly, age ten, who suffered from Down Syndrome. Alice was admitted to the hospice dying of colon cancer. Molly was her main concern. Alice knew that her husband, Jonathan, was not only struggling to come to terms with the fact that she was dying, but was extremely anxious about caring for Molly on his own. Alice wanted to prepare everyone as much as she could before leaving them, so that was the focus of my work. I saw Alice most days over a period of a few weeks and supported her to make plans and put strategies in place to help both Jonathan and Molly after her death. I lent Alice a wide selection of children's books with stories about dying, which Alice wanted to read so that she could choose the ones she wanted. These included a book for people with intellectual disabilities that tells the story of the death of a parent using pictures in a simple but moving way (Hollins & Sireling, 2004a, b). Alice gave her selected books to Molly's school support worker, who visited the hospice on several occasions to meet with Alice and myself to improve Molly's support.

Alice made Molly a memory box (see Chapter 6) and also, helped by friends, constructed a book to tell the story of her life to help Molly as she grew older. This included photographs of her in her hospice bed, to avoid confusing Molly later, since all the other photos were of Alice looking well. She involved her friends in several ways, hoping to strengthen wider future help with Molly. Alice wrote down important information about

Molly that she thought Jonathan might need, including immediate matters such as hospital appointments; some people prepare a guide to the things they usually do around the house. Jonathan brought Molly to visit Alice most days; usually they played card games with Alice at her bedside. Each time they told Molly exactly what was happening in words that Molly could understand. As Alice became weaker and sleepier, Molly knew that her mom was dying.

Case example: Mary and Alan

The practitioner's account follows. Mary age forty, with advanced breast cancer, was admitted to hospice for terminal care with rapid deterioration after intensive treatment. On admission, Mary's husband, Alan, requested urgent referral to the hospice social worker for help with breaking news of Mary's imminent death to his daughters, age ten and thirteen. I arranged to see Alan the following morning when he planned to bring the girls for a brief visit to Mom and to see the hospice.

I began by asking Alan about his wife and their journey through her illness and treatment [an example of the approach of asking for a narrative to put the jigsaw puzzle together at the engagement and assessment stage; see Chapter 4]. Alan gave a clear account and was keen to explain to someone in detail all that had happened over a relatively short period of time. Despite many setbacks, they had maintained hope that Mary would be well again; this was also the message they had given the children. However, Mary had reached the end of all possible treatment at the hospital where she had been an in-patient prior to transfer to hospice the day before. I asked Alan how much the children knew about their mother's recent deterioration and reasons for admission to hospice care. Alan did not know what or how much Mary had told his daughters. He was not sure what Mary might have said earlier and now she was too ill for him to be able to ask her. Alan acknowledged that he "may have held things back" from the girls. He thought the older girl might know more, because she wanted to be a doctor, watched TV hospital programs, and looked for information on the Internet. I asked about whether he thought the girls had discussed with each other how ill their mother was. I suggested that perhaps they both already knew more than he thought. Alan said he had no idea what they might have said to each other.

I talked about what children need to know, why it is important to be up front with them, and how they need time to prepare themselves for the death of someone close to them in just the same way as adults do. I also commented that parents naturally want to "protect" their children from upsetting situations. But, in this situation, nobody can change what is happening; we cannot protect children from something that we cannot alter. Furthermore, children are very likely to know more than adults realize because they overhear telephone conversations, see distressed adults and grandparents, perhaps look on the Internet, and work things out for themselves. However, this "working out" is not always accurate, and it is also important for parents to ensure that their children do not misunderstand what is happening.

Initially, Alan wanted to leave telling the children until the following day because one of the girls was going to stay overnight with a friend who was only in the country for a brief vacation, and he did not want her to be upset before setting off. I said that I respected his decision not to tell the girls yet; he knew them better than anyone, whereas I had never met them. However, I then talked more about what can happen when children are not included in important family communication and discussion. For example, sometimes children subsequently feel angry that they were excluded and may feel they can't ask questions or even trust adults to be honest with them. I asked Alan how they had dealt with other important events as a family in the past. He said they had always been open, sharing important information with the children.

Following this, Alan said clearly that he did not want the children to be angry with him; he would have enough problems later. He now wanted to talk to the children that day. His plan was to take the girls home, read the leaflets and book I had given him (Stokes & Crossley, 2001), and then tell them. We talked about how they would be upset and that it is OK to cry and to share the extreme sadness they will express at the news that their mother is dying. I added, however, that once Alan had told them, they would be much more able to support each other. I thought that the child who was going to stay with a friend later that day would quite likely still to want to go, but that if Alan gave her the choice, she would be able to make her own decision; this would mean that Alan did not need to worry about what to do.

During this conversation, the children were absorbed in making cards for their mother in the children's activity room at the hospice. Alan's thinking changed again and he decided not to wait until he got home but to tell the children straight away. Later in the day, Alan called me to say that he felt so much better because, having told the children, everything was out in the open. He had explained the situation to the mother of the friend, who wanted to help. The younger child went ahead with her sleepover, but returned home early the next morning. Alan brought the girls to visit Mom the following day. They brought their birthday presents for her early, told her they loved her, and gently said their goodbyes. Mary died peacefully later that day.

Financial Issues

When people become caregivers for family members with a serious illness, their family's financial affairs are likely to change. If the sick or disabled person then dies, there are at least two further stages of change to cope with, set out in table 5.4.

TABLE 5.4   Financial issues for caregivers at different stages in the illness

Stage	What happens financially
1 Disease progression creates financial stress for patient and family	Employed patients and caregivers may lose some or all of income; long-term disability may lead to changes in social security, pensions, insurance or other benefits.
	Retirement pensions or other insurance or social security rights may be triggered.
	Additional costs of condition, treatments, travel to hospital.
2 Death	Additional costs for funeral. Death or bereavement insurance or benefits compensate.
	Caregivers no longer receive financial support for their role.
	Caregivers may become entitled to widows', dependents or other insurance or social security benefits.
3 Post-death	Long-term costs of illness or funeral.
	Long-term financial reconstruction for family.

Source: Developed from Bechelet, Heal, Leam, & Payne (2008).

The responsibility for financial management often falls to the spouse or close family member of a patient, as the primary caregiver, since patients are often too ill or fatigued to deal with difficult and complex matters that are often beyond their normal experience. Also, caregivers who will shortly become bereaved are affected directly by the financial consequences of the illness and death and may want to take early preventive action. Therefore, social workers may help by careful discussion about changing family finances, talking through each stage with the patient and caregiver. One of the difficulties in doing so may be that the dying person may be the family member who has organized financial affairs, and caregivers may have to learn quickly about the circumstances that the family is in.

Another possibility is to take a more educational approach. Bechelet and colleagues (Bechelet, Heal, Leam, & Payne, 2008) describe a seminar for people at referral to a hospice, which offered a program of education and discussion about:

- Social security and other public benefits, including tax benefits for service users and caregivers
- Various relevant grant applications that they could make for charitable or other help
- Ways of dealing with debt problems and unexpected financial demands of illness
- Pensions and investments
- Wills and probate
- Financial planning, including the potential to release capital from insurance policies when given a terminal diagnosis
- Registration of deaths, arranging and paying for funerals
- Help for widows and others in bereavement

The program was positively evaluated by attendees, who either had been unaware of the help available or were given added confidence in dealing with their financial affairs. Although groups included patients with terminal diagnoses and their relatives, there was little distress about discussion of funeral and bereavement issues.

Pause and reflect—Case example: Ethel and Jim

Jim had advanced prostate cancer, and spinal cord compression caused paralysis from the waist down. He spent most of his time in bed, unable to tolerate more than an hour at a time in a chair before becoming short of breath and feeling dizzy and lightheaded. He was now incontinent. At times he was confused, at other times angry and frustrated because of his situation. Yet he remained optimistic that he would get stronger and be able to drive his car again. Meanwhile, Jim's wife, Ethel, could see that Jim was increasingly weak and understood that his prognosis was likely to be short. Both Jim and Ethel were in their eighties, but Ethel was several years older than Jim and had suffered from ill health for many years. Jim had been Ethel's caregiver and had always undertaken the domestic chores and attended to the household finances. Jim and Ethel had become quite isolated in their community, with few friends. Both their daughters and grandchildren lived far away, in Australia.

Ethel's role in the marriage had already changed, she was dealing with the bank and the tax office but found it a source of anxiety. She was unable to drive and was frightened about coping after Jim's death. She was also terrified by the responsibility for looking after him. She was struggling to cope both on a practical and emotional level. She was exhausted because of attending to her husband several times a night and being unable to sleep because of anxiety.

What are the issues and how might you approach them with both Jim and Ethel? The couple's daughters are worried about both parents. What can you do to help them?

Discharges from Care and Care Homes

Many people feel that the most important decisions in end-of-life care are the arrangements for care, particularly when there has been a period in a hospital or hospice for treatment or respite. The process of discharge from hospital or hospice often leads to great anxiety, both because it raises again the level of uncertainty that people face and also because it means a move that focuses attention on the client's increasing dependence, and the financial costs of care and depletion of family financial resources (Reith & Lucas, 2008). It may be useful to see the process not as a discharge but as a transfer of care to a new setting.

Social workers are often the major professional group dealing with discharges where they involve care arrangements, and a number of the case examples in Chapters 4 and 5 involved this common social work task. We stress the importance of allowing people time, space, and flexibility to work out their own destiny. To help them do so, it is often helpful to think through what information the practitioner can usefully provide and the areas of discussion that might help, either with the client or with family members. These might include:

- What knowledge will clients and the people around them need to make a decision about what they want?
- In turn, what do we need to know to help them prepare?
- How might they prepare for this change in their lives?
- What will be the personal implications of the change?
- How will the transition take place?

- How might they best feel integrated in the new situation?
- How will they recover from the change?
- What elements of the process will feel forced upon them, compulsory?
- What losses and gains will they experience?
- What will help them adapt?
- In the new situation, what is the balance between freedom and independence and between risk and safety? (Payne, 2008a)

CONCLUSION

This chapter has explored what may be involved for practitioners in a number of end-of-life care interventions that social workers often deal with. We started looking at psychosocial needs, which are the responsibility of all practitioners in end-of-life care, but where social work has a particular role. Enabling families and caregivers to develop successful responses as they experience the major life transition of death, dying, and bereavement is an important contribution made by end-of-life social work to social resilience in the community.

End-of-life social work therefore must concentrate on empowering people's control over end-of-life situations and their capacity to make decisions that meet their emotional, practical, and social needs. The experience of loss leads to uncertainty and, loss of confidence; the experience of approaching the end of life requires people to "come to terms" with death in a way they have not had to before, and people need to prepare for death. This requires a repositioning of the family and social networks around the dying person. As this process goes on, some members of the family, very often those who are less powerful in family and social relationships, may be excluded, and social workers need to help people deal with such exclusion.

Interventions may use a range of specific therapeutic techniques, selected both for their appropriateness to the problems a client is facing and to the practitioner's capacity to implement them effectively.

The social work's role usually includes providing help to family members and informal caregivers to play the roles in caring that they choose, and also helping them to avoid being overburdened. In family relationships, it is important to be aware of the possibility of neglect and physical, financial, and other forms of abuse of clients and other vulnerable adults; the situation of clients and caregivers is stressful and rapidly changing, and may raise the risk of existing relationships unraveling.

It is also valuable to help people plan for and implement important life decisions. Planning a future for children and vulnerable family members will be an important focus for many people at the end of life; there may be financial issues to be resolved, and this will take people through three stages of financial reconstruction. Finally, changes in the way people's care needs are met by care services will also change at the end of life, and clients and practitioners need to think through their needs and plan carefully.

FURTHER READING

Berzoff, J., & Silverman, R. (Eds.) (2004). *Living with dying: A handbook for end-of-life healthcare practitioners*. New York: Columbia University Press. This edited collection of articles from leading American writers on palliative care (there are two contributions from other countries), is an advanced text originally edited for leaders in palliative care, and its coverage of practice issues is useful but perhaps too extensive for new or nonspecialist social workers in end-of-life care.

JOURNALS

The only journal specifically concerned with end-of-life and palliative social work is:

- *Journal of Social Work in End-of-Life and Palliative Care*, Haworth Press.

General journals on social work in health care sometimes publish papers on end-of-life and palliative care. These include:

- *Health and Social Care in the Community*, Blackwell.
- *Health and Social Work*, National Association of Social Workers (United States)
- *Social Work in Health Care*, Haworth Press.

WEBSITES

Listings of organizations for palliative and end-of-life care social workers are provided in the Websites list.
Organizations for caregivers:
Australia: Carers Australia: http://www.carersaustralia.com.au/
Canada: Canadian Caregiver Coalition: http://www.ccc-ccan.ca/
UK: Carers UK: http://www.carersuk.org/Home; the Princess Royal Trust for Carers: http://www.carers.org/
U.S.: National Family Caregivers Association: http://www.nfcacares.org/

Chapter 6

GRIEF AND BEREAVEMENT: IDEAS AND INTERVENTIONS

CHAPTER AIMS

The main aim of the chapter is to introduce ideas about grief and bereavement and helpful interventions in bereavement.

After working through this chapter, readers should be able to:

- See preparation for bereavement as an issue in the helping process throughout engagement and intervention with people approaching the end of life;
- Review psychological and sociological models of bereavement and how it affects individuals and families;
- Assess risk and preventive factors in serious problems of bereavement;
- Identify appropriate interventions with bereaved people and families;
- Engage with and intervene with bereaved people to assist them with emotional and practical issues in their bereavement;
- Assist children in dealing with bereavement; and
- Help bereaved people evaluate appropriate memorialization.

LOSS, GRIEF, MOURNING, AND BEREAVEMENT

When we die, other people close to us may experience grief, an emotional and physical reaction to loss. Mourning and bereavement are social processes allied to grief, in which people change their expectations and relationships to respond to their loss. Mullan and colleagues (Mullan, Pearlin, & Skaff, 1995) suggest that the bereavement process starts from loss, moves through grief for the loss, and ends with recovery. This is a natural process, which most people move through with the help of families and friends; help with grief and bereavement aims to help people move through the process if they have any difficulties. A small proportion of people may experience severe difficulties as "complex bereavement," needing therapy or psychiatric treatment. However, this should not prevent us from seeing bereavement as a normal social process.

Among the losses that people experience are:

- Loss of persona, their own, or the persona of the deceased person. A bereaved person has a social being, the collection of roles and contributions he or she made to relationships. When someone dies, those relationships are altered
- A reduction in loving support in their lives
- Companionship, someone to do things with, "my best friend"
- Instrumental support—the person who did the shopping, cooking, organized the garden or finances
- The feeling that there is no one to whom the bereaved person matters
- Loss of contact with social ties that came as part of the loved one's social network
- Loss of material resources, including income or pension
- A loss of history, a joint knowledge about a shared past, including a personal history and a family history
- Loss of a planned future together

Bereavement has consequences for the health of the people experiencing it. Stroebe and colleagues' (Stroebe, Schut, & Stroebe, 2007) systematic review identifies:

- Increased risk of mortality, including suicide
- Increased rates of disability, medication use, and hospitalization compared with similar nonbereaved people. Widowed people consult with doctors more frequently than other similar people
- Failure to seek help for feelings of intense grief
- Psychological reactions, which may range from mild and short-lived to extreme and long-lasting
- Other medical consequences, including impaired memory, nutritional problems, work and relationship difficulties, and difficulties with a reduction in social participation

These are the serious consequences that, if they occur, care for bereaved people seeks to alleviate.

Is Grief Universal?

Loss is a universal experience, because, as we saw in Chapter 1, we all lose things and other people, and aspects of our own identity, which other people may be part of. We also lose people continually as we experience change. We sometimes neglect the fact that change is always a movement away from events, people, and things in the past because we concentrate on the new. Loss therefore goes alongside growth: since all growth involves change, it must therefore bring loss with it.

However, while loss is universal, the reaction to it varies. Smith (1982) argues that how we experience and express grief through rituals of mourning and bereavement are constructed by social expectations in a particular society. People from different cultures may react to loss in different ways (Howarth, 2007). Losses may be minor, or they be major turning points in our lives. Smith (1982) argues, however, that although there may be variations in reactions to change and loss, there are patterns that we can identify and that enable us to help people deal with loss. The way we prepare for and experience loss can have significant or lasting consequences on our lives.

Loss because of a death disconnects us from the person who has died. Bowlby's (1973, 1980) groundbreaking work argues that a person's need for secure attachment to other human beings is fundamental to emotional development and well-being. In this view, a significant loss of someone close means losing part of our security. How we deal with disconnection has profound consequences for our own development and for connecting with people in subsequent relationships.

Pause and reflect

Build upon the reflection you may have worked on in Chapter 1 about loss. In Chapter 1, you looked at typical situations in which you lost things: now consider situations in which you lost people from your life; this might include deaths, but you may have had other experiences such as divorce.

Some suggestions

We argued in Chapter 1 that loss is central in understanding social work practice in end-of-life care, and also in much other social work. We saw that all social workers need skills in responding to loss, grief, and bereavement because loss affects all our clients in different ways and is one of the major recurring themes across all social work areas of specialization. Social workers all work with people who face abandonment, rejection, and separation along life's journey. Such situations might include going to school, thereby losing full-time contact with a parent; leaving home to go into residential care as a child or adult; leaving home for the first time to work or go to college, leaving home to get married; divorce; loss of health, either physical or mental; and imprisonment.

And, of course, it includes deaths of people around us. How previous losses have affected people influences reactions to the present bereavement, and, similarly, current bereavement experience affects responses to future losses.

LOSS AND END-OF-LIFE CARE

Providing a bereavement service is integral to holistic end-of-life and palliative care. It supports families and caregivers both before a person dies and afterward. Caring for someone at the end of life should include the needs of both patient and bereaved family. Individual bereavement is affected by the person's experience of death (Kristjanson, Sloan, Dudgeon, & Adaskin, 1996). According to Kristjanson and colleagues, "care experiences, perceived as stressful by families, may complicate the recovery of members during the grieving period" (p. 10). These authors evaluate the quality of good end-of-life care as being possibly more significant for the family than for the person who is dying. If, perhaps, a family believes that their loved one received inadequate symptom relief, or lack of care when dying, their bereavement is likely to be complicated by regrets and unanswered questions.

If someone dies suddenly or has a traumatic death, such as one resulting from a traffic accident, homicide, or suicide, close family members often experience greater distress than if someone dies peacefully from natural causes at the end of a long life (Worden, 2003; Jeffreys, 2005). However, caring for someone suffering from a long or chronic illness may be exhausting and demanding for the person who will be bereaved, and can cause other difficulties. For example, caregivers may have put their own lives on hold and may resent the sick person for causing major family adjustments and changes. People may experience a sense of relief at the death, often accompanied by guilt rather than grief (Elison & McGonigle, 2003). Such experiences may exacerbate feelings such as anger and guilt in bereavement (Reith, 2007. p. 22). People may experience anticipatory grief, if they have time to prepare emotionally for their loved one's impending death (Worden, 2003). Such grief may be further complicated if the dying person suffers from a progressive neurological condition or brain tumor causing personality changes and deficits, since the person that family members and friends knew may already be lost to them.

Whatever the circumstances surrounding a person's end-of-life situation, it is crucial to remember that supporting dying patients, their caregivers, and families "helps relatives recover from bereavement" (Reith, 2007, p. 26).

UNDERSTANDING GRIEF

Conceptualizing grief, thus making sense of people's reactions to loss, is prerequisite to identifying helpful supportive interventions. There are two main approaches to conceptualization (Howarth, 2007, ch. 10).

Psychological models propose understanding grief by seeing the grieving process as having tasks or stages that individuals need to accomplish or work through; the problem with these models is that if we see extreme reactions, we may focus too much on the individuals' internal emotional reaction, seeing them as having deficits in how they are dealing with their grief. It is also important to examine social factors that may be exacerbating their reaction. More recently, sociological ideas consider how people reconstruct social relationships between the deceased person and the bereaved person; these views help us to focus on positive changes as well as losses.

Psychological Stage and Task Models

Table 6.1 analyzes some well-known stage and task models. They all propose a period of disorientation, differently described, leading up to a recovery of some kind from the disturbance. Even though the models are not intended to be equivalent, we have juxtaposed the various stages and tasks to show how they differ in the amount of detail provided about different stages. Bowlby's (1980) attachment theory explored how adult loss and separation reflect previous experiences, especially in childhood. Kübler-Ross (1969; see also Chapter 1) interviewed people facing their own death rather than bereaved people. Her detailed account of the stages of loss in the dying process has subsequently influenced ideas about bereavement. Glick and colleagues (Glick, Parkes, & Weiss, 1974) aimed to identify determinants of grief using a sample of young American widows and widowers, building on Bowlby's ideas. They differentiate the recovery phase more fully, perhaps because as psychiatrists they focused on what would lead to improvements.

By using tasks, Worden "implies that the mourner needs to take action and can do something . . . giving the mourner some sense of leverage and hope that there is something that he or she can actively do" (Worden, 2003, p. 26). He argues that by using his model, practitioners can offer hope to bereaved people that grieving will not last forever, and help to counter the feelings of helplessness experienced by most mourners. While Worden's tasks are described extensively, he does not differentiate stages as the other models do, since he views the tasks being carried out as part of an integrated process; he does not see them as needing to be done sequentially. "Tasks can be revisited over time. Various tasks can also be worked on at the same time. Grieving is a fluid process" (Worden, 2003, p. 37).

Most modern writers recognize that many emotions and responses are present for some people but not others and people do not experience them in order. Rather, these formulations help practitioners to be aware of and accept common reactions to bereavement.

TABLE 6.1 Stage and task models of grief and bereavement

Bowlby (1980)	Kübler-Ross (1969)	Glick, Weiss, & Parkes (1974)	Worden (2003)
Phase I: numbing	**Stage I:** Shock and Denial. Disbelief is common immediately after a loss or the threat of a loss.	**Task I:** Intellectual recognition and explanation of loss. The bereaved person needs to understand his or her loss and make sense of it.	**Task I:** To accept the reality of the loss. Initially after someone dies the bereaved person cannot believe it has really happened. Bereaved people must recognize intellectually that the person has died and will not return before they can make sense of their world and begin to move forward.
Phase II: searching and yearning	**Stage II:** Anger. Rage, resentment, bitterness, irritability, hostility, and aggression are all expressions of anger that the bereaved person may experience.		**Task II:** To work through the pain of grief. Worden states that, while the intensity of the pain felt varies, it is not possible to have a close attachment to someone and not experience some level of physical, emotional, or behavioral pain when the person dies. "One of the aims of grief counseling is to help facilitate people through this difficult second task so they don't carry the pain with them throughout their life" (Worden, 2003, p. 32).
Phase III: disorganization and despair	**Stage III:** Bargaining. People may try to find more time or relief from pain and suffering by bargaining. "If I start praying again or pray more, I will get well."		**Task III:** To adjust to an environment in which the deceased person is missing. Worden describes three areas of adjustment: • External • Internal • Spiritual
	Stage IV: Depression. Some people will withdraw as they face their own death, spending time thinking about their lives, the meaning of life and death and other spiritual issues.		

TABLE 6.1   Stage and task models of grief and bereavement—(Continued)

Bowlby (1980)	Kübler-Ross (1969)	Glick, Weiss, & Parkes (1974)	Worden (2003)
			First, bereaved people have to cope with the functions of daily living, often taking on new roles previously undertaken by the deceased person. This is especially obvious when the death is of a partner. Second, the bereaved person has to develop a new identity in a changed world. This is not just about seeing oneself as a widow or a bereaved parent but also about self-esteem and confidence. Third, the bereaved person has to adjust spiritually to finding a new sense of purpose in his or her changed world. Some deaths particularly challenge a person's beliefs, values, and assumptions about the world. (Worden, 2003, p. 34).
	Stage V: Acceptance. Some people who are facing the end of their life may intellectually accept the unavoidable reality while at the same time remain depressed, angry, and frightened.	**Task II**: Emotional acceptance of the loss. In this stage, bereaved people can recall the deceased person without a resurgence of pain.	**Task IV**: To emotionally relocate the deceased and move on with life. This involves being able to hold on to the inner picture of the person in a changed world. The connection with the deceased changes but continues in the new world. Worden suggests that, "for many people, Task IV is the most difficult one to accomplish" (Worden, 2003, p. 37).
Phase IV: reorgani-zation		**Task III**: Assumption of a new identity. This transition to a new way of thinking of oneself is often a difficult process involving painful reality testing.	

Case example: Gordon

Elements drawn from different stage and task models often help practitioners to position themselves in clients' experiences. Gordon, whose wife, Cynthia, had died eight months previously, had weekly counseling sessions and for six weeks showed no signs of feeling less bereft. He cried throughout sessions and seemed totally preoccupied with Cynthia and how he could not exist without her. Between sessions, Gordon visited all the places he and Cynthia had lived since they were first married forty years previously. He described how he would sit in his car outside each house in different parts of the country and hope that he would see her. He seemed stuck in his grief and could see no way through it. However, at the next session, he said he was feeling a little better. The practitioner explored what had changed: Gordon said he now accepted that Cynthia really had died. Gordon said that until then he had hoped that if he cried or prayed enough it was possible that she would return to him, an example of bargaining. Gordon clearly articulated accomplishing the first of Worden's tasks, "to accept the reality of the loss." Seeing the pattern of his grief helped the practitioner to make sense of it.

Sociological or Process Models of Grief

These models of grief see people as going through a social process in which they reconstruct the relationship with the deceased person as part of their present social relationships. They do this by taking part in various social processes that may be influenced by the bereaved person's culture, faith, or beliefs. Lloyd (2002) argues that the multicultural context of many populations and the postmodern context of service, which gives priority to flexibility and responsiveness, require a practitioner to include the diverse social and cultural lives of people experiencing bereavement. Three ideas influential in bereavement work are:

- The continuing bonds model of grief (Klass, 1996)
- The dual-process model of grief (Stroebe & Schut, 1999)
- Understanding loss as a process of meaning reconstruction (Neimeyer, 2001).

Continuing Bonds. Klass (1996) explains the healing of bereaved people as a unique process in which bereaved people integrate the deceased person into their life while, at the same time, redefining themselves in the present. The continued bond with the deceased person is a healthy part of the survivor's ongoing life in two ways:

- *New inner representation*: the bereaved individuals revise the way they see the person who has died, creating a new reality. It is then possible to form a bond with this new image of the person who has died.
- *Reestablishment of social equilibrium*: bereaved people must evolve a new equilibrium in their lives, a picture of who the person they have lost is now and who the bereaved person is to the outer world. (Klass, 1996)

This model is useful when working with children to help them retain a sense of who the person who has died was and their own connections and memories with the person. See the section on assisting bereaved children below. A caution in using continuing-bonds ideas is that, of course, reflection on past experiences may lead a bereaved person to move away, reject, or realize that there were unsatisfactory aspects of the relationship. Even though the new bond may acknowledge negatives, its achievement is still a healthy development. Experiencing new relationships may be part of that realization. For example, a woman whose husband was violent formed a new partnership with a man with different behaviors, and this led her to reject good things about her previous marriage, which before she had focused on, in order to balance her rejection of the violence. This illustrates a complicated grief; continuing-bonds work may lead to negative rather than positive assessment of past relationships. Also, the relationship with the deceased person is continued in the context of new relationships, which may lead to a reassessment of the past.

Dual-Process Model. Stroebe and Schut (1999) developed the dual process model as an alternative to stage-based models of grief. Responses to grief have two aspects, both necessary for grief resolution. The bereaved person must cope emotionally with the loss but also adapt to the consequences of the loss, changes, new roles, and adjustments.

- *The loss-oriented focus* involves behaviors that focus on emotional reactions including missing the person who has died, yearning, reminiscing, and reviewing.
- *The restoration-oriented focus* involves behaviors that attend to solving practical problems. These include learning new skills to enable the person to construct a new identity to be able to live in the post-loss world.

Stroebe and Schut (1999) emphasize that the bereaved person oscillates between these coping behaviors, both being necessary for successful adjustment. In the early stages following bereavement, people concentrate more on the loss aspect and may be unable to contemplate a future without the deceased. The restoration focus is more likely to become significant later in the bereavement journey. However, people still move between the two and can experience both at the same time (Thompson & Thompson, 2004, p. 352). Both should be present, and if one is absent there may be difficulties that need to be worked out. One factor, addressed by Stroebe and Schut, helpful to social workers is the recognition of gender and cultural differences in the grieving process. Currer (2001, p. 102) points out that the model allows for women to be more likely to express emotional responses to loss and men to be more oriented to restoration. However, there is no evidence of gender difference that excludes one or the other focus; both men and women may have a leaning toward one or the other.

The process of oscillating between the two dimensions to grief can be helpful both when working with bereaved children and helping adults to make sense of children's apparent ability to switch rapidly between intense sadness one minute and wanting to play or be with their friends the next. It is not that the child doesn't care, as a bereaved parent may feel, it is simply that children cope with their emotional responses by switching more rapidly than adults between the two states and also by taking time out from grieving. This model also allows for understanding complicated grief by seeing it as "disturbances of oscillation" (Stroebe & Schut, 1999, p. 217). This may involve someone avoiding the focus on loss or it may be that the bereaved person is totally wrapped up in his or her emotional response and unable to consider the restoration behaviors needed to move forward.

Meaning Reconstruction. Robert R. Neimeyer's ideas are a form of social-construction theory. He is critical of "traditional grief theories," arguing that instead "meaning reconstruction is a central process in mourning" (Neimeyer, 2005, p. 27). He allows for the uniqueness of grief and avoids the dangers of other theoretical models seeking similarities between patterns of grief. He emphasizes the need for bereaved people to find new meaning in their lives, which requires them to reorganize their identity, purpose, and role in life following their much-changed personal and social situation. The meanings people give to their life stories provide the existential, spiritual, social, and personal basis for their sense of identity. When a loss is experienced, these meanings are challenged and often profoundly disrupted, and must be adjusted to the new reality of the post-loss world.

Neimeyer and colleagues feel that bereaved people should ask questions such as: "What do the life and death of this person mean to me?" "Who am I now?" "What can I no longer take for granted in this changed world?" "What do I need to learn and who do I need to become in order to integrate this loss and move forward with my life?" He does, however, acknowledge that not "all bereaved persons undertake an agonizing search for philosophic meaning in their loss, or that professionals should instigate such a search when the bereaved themselves do not do so" (Neimeyer et al., 2002, pp. 63–64).

Gender Differences and the Grieving Process. Gender stereotypes abound in our society and easily become gross generalizations accounting for behavior differences. Many other factors influence grieving patterns, but gender differences should be included in assessing grief responses and difficulties. "Men and women, because of their socialization into sex roles, are likely to exhibit different grieving patterns. Men are more likely to be found on the instrumental end of the continuum, while women are more likely to exhibit an intuitive style" (Martin & Doka, 2000, p. 99).

- *The intuitive pattern* expresses intense feelings, sadness, crying, and talking about the loss.
- *The instrumental pattern* identifies problem solving as a predominant feature with a general reluctance or difficulty to talk about feelings. (Martin & Doka, 2000, p. 53)

ASSESSING GRIEF

Natural Responses

Grief is a natural human process, and people should be reassured if their experiences are commonplace reactions. There may be widespread physical and emotional reactions. As well as the health consequences discussed above, Stroebe and colleagues (Stroebe, Schut, & Stroebe, 2007) identify the following:

- *Cognitive manifestations* of grief include disbelief and a sense of unreality. There may also be elements of denial. Preoccupation with thoughts of the deceased person are common. Similarly, it is not unusual for bereaved people to experience a sense (visual or auditory) of the deceased person's presence. Concentration is often poor; short-term memory is also affected, and finding a sense of purpose is often more difficult following a bereavement.
- *Physical manifestations* include lack of energy, hollowness in the stomach, tightness in the chest or throat, oversensitivity to noise, a feeling of shortness of breath, muscle weakness, a dry mouth, and a sense of depersonalization.

- *Emotional manifestations* include a range of reactions, all of which may help someone to absorb gradually the finality of the death. Among these, people may experience a sense of shock or numbness—not really believing the death has happened. There may also be an element of denial. Anger may be directed at medical staff, God, the deceased person themselves, family, friends, or no one in particular. Anger may have a legitimate basis, in which case, complaints should be resolved quickly. Guilt in the form of self-blame and regret are common, both real and imagined. "If only I had done more . . . if only I had not gone to work that day . . . it was my fault he got sick/fell/died." Real guilt is more difficult to address. Anxiety is a likely reaction because of the intensity of change and general feelings of an inability to cope. A sense of helplessness and disorganization may also be present. The most common reaction is usually a profound sense of sadness. This can be prolonged and may appear similar to depression. Feelings of relief and freedom may be accompanied by guilt.
- *Behavioral manifestations* include appetite disturbance—both not eating and overeating. Sleep disturbances, including dreams about the deceased person, may occur. Social withdrawal is not unusual, partly to avoid reminders of the deceased. Restless over-activity, searching for the deceased, or carrying objects that hold reminders of the dead person may also be present. Sometimes, people want to make sudden and major changes in their lives as a way of avoiding painful memories, but rapid lifestyle changes are not usually advisable because running away from memories is unlikely to work—you cannot run away from yourself.

Unresolved and Complicated Grief and Depression

Unresolved grief can cause additional stress and makes people more vulnerable to subsequent losses, increases the risk of suicide, and can lead to such problems as mental health difficulties, depression, anxiety, alcoholism, and agoraphobia. People may experience increased physical problems such as heart disease, arthritic disease, and other symptoms. Long-term risks of incomplete mourning include depression, suicide, drug and alcohol dependence, physical symptoms, and antisocial behavior.

These serious complications in a minority of people make it useful to identify unresolved and complicated grief. Most bereaved people describe themselves as feeling as they would have expected given the circumstances. However, most bereaved people who are depressed see themselves as being different. Younger people tend to experience more severe symptoms of sleep, appetite, and memory disturbances initially. They are also likely to be more restless, lonely, fatigued, and weepy. Regular daily routines and structure may, however, act as a protective factor that helps counter depression.

When a person's grief is outside normal limits, this is regarded as complicated grief. Treatment for depression is indicated, and psychiatric assessment may be required. Delusions or hallucinations in addition to hearing or seeing the deceased person, and actively suicidal thoughts may indicate that depression has overtaken grief. Among factors to consider are guilt that is not solely focused on things done or not done in relation to the person who died. Depression may be indicated if the bereaved person has thoughts of death other than feeling that they would be better off dead or should have died with, or instead of, their loved one. Other factors include a morbid preoccupation with worthlessness, marked psychomotor retardation, and prolonged and marked inability to get on with the daily tasks of life.

BEREAVEMENT ASSESSMENT

Risk or Need, Prevention, and Responsive Services

Four main aspects of the situation affect how people react to bereavement. These aspects may increase the risk or protect people from adverse reactions, and are among risk factors that suggest a need for referral to a helping service, identified by Stroebe and colleagues' (2007) systematic review:

- The nature of the death. There are inconsistent results for many factors, but issues to think about include: sudden death where people are already vulnerable, multiple losses, and extreme distress during the dying process make things worse, while "dying well" (see Chapter 2) improves reactions; pre-bereavement caregiver strain may make bereavement worse, but relief from the strain may be helpful; having a kinship relationship reduces bereavement distress, but loss of children may lead to more intense grief than death of a spouse; concurrent stressors such as relationship conflicts or financial problems increase hardship.
- Intrapersonal risk or protective factors are also relevant. Research shows that optimism, people's perception that they have control over daily activities, high self-esteem, and a secure attachment style are all helpful. Prebereavement depression is a risk factor. Bereavement in childhood or as a young person may produce mental health problems later, but adequate parenting reduces these problems. Many studies show that religious faith reduces bereavement risk. There are some sociodemographic variables:

widowers are more vulnerable than widows, mothers than fathers; anger and despair are higher in black populations.

* Interpersonal or nonpersonal resources generally protect people from adverse reactions. People with good social support are less at risk while socially isolated people are more at risk, material resources protect against other stressors, but distress is comparable across socioeconomic groups.

* Coping styles and strategies may be less important than earlier studies suggested. Grief work, sharing, and openness do not predict a good result; avoidance is not necessarily detrimental. However, ruminating on the loss leads to poor outcomes while positive reappraisal of life brings good outcomes. Regulation in grief is helpful, that is, balance between positive and negative appraisals of the situation.

The evidence is so mixed that the weight given to bereavement risk assessment tools in some palliative care services needs to be treated cautiously. Parkes developed a bereavement risk-assessment index (BRI) that has been used to target people considered most in need of bereavement services (Parkes & Weiss, 1983, 308–315; Parkes, 1993). Kristjanson and colleagues (Kristjanson, Cousins, Smith & Lewin, 2005) tested Parkes's BRI and found that using a shorter, modified version produced an acceptable level of reliability and validity. However, as Sheldon points out: "Studies of its reliability have shown it to be predictive of outcome at three months, but not at other times in the bereavement" (Sheldon, 1997, p. 102). U.K. official evidence-based guidance is unequivocal: "Individual clinical judgment is currently the most effective way of identifying those at risk, as risk assessment tools cannot be relied upon as a predictor of outcome" (NICE, 2004, para. 2.53). More recently, attempts have been made to identify "bereavement needs" (Machin & Spall, 2004) and the outcomes have been used to create an assessment document (Relf Machine, & Archer, 2008). People are classified into four categories: overwhelmed, balanced, controlled, and resilient, using a combination of factors.

The nature of the relationship with the deceased person affects bereavement. A very dependent or ambivalent relationship makes grief after death more difficult to resolve. Kissane has demonstrated the importance of family functioning and suggested this may be a strong predictor of bereavement outcome (Kissane, Bloch, & MacKenzie, 1997). Personality factors, including individual resilience and strengths, are also an important determinant. How someone has coped with previous losses can indicate future coping patterns. Unfinished business may be troubling. Similarly, concurrent environmental stresses including multiple losses make it harder to cope. All these factors can help identify where someone may be more likely than most people to suffer adverse effects.

As we have seen, effective symptom and pain management and good care at the end of life for a dying person helps people's bereavement. Involving people in the death in the way they wish is central to achieving a good bereavement outcome. Effective communication before death, which enables people to resolve unfinished issues and to say goodbye also minimizes bereavement risk. Viewing the body, attending the funeral, and other culture-specific rituals will also help. For some people, organ donation to give life to another person can be supportive and consoling. All these supportive measures may help forestall difficulties in bereavement.

Bereavement literature has emphasized the importance of social networks as a protective factor in bereavement, but it is often the bereaved person's perceived lack of social support that affects his or her reaction, rather than the actual support available. A person's social, cultural, and religious context is important. Understandably, adults are particularly at risk if it is their child who has died.

Critical Review of Bereavement Risk Assessment Tools

Not only is the reliability of risk assessment tools in doubt, but using such tools may be flawed practice for other reasons. First, the idea of risk or need takes a deficit view of grief and bereavement: it sees bereavement as a psychological "problem" rather than a natural reaction, constructed by social and cultural expectations. Assessing risk and need prior to or at the death therefore raises ethical issues that may lead to practical consequences. The assessment is rarely undertaken in an open and transparent way with the full knowledge of the bereaved person. Nurses may see the assessment as intrusive (Payne et al., 1999, p. 96). The validity of the tool is in question, especially in nonspecialized end-of-life care settings, where the staff's focus is on treatment or care over the long term rather than preparation for death, as in palliative care, or where staff may visit the patient's home or see the patient in a care-home setting and not meet many family members (being therefore unable to assess them). Nurses or other staff completing the assessment often have limited knowledge of the family and may only see family members in crisis rather than over a period of time. They may never see a child, for example, who is kept away from the dying person, but who may be strongly affected by his or her loss. If the assessment is based on the subjective observations by staff at a time when people are particularly stressed and distressed, it may not give an accurate reflection of bereavement needs.

A further ethical issue is ownership of the assessment and the record of it—it does not belong to the patient, but have relatives, who are being assessed given consent for assessments and records to be kept about them? Are they even aware that practitioners are observing them or checking their background details for signs of possible bereavement problems in the future? Relf et al. (2008), in the recently published bereavement needs-assessment guide, prefer that the assessments made by nurses in palliative care settings be discussed openly, but suggest that this is often impossible. This approach seems at odds with the general policy of openness and transparency within palliative care. Palliative care has been criticized for assuming consent when patients may not be aware of the assumption that treatment will go beyond medical and nursing care (see Chapter 8). This applies even more to covert observation and recording of nonpatients' reactions to the patient's death, particularly as most people will not require help. Bereavement risk or needs assessment in the context of services particularly for people at the end of life seems, therefore, to be a disproportionate intervention.

Relf and colleagues (2008), Machin and Spall (2004), and many bereavement service providers argue that there is a duty of care to identify and treat the exceptional needs of people with complicated bereavement. The question here is the point at which this duty applies: most psychological and social care is offered when the person concerned recognizes the need for help; usually that is the point at which it is most effectively offered. Indeed, Machin and Spall (2004) suggest that the most useful application of the "adult attitude to grief scale" may be in starting off the process of counseling and opening up topics for discussion.

Using an assessment tool at a very early stage in the bereavement may seem to make best use of scarce resources; however, as a rationing process, it may easily miss those most affected by the bereavement. A more equitable approach is to offer the service to all those who are bereaved, leaving the individual to determine if he or she wishes to take up the service. The offer may be repeated at intervals through reminder letters or telephone contacts. These can also ask if there are other members of the family affected. In this way, the service can be offered in a way that respects the capacity of bereaved people to determine the point at which they are ready to use it. People with severe complications are likely to come to the notice of health and other community services. This approach is less likely to create a stigmatizing service based on a deficit model of assessment. The individual complexities of bereavement are such that it seems arrogant for professionals to decide who needs bereavement support. In general, the majority of people recover from bereavement without professional help, and in the United Kingdom; for example, the take-up rate of most hospice-based bereavement services is around 30 percent (NICE, 2004).

Disenfranchised Grief

Doka has written extensively about disenfranchised grief, which occurs if the death cannot be openly or publicly mourned, and can lead to difficulties in bereavement (Doka, 1989, 2002). Disenfranchised grief arises where the death is either stigmatized or hidden. Stigmatized deaths include suicide and homicide. Hidden grief may arise following the death of a partner in a same-sex relationship, or an extra-marital affair, for example. Glackin and Higgins (2008) in a study of Irish same-sex couples one of whom died found that where the couple is "out," that is, people around them are aware of the relationship, grief may not be disenfranchised. In many instances, however, the bereaved person was unable to fully acknowledge his or her grief. But disenfranchised grief can also occur when the death is of a friend or a neighbor. It may be difficult to mourn an ex-partner, or stepparent, stepchild, an in-law or caregiver. Loss arising from stillbirth and abortion is often hidden, and in the case of the latter may also be stigmatized.

Corr's (1999) more complex understanding of disenfranchised grief includes:

- *Disenfranchised relationships*—where the relationship with the deceased person is not recognized
- *Disenfranchised losses*—the loss is not recognized socially as a loss, for example, the loss of people whose dementia has changed their personality
- *Disenfranchised grievers*—where the grief of young children and people with intellectual disabilities is not recognized
- *Disenfranchised deaths*—where stigmatized deaths from, for example, AIDS or suicide, cannot be openly discussed

Corr suggests the concept of disenfranchised grief enables a more complex understanding of feelings and social reactions to bereavement, grief, and mourning.

Case example: Ella

Ella sought bereavement counseling after the death of one of her husband's friends, Alberto, who had become a family friend. He lived near the family, had often participated in family events, and had joined the family on holidays. People in the family's network of friends had begun to see Ella's distressed reaction as excessive, since although there had been a close relationship, they felt her grief was extended and overemotional. She had said to her husband and friends that she was particularly affected because she had provided a lot of personal care for

Alberto and had left his house shortly before he had died, and she did not like to think of him dying on his own. This appeared to be an example of disenfranchised grief, because her feelings were thought to be inappropriate to normal grieving within her social circle.

However, during counseling Ella disclosed that she had been having an illicit sexual relationship with Alberto for the last year of his life, a different aspect of disenfranchisement. As counseling proceeded, she said they had planned to marry, but when he became ill, they decided to maintain secrecy and not disturb Ella's existing marriage. However, she had disclosed the affair to Alberto's parents, who had been sympathetic. Ella's behavior was such that she almost seemed to want to display her grief publicly so that people would realize and recognize the importance of this illicit relationship. She seemed ambivalent about continuing her marriage; rationally she saw this as the least disruptive course for her and the children. However, the counselor recognized that to incorporate Alberto's death into her own future life, Ella wanted the relationship publicly acknowledged. Applying Klass's (1996) model, discussed above, she could not arrive either at a reconstruction of the meaning of the relationship with Alberto, or a new social equilibrium, which incorporated the relationship into her continuing life. The disenfranchised character of the bereavement seems to have led to an inability to move forward.

Cultural, Ethnic, and Faith Dimensions

To reduce misunderstandings, practitioners need to respect and seek to understand grief reactions of people from different cultural backgrounds and faiths. "Grief is expressed so differently from culture to culture that it is absurd to use notions of pathology derived from one culture to evaluate people from another" (Rosenblatt, 1993, p. 18). Written information is often helpful, but all faiths and cultural groups have many interpretations and subgroupings, and general guidance about "what Muslims do," for example, may not represent the beliefs of a particular family. Therefore, practitioners might best approach patients and their families with genuine caring and sensitivity to ask them about customs and beliefs so that their needs may be met (Neuberger, 2004, p. 96).

For example, we have seen in Chapter 3 that open discussion about prognosis may be impossible if maintaining hope of life is fundamental to someone's belief system. In some cultures, the unit of importance may be the family rather than the individual (Dein & Thomas, 2002). Resuscitation, feeding, and hydration issues need to be addressed sensitively.

Pain-relieving medication may also be an issue, since over-sedation can leave people feeling cheated of opportunities to share last moments.

Similarly, "factors such as gender and culture powerfully affect our understanding both of what counts as loss and of what should be done about it" (Currer, 2007, p. 47). The process of mourning is culture-specific with very different rituals, customs, and expressions of grief according to culture and religious practice. It is important for social workers to clarify their clients' cultural needs and expectations to avoid inaccurate assumptions.

Case example: Winston

The practitioner's account follows. Winston, an African-Caribbean man, lived in a multi-ethnic community in a city in England. After his young wife, Bertha, died, Winston arranged her funeral through a local funeral director. At the cemetery, Winston's brothers became upset and subsequently angry because the undertakers were unwilling or unable to allow them to fill the grave with earth after Bertha's casket had been placed in it; this is also a requirement of many Jewish burials. Winston became distressed and embarrassed at the ensuing scene and asked me to mediate to calm the situation.

Later, Winston asked me how he might ensure that such a situation did not arise for others in the future. Together, we composed a letter to the funeral director requesting sensitivity to people's cultural customs, particularly at such an important time. Here the social work role was to advocate on Winston's behalf to empower him to seek redress and change for his minority ethnic group. Winston felt excluded from a system that did not respect his culture and customs, and yet, at the same time, he wanted to achieve change without alienating what he perceived to be the more powerful white majority. The outcome of his letter was to receive an apology and a cash refund for part of the funeral costs. Winston, not wanting to profit from this, donated the money to the hospital that had cared for Bertha.

BEREAVEMENT INTERVENTIONS

In a disappointing systematic review of bereavement care interventions, Forte and colleagues (Forte, Hill, Pazder, & Fendtner, 2004) suggest that, except for pharmacological interventions in depression, which are effective, the wide range of theoretical models of bereavement means that studies vary in terminology and helping approach. This makes it hard to build up a clear picture of effective bereavement interventions.

Forte et al.'s (2004) different types of intervention were:

- Pharmacotherapy, mainly for depression and/or anxiety
- Support and counseling
- Psychotherapy, which mainly incorporated cognitive-behavioral and psychodynamic approaches
- Systems-oriented interventions with bereaved people or families, mainly concerned with improved care coordination in connecting services with palliative care services

Stroebe and colleagues' (2007) systematic review divides interventions into three groups, which helps us identify where efforts will be most useful:

- Primary interventions are available to all of a bereaved population; these are found to be ineffective, except where bereaved people request services, and where there are evident mental health problems; this again supports the widespread caution about risk and need assessments.
- Secondary interventions are designed for those who have been assessed as at risk and who want help. These are more effective than primary interventions, provided there is careful assessment and strict criteria for help.
- Tertiary interventions are those providing for complex grief reactions and post-traumatic disorders, where psychological or psychiatric help has generally been effective.

ASSISTING CHILDREN TO DEAL WITH THEIR BEREAVEMENT

Much of the work described in earlier chapters, on working with children preparing them for the death of someone close to them, is relevant here also. The death of someone close is just as hard for children to face as it is for adults. While protecting children from sadness and pain following someone's death is not possible, adults can do a lot to help children cope. Parents and grandparents may find it hard to deal with their own grief at the same time as helping children with theirs; however, supporting bereaved adults to reach out to their children can help adults with their own grief. Honest, open communication with bereaved children is very important, and Christ's (2000) significant qualitative study of American childen shows that most successfully adapt to the death of a parent, but that the grief processes are different at different ages. It is natural to be sad and to cry, but sharing this expression of grief can help children by giving them permission to express rather than hide feelings.

As we have seen in previous chapters, death is hidden and medicalized, and, therefore, many adults feel awkward talking about death, especially to children (partly because they have not addressed their own fears about death). However, generally, children are resilient and better able than adults think to cope with an honest attempt to explain death. They also value the attempt at openness; it is important to help people see that their help to their children does not have to be perfect. We have seen from several of the case examples that if children are not told the truth, they are likely to draw their own conclusions, which may be more disturbing than reality and may lead them to blame themselves. They may also be angry or distrust adults when they subsequently learn what has really happened. As Silverman says, "If we exclude children or protect them from death and bereavement, what we are really doing is not preparing them to deal with life. We are not teaching them anything. We are not helping them to grow and develop" (2000, p.73). A summary of typical reactions to death at different ages is set out in table 6.2.

TABLE 6.2 Children's understanding of death, and possible reactions in relation to age

Age	Concept of death	Reaction
0–2 years	No concept of death	4–7 months—protests at separation, despair, detachment
		stranger anxiety
		regression
		feeding and sleeping difficulties
2–5 years	Death seen as reversible	Fears: abandonment, separation, intrusive procedures, mutilation
	May feel they have caused death	Loud protest
	Magical thinking	Despair
		Indignant of any change in routines of living
		Sleep problems
		Regression
5–11 years	More permanence	Withdrawal, sadness, loneliness, depression
	Exposure to death	Anger—behavior, learning, school problems
		Perfect child, being brave, being controlled
		Regression
Adolescence	Death permanent	Withdrawal, sadness, loneliness, depression
	Denial—it can't be true	Anger, rejection
		Joking, sarcasm
		Regression, dependence

Source: Developed from Marie Curie Holme Tower (2001).

Very Young Children

Children under the age of two will not have an understanding of death, but they will be aware that things are different and that the person to whom they are attached has disappeared (Dyregrov, 2008). They will react to this loss as separation even though their limited language skills make it impossible for them to verbalize their distress. They may become withdrawn, unhappy, or distraught and will need extra reassurance and comforting from an adult whom they know well. If the adults around them are displaying their own distress, this will affect them. As young children develop language, they need to be given information and explanations about the person who has died so as to enable them to integrate this history into their own life story. Letters from the deceased person, photographs, and life stories may be helpful, and may be picked up again in later years and reintegrated in a different way.

Viewing the Body

Parents and grandparents sometimes ask social workers whether to allow or encourage a child to see the body of the deceased person. It is a very individual decision to which there is no right or wrong answer. However, some guidelines may be useful. By viewing the body, children may be helped to believe that the person has died, if they express doubts; but they should never be forced to see the body if they don't want to. Parents might make it clear that this will be the last opportunity to say goodbye. Children need to be prepared for what they might see and experience. They need clear explanations in advance about how the person may look; that they will not be breathing and will feel very cold. "Preparation and sensitive handling are the keys to this being a success. The child needs to know what smells, sounds and other sights the funeral director's rooms will hold for them" (Smith, 1999, p. 55). It needs to be made clear to children that they do not need to touch the body, but they can do so if they wish. Careful consideration should be given as to whether a child will benefit if the body has been badly disfigured following a violent or traumatic death. It may be useful for the adult to see the body first to inform the decision and to give specific information to the child. The child might be prepared by thinking through what they might like to do, for example, leaving a toy that they have shared with the deceased person or a goodbye card.

Attending Funerals

Funeral rituals are probably as important for children as for adults. They have lost someone and need the chance to express their loss and have it recognized by others. Children can be encouraged to take part in funerals. They can choose their own flowers or perhaps a single flower to put in or on the casket. They can draw a special picture or write a letter or poem or make a goodbye card. Worden's report on the Harvard Child Bereavement Study found that, "being included also helped children to feel important and useful at a time when many were feeling over-whelmed" (Worden, 1996, p. 23). Children need to have the funeral service explained in advance and to be as prepared as possible for what to expect, particularly if they are not accustomed to church attendance.

Case example: Charlie

The practitioner's account is as follows. Once when I was working with a family before the death of the mother, the father asked me immediately after his wife's death for help because their son, Charlie, while he had been close to his mother, was reluctant to go to her funeral. The family wanted Charlie to attend his mother's funeral on the grounds that it was an impor-tant experience that he could not retrieve at a later date. The father recognized that it was difficult for Charlie to contemplate the funeral and told me that it was unimportant whether he joined the family in the funeral car or merely wanted to slip into the church at the back in his jeans, just so long as he was there. Dyregrov advises that a child attending a funeral should be accompanied "by a trusted adult," but one whose own needs would not get in the way of supporting the child. The adult who is there for the child should "be someone who can explain what is happening, who can support and console, and who can fol-low the child outside if needed" (Dyregrov, 2008, p. 95).

I visited the family twice in the few days preceding the funeral and read children's stories with pictures that explained funeral services and burials (e.g., Thomas, 2000; Brown & Brown, 1996), but Charlie remained adamant in refusing to attend his mom's funeral.

The day before the funeral, I visited again in a last attempt to see if I could understand what was stopping him. I asked if he would like to drive with me to the church where the funeral was being held and check out parking for the following day. I explained that parking would be difficult because so many peo-ple would be coming to the funeral as his mother had meant so much to so many. There was an attractive public garden next to the church. I suggested that we could go to the garden rather than the church if he wished and hold our own special service at the same time. Would that be easier for him?

I asked what he was most afraid of about the funeral and he said he was afraid that his grandparents would be very distressed and cry uncontrollably; he would find this embarrassing and upsetting. I said that undoubtedly people would cry because they were so sad at losing his mom, but that if he wanted, I would stay with him and would also be sad but would not break down in tears. Also, I made sure he knew he could, if he wished, leave the service before it ended and I would go outside the church with him. Charlie asked what happens in funeral services, how long they last, and other similar questions. We talked about what people wear to funerals and how his younger sister had a special new dress for the occasion. Charlie asked what boys and men wear to funerals; I said that often they dress up in their best clothes and wear black ties as a mark of respect. He then moved from talking about funerals in the third person and asked if it would be OK to wear a blue and orange striped tie. I replied that I thought his mother would be very pleased if he wore this tie, realizing that he only had one tie. He then asked if we could drive to the cemetery so that he could see where his mother would be buried.

Once Charlie felt reassured that he could go to his mother's funeral and at the same time feel safe, he quickly entered into a plan that I could follow through on. Returning to the house after our drive, I explained that Charlie and I had agreed to go together to the funeral and I hoped this would be acceptable to the family. Dad was delighted and offered Charlie a black tie that he had bought specially for him. On the day of the funeral, Charlie and I arrived early but found the church already full, so we sat at the front of the church reserved for the family. We shared a hymnbook and service sheet. We both had tears in our eyes but I kept to the agreement that I would not cry in an uncontrolled way. At the end of the funeral, Charlie was quite content to join the rest of his family in the funeral cars and go to the cemetery for the burial service.

MEMORIALIZATION

We saw in Chapter 2 that memorialization is an important social process in death and dying. People may be uncertain about what is appropriate, particularly since current conventions are usually more informal than in the past. Visiting graves, or sites that were important to the deceased and bereaved people, planting a tree, keeping mementos, building up photo or DVD libraries of memoirs, or writing a poem or life story are all possible options even if the deceased person has provided some memorials themselves. Bereaved people may carry on particular social tasks that they shared with the deceased. Anniversaries may be important. For example, a recent newspaper report described how two sisters had a memorial shopping spree on the anniversary of their mother's death every year. The only limit is bereaved people's imagination. The following suggestions for helping children applies also to adults, as Hector's case example, toward the end of this chapter, shows.

Interventions for Helping Children Develop and Keep Memories

After a significant death, it is helpful to encourage children to choose a memento belonging to the person who has died. Looking through old photographs or perhaps making a scrapbook can help children talk about their memories, thoughts, and feelings. Keeping an object that reminds a child of the person who has died gives a child an important way of connecting and remembering. Encouraging children to make their own memory box, which they can personalize and decorate, that keeps together items that have special meanings or memories for them can be beneficial. There is no right or wrong way of grieving. Each child is unique and special and needs to feel loved and secure in the face of loss, change, and uncertainty.

Table 6.3 lists a range of interventions that may help a bereaved child. Some are activities that children can pursue alone, though stimulation and support from adults who are close to them may be beneficial. Many of these are helpful around the time of death or soon afterward. Others are joint activities, with brothers, sisters, and relatives, and may be carried on for some time, including marking the anniversary of the death. It is also important to prepare organizations that the child is involved with, particularly school, but this may also include youth organizations. The child's experiences will raise fears and concerns for other children, and the experience may lead to a useful program activity to stimulate education for a wider group of children. It is important, however, that the bereaved child does not feel that he or she is responsible for the activity, or for distress and anxiety that other children experience.

Similar interventions may usefully be used with individual children where there has been a multiple loss, for example a road traffic accident affecting a bus or van involving children known to a class, a terrorist incident, or a shooting event. Group approaches may also be used to facilitate first information, then discussion, and finally emotional release, followed by discussion about the meaning of the events to the school and

TABLE 6.3   Activities to help a bereaved child

Individual activities about the time of the death, to help deal with grief and promote constructing the deceased person in a new way. May be helped by an adult demonstrating or helping	Make a memory box.
	Make a memory book, a scrap book with pictures, drawings, photos, writings.
	Write a letter or poem to the person who has died.
	Make your own photograph collection.
	Make a salt model to create a jar of memories.
	Make a calendar of important and special dates.
Activities that may be done jointly with brothers and sisters and relatives	Read children's story books that focus on bereavement.
	Remember anniversaries and birthdays in a special way.
	Light a candle on special days.
Professional help	Attend a children's bereavement group to meet other children who have had similar experiences.
	Seek individual bereavement counseling for children if they want this.
Community involvement and environmental support	Involve the child's school and make the school aware—it may have its own program of activities for bereaved children.

people affected. Building on existing social networks is also important (Dyregrov & Dyregrov, 2008).

1. Making a Memory Box. A memory box is a collection of significant items, including writings, drawings, recordings of favorite music, and pictures that will remind a bereaved child or adult of important shared experiences. Usually a memory box will contain photographs, details of special family events, information about the person who has died as well as particular items that help a person to understand more about the dying family member later. A memory box helps people to understand their own life story by giving information about the past and so helps the person to feel more confident about themselves, their identity and roots.

Any box can be used but it may help if the box can hold standard documents and is not too big. Children can personalize the box by decorating it with pictures, stickers, and perhaps a photograph to make it their own special box. Adults should help children to think of what they might want to include. The dying person may want to make a memory box as one of his or her end-of-life tasks. It can also be very special for parent and child to make one together. This may be done at any time, not necessarily when approaching death.

Think about objects that hold memories not only of the person who has died but also the relationship between the two people. Shared activities that connected two people can be represented in different forms. For example, if cooking was a shared pastime, a special family recipe can be included or the recipe for the family's favorite birthday cake or special cookies. A child might like to think of the person's favorite foods, color, garden flowers, or sport or other hobbies, and how these can be represented.

It may help the child to construct an account of important information about his or her own early life as well as that of the person who has died. Making a disk of the person's favorite music can be a wonderful way of making connections. If it was a father who has died, objects that represent his favorite sport, perhaps his old college tie, an old pair of cufflinks or his favorite pen, a movie, or book might be used. If a mother has died, it might be good to include some of her favorite perfume, or a scarf, or a small piece of her jewelry. Attaching a label or gift tag with a short message or explanation noting the meaning or significance of the object will help children remember or to construct a story for themselves. If items are small and easily lost in a big box, it is worth using a series of smaller boxes inside the large one to ensure that treasures are kept in an organized way. Special photographs, letters, old birthday cards, a passport, or certificates and reports from school or college can all help to create a personal memory store that enables a child to retain and retrieve memories. "A memory box can be a real comfort, and can be used to collect and treasure things that help people connect with someone who has died . . . Looking through the memory box can help with the process of grieving for all the different aspects of the person who died—who they were, what they liked or did not like, what they were good at and not so good at, as well as the things that were important to them" (Stokes, 2004, p. 81).

Obviously, adults can also make memory boxes—although it seems particularly helpful for young children who may not have a lot of their own memories and may need help to hold on to significant connections. A U.K. children's bereavement charity, Winston's Wish, accessed through its website, produces a range of materials to guide adults through a child's bereavement, including "Developing a Memory Store for Your Child." More recently, Winston's Wish has produced a guide for older children, subtitled: "Making Memories Last When Someone Has Died" (2006). (www.winstonswish.org.uk)

2. Making a Memory Book. Memory books or activity books can be made by the child (with adult assistance if required) by using a scrapbook. Alternatively, books designed for this purpose are available from several sources (e.g., Crossley, 2000; Silverman, 1999). Silverman writes: "Every family should have such a book dedicated to the deceased . . . The focus of memory books should be on helping children develop a sense of who died. As children grow, they need help in developing a more mature sense of the person who died" (Silverman, 2000, p. 232).

3. Making a Salt Model, or Salt Sculpture. This is an activity that can be done either with one child on their own or with a children's bereavement group, which is perhaps more usual. In our experience, it is an activity that is both fun and serious at the same time and gives adults an opportunity to engage with children communicating about the person they are remembering in a nonthreatening way. Making a salt sculpture provides a vehicle for remembering important things about the person who has died.

Each child needs a small jar with a lid and a wide neck that is completely filled with salt, several strongly colored chalks, and five sheets of paper. Divide the salt from the jar onto the paper. Encourage or help each child to think of five things he or she remembers about the person who has died. A different color salt represents each memory. To obtain the colors, rub the chalk into the salt until it takes on the chalk color. Pour each pile of colored salt back into the jar. Make sure that the jar is completely full so that there is no space for the salt to be mixed up. Secure the lid firmly and you have a jar of memories. It helps to write on another piece of paper or small card what each color represents.

Case example: Hector

The practitioner's account is as follows. I was approached some time after the death of a woman by her adult son, Hector, who had intellectual disabilities. He had been abroad with his father at the time of the death, and had been separated from his mother for some years. I used the health care records of his mother's death to talk about his mother, and Hector was very distressed. I got out the salt and provided a jar. Hector said that he wanted his memories to be highly colored, to remember their home island in the Caribbean where the flowers were so colorful, so he rubbed away at the salt for a long time—the more you rub the stronger the color. Hector left the office clutching his jar; he had cried a lot, but now seemed pleased with his memorial.

4. Using Children's Literature to Connect with Memories.
There are many children's books available that can be read aloud with
young children to help them make sense of what has happened. *Badger's Parting Gifts* (Varley, 1984) tells the story of Badger's friends being
very sad when Badger dies. The friends, Mole, Frog, Fox, and Rabbit,
think they will be sad forever. "Mole especially felt lost, alone and des-
perately unhappy" . . . "Badger had always been there when anyone
needed him." Slowly, through reminiscing and sharing with each other
their stories and memories about Badger, the animals each remembered
the skills Badger had taught them. "Each of the animals had a special
memory of Badger—something he had taught them that they could now
do extremely well. He had given them each a parting gift to treasure
always. Using these gifts they would be able to help each other." This
story and others like it can be used as a gentle and sensitive way to help
children find a way of developing continuing bonds with the person who
has died.

There are also many books for older children to read themselves.
Some are fiction, whereas others are stories that are purpose-written to
address difficult issues and experiences facing children. Reading lists are
available from, for example, the Winston's Wish website or may be found
by Internet search. More detailed guidance on age appropriate books and
their content with brief summaries of the story and underlying message
can be found in Jones's work (2001). She also explores the value and
benefits of using literature to help both young and older children think
about death. "The strength of using fiction lies in the fact that the child
can become his own therapist, reading and re-reading a book, perhaps
discovering new levels of meaning, interpretation, understanding and
relevance to his own situation" (Jones, 2001, p.124).

A POEM FOR MARK: A COLLECTIVE POEM

This is a collective poem written by the Thursday group in the Creative Living Center at St. Christopher's Hospice in May 2008. A collective
poem is created by the group deciding on a topic that is important to
them, with each person contributing a thought; the thoughts are put
down in order, and a flow of thoughts often emerges. There may be some
reordering at the end. On this day, a member of the group, Mark, who
liked to paint, had died. Among the possible interpretations, this poem
could indicate some of the features of the dual process model of grief.

Sorrow . . .
  Perspective . . .
    Happy for Mark, at peace
      Calm
        Resting 5

No more pain
　No more suffering
　　His beautiful colors
　　　Looking for the positive

Wishing he is in heaven　　　　　　　　　　　　10
　In God's memory
　　Everlasting eternal life
　　　Blessed

Making the most of life
　Privileged to be here　　　　　　　　　　　　15
　　Sharing . . . Caring . . .

CONCLUSION

In this chapter, we have introduced bereavement care, picking up the discussion of issues of loss started in Chapter 1. In many end-of-life services, bereavement care is a role of social workers and counselors, who often organize groups of volunteers. We have examined psychological and social models of grief and bereavement that are the foundation for practitioners' interventions. In addition to work addressing emotional and social reactions to bereavement, we have also examined some practical ways of helping people to memorialize the deceased person.

In addition to specialized bereavement services, many social workers will come across people who need help with bereavement in the course of their everyday practice, and being able to respond with appropriate help is an important aspect of social work, which will help families deal with other life events.

FURTHER READING

In addition, to the general books on palliative care social work, the following more specialized texts are helpful:

Jeffreys, J. S. (2005). *Helping grieving people: When tears are not enough.* New York: Brunner-Routledge. A comprehensive and approachable introduction covering a full range of bereavement services.

Lendrum, S., & Syme, G. (2004). *Gift of tears: A practical approach to loss and bereavement counselling and psychotherapy.* (2nd ed.) London: Routledge. A good general book on bereavement work with a counseling and psychotherapeutic approach.

Christ, G. C. (2000). *Healing children's grief: Surviving a parent's death from cancer.* New York: Oxford University Press. An important and moving study, which provides rich information for people working with children's grief.

Currer, C. (2001). *Responding to grief: Dying, bereavement and social care.* Basingstoke, England: Palgrave. Useful because it focuses on helping practitioners who are not in a specialist end-of-life service.

Monroe, B. & Kraus, F. (2005). *Brief interventions with bereaved children*. Oxford, England: Oxford University Press. An edited collection of useful practical and conceptual articles on helping bereaved children.

Read, S. (2007). *Bereavement counselling for people with learning disabilities: A handbook*. London: Quay. A useful, practical guide to working on bereavement issues with a special client group.

Nadeau, J. W. (1998). *Families making sense of death*. Thousand Oaks, CA: Sage.

Kissane, D. W. & Bloch, S. (2002). *Family focused grief therapy*. Maidenhead, England: Open University Press. Two useful books looking at families as groups. Although Kissane and Bloch's work describes a very resource-intensive model of practice that may be beyond the reach of many services, it offers useful ideas about approaching family bereavement work.

JOURNALS

In addition to palliative care journals about aspects of death and dying recommended in previous chapters, there are journals specifically concerned with bereavement care:

*   *Bereavement Care,* Cruse Bereavement Care, PO Box 800, Richmond, Surrey TW9 1RG, UK; http://www.crusebereavementcare.org.uk/ber_care.htm
*   *Grief Matters: The Australian Journal of Grief and Bereavement*, Australian Centre for Grief and Bereavement, McCulloch House, Monash Medical Centre, 246 Clayton Road, Clayton VIC 3168, Australia; http://www.grief.org.au/grief_matters.html

WEBSITES

The Dougy Center for Grieving Children and Families: http://www.dougy.org/ An important U.S. website.

Winston's Wish: www.winstonswish.org.uk
A U.K. child-bereavement organization offering a wide range of resources.

Chapter 7

MULTIPROFESSIONAL
END-OF-LIFE CARE

CHAPTER AIMS

The main aim of this chapter is to review practice in working in different forms of partnership to promote holistic end-of-life and palliative care.

After working through this chapter, readers will be able to:

- Evaluate ways in which they can implement holistic end-of-life care in their work;
- Identify difficulties and opportunities of the social work role in end-of-life care teamwork;
- Identify ways of engaging in and developing effective multiprofessional teamwork through making their team a practice community;
- Examine the possibilities offered by various forms of review and education processes in developing multiprofessional work;
- Examine the settings of and relationships with other practitioners, disciplines and professions in end-of-life care; and
- Consider the impact of accumulated loss in their work on their stress, need for support, and the role of professional supervision.

PARTNERSHIP TO WORK HOLISTICALLY
IN END-OF-LIFE CARE

Practising end-of-life and palliative care aims to be holistic, dealing with the whole of an individuals' health and social needs, including the impact of their needs on their family and community and the influences of family and community on their health and social care. Therefore, its practice involves partnership

- Between practitioners, clients, their informal caregivers, and families
- Between different professional groups
- Between professionals, paraprofessionals, and volunteers

- Between agencies with different roles in the care system
- For social workers particularly, between health care and social work and social care agencies

Pause and reflect

Why do you think so many different forms of partnership are important in end-of-life care?

Some suggestions

To be holistic, end-of-life care must involve a range of expertise and organizations. Toward the end of life, people's care needs are significant, and so a response out of normal agency hours and sometimes round the clock is required. Since we are dealing with both physical frailty and psychological and social distress we need practitioners who can deal with the body, mind, and spirit, and families and social networks.

In Chapter 2, we saw that there is a risk that end-of-life care may be medicalized and focus too much on individualized care for physical symptoms, rather than broader care for the whole person in his or her social networks. The focus of social work on the social and the system counterbalances this tendency. Social workers also play an important role in structures that enable practitioners from different agencies and professions to work together, in family meetings/conferences and in protecting vulnerable adults from harm, as we saw in Chapters 4 and 5.

However, social workers also face a number of difficulties in taking part in these partnership processes. Reese and Sontag (2001) identify potential barriers in hospice settings to social workers' involvement in multiprofessional teams, which will feel realistic to many social workers in wider health care settings. These include:

- Lack of awareness and expertise about the potential role and skills of social workers
- Role blurring, leading to other professions taking on roles that might be better undertaken by social workers
- Conflicts arising from theoretical and disciplinary focus of different professions
- Negative team norms, including some members having little commitment to working on the team process and little willingness to share work; blaming behavior when things go wrong; and power, gender, and salary disparities
- Clients who resist referral because they stereotype such practitioners as psychiatrists, psychologists, social workers, and spiritual care staff as members of authoritarian or stigmatizing professions. However, this may be exaggerated, since clients may dislike or

resist any profession or individual; it is often possible to overcome uncertainty by introducing yourself and explaining your role in such situations
- Administrative and financial issues in services that lead to reductions in social work provision

Although social work is an established profession and has been part of health care for more than a century, it is peripheral to many health care teams and needs to empower itself and be empowered to play its role effectively. It is peripheral because:

- The leading professions in end-of-life care, medicine, and nursing have a biomedical focus. The social science focus of social work gives it a different perspective, which is easy to overlook in daily practice. As a result, we propose that, although they will contribute to group-relations teamwork, social workers focus on the knowledge-based form of teamwork, which emphasizes these issues.
- Among the leading professions, medicine has a high social status and nurses are large in numbers. Consequently, end-of-life and palliative care organizations have to pay attention to their needs and interests. The requirements of social work may seem a lower priority.
- Social workers are often on their own or in small teams in end-of-life and palliative care organizations, and they may be aggregated for administrative purposes with other similar groups, so their professional concerns need to be carefully preserved and balanced with the needs of other professional groups.
- Medicine and nursing are individualized professions, focusing on the care needs of a particular patient, who can be seen as the source of professional and ethical authority to act. Social workers have a system and family focus, so that their professional and ethical responsibilities have particular complexities that are not always clear to colleagues and clients.

Pause and reflect

Try drawing a team eco-map—a social network diagram that takes account of physical locations and environmental factors—of an end-of-life team you know. List the team members; who would be core and who would be on the periphery? Do they have responsibilities of support outside the care team?

Some suggestions

A core and periphery pattern of team organization is common in many health care agencies (Miller, Freeman, & Ross, 2001). This is illustrated by the team eco-map in figure 7.1, which describes a typical ward team in St

Christopher's Hospice and is similar to the arrangement in many in-patient units in hospitals and hospices. A similar eco-map could also be drawn of many home care services. Here there is a group of nursing staff who are part of a hierarchy, so that the ward manager, who is always a senior nurse, is responsible to a more senior manager outside the ward for the work of the group. The doctors do not have quite such a hierarchy of responsibility and are independently responsible for their practice, but they are connected to a group of doctors who work in different settings across the hospice. The ward clerk does the ward team's administrative work and is responsible to the hospice administrator, again outside the ward (but another common pattern would make the administrator responsible to the ward manager). These are the staff who work every day in the ward and therefore form the core team. Another group of staff are part of the ward team, but on the periphery; at St. Christopher's they include the social worker, the physical therapist, and the spiritual care team member. Although these staff are attached to the team, their work base is elsewhere and they visit the ward. Moreover, they do not work with every patient on the ward, but only those referred by the core team. Because they are on the periphery of the ward, they have to work hard at building relationships.

FIGURE 7.1   Core and periphery ward team

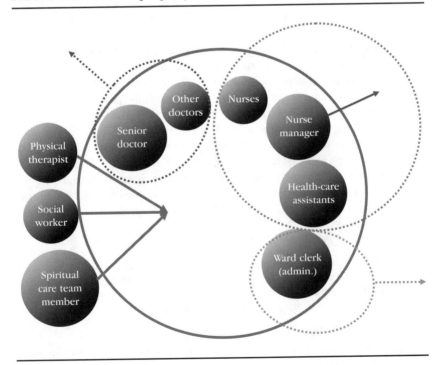

They do this through various means in "everyday teamwork" (Payne, 2006a):

- Informal and social relationships, such as taking breaks with core team members, taking part in shared outings, parties, and other social events. Peripheral team members have to work harder at these social connections than core team members.
- Informal interpersonal help with the stresses of work. Social workers and others who have work based away from the daily pressures of a ward may be particularly helpful for this reason.
- Participation in "patient teams," groups of people planning work with particular patients.
- Participation in dealing with particular difficulties presented on the ward, for example, responding to help with difficult behavior from visitors or relatives. Since core team members are, in a sense, trapped on the ward with any problems, it is important that they are supported in dealing with challenging or difficult behavior.

In addition to everyday teamwork, most organizations with complex groups of staff make arrangements to group people in teams and promote their collaboration. They do this through:

- Regular planning and decision-making forums based on teams that often work together, such as ward or home care team meetings
- Reviews of particular aspects of practice, such as debriefing when there have been accidents, violence towards practitioners or between patients, or suicide or self-harm
- Educational structures to promote teamwork such as journal clubs
- Formal team-building activities

Many organizations reserve more formal team-building for occasions where there have been relationship difficulties between members of a team, a change in organizational structure, a new development in work practice, or a substantial change in team membership (Payne, 2006a).

Different situations require different forms of teamwork. Three commonplace forms of teamwork are:

- Coordinative teamwork, as in the core team, where all members work as a group, but have different roles; this is like a football or baseball team where everyone is on the field at once but take on different roles.

- Cooperative teamwork, as a professional team of nurses, doctors, or social workers, where all members do similar things in similar roles but in different wards or localities; this is like a tennis or golf team, where people can support each other in their separate matches because "they've been there."
- Network teamwork, as in a multiprofessional home care team, where all members do different things, separately, working in different places such as care homes and people's own homes; this is like an athletics team, where people support each other in their different sports.

Research (Payne, 2000; Borrill et al., 2001) shows, however, that teamwork usually has several important aims:

- Clear team objectives (a team mission or statement of objectives)
- Participation (an informal and cooperative atmosphere)
- Commitment to quality (always seeking to improve practice)
- Support for innovation (always seeking to identify new ways of doing things)

Much team-building work seeks to work on these issues through two different processes:

- relationship-building work
- knowledge-based practice (Payne, 2006a)

Relationship building tries to deal with conflicts, poor communication, and difficulties in making agreed decisions by getting team members to participate in agreeing procedures and communication processes for transferring work and making decisions between team members. A recent German palliative care study (Jünger, Pestner, Eisner, Krumm, & Radbruch, 2007) found that good communication was the most important factor in achieving successful multiprofessional work, and role ambiguity and conflict important factors in obstructing it. By working on these issues, teams develop an easy form of relationships in everyday teamwork. An important aspect of this is mutual support. West (2004, p. 155) identifies three forms of support that team members can work on:

- social support: this includes emotional support, noticing when someone is distressed and upset and offering help; informational support, being prepared to offer information to help a colleague, rather than keeping it to enhance your power; instrumental sup-

port, practical help such as giving someone a lift on a journey; and appraisal support, taking time to help people think through issues in their work
- developing a positive and friendly social climate
- support for individual team members' growth and development through training and staff-development processes

Knowledge-based teamwork starts from the proposition that each team is a practice community (Wenger, 1998) that shares learning as they practice together, each contributing their particular knowledge and skill to the overall task. The role of leadership in this form of team development aims to help different people "speak" their expertise, rather than cutting it off because it does not fit with others' understandings. The team should aim to help different professionals pursue the tasks required to achieve good practice within their profession, and put the different tasks together in an overall plan that includes everyone (Opie, 2003). Each patient's or client's plan therefore would consist of some overall objectives that all team members would contribute to and agree with, and then would record specific plans that would meet the professional duties of particular team members, so that others would understand what they are trying to achieve in their work. As well as recognizing minority forms of practice, this particularly inclusive form of teamwork practice is good for recognizing and dealing with strain that arises because of ethnic, social, and gender differences between team members.

Case example: Hospice Team

In one hospice, the regular ward meeting reviewing the plans for each patient took the form of the report on the diagnosis and any medical tests and focused on nursing plans to deal with different symptoms and physical therapy to help with pain control and mobilization of patients, so that they could move around more easily. If nurses or doctors reported psychosocial or spiritual issues, the decision was made to refer these to the relevant professionals, who were not able to attend every meeting. The core team assumed that these issues were dealt with, unless difficulties with them obstructed discharge from the hospice. If this happened, it was usually social workers who were specifically asked to the meeting to explain why they had failed to meet the medical objectives for discharge. Sometimes, great concern was expressed where extra costs were incurred for the hospice because discharge was delayed, and the social workers felt blamed for not being able to meet the objectives, and also that the core team failed to recognize their difficulties in achieving the required outcomes.

A new nurse manager instituted a knowledge-based process. This meant that the review meeting set overall objectives for symptom management and discharge dates, and included where necessary psychosocial and spiritual care objectives. Thus, in addition to listing medical and nursing plans, the meeting also asked the social worker attached to the team to list what he or she would have to do in order to meet the psychosocial aims. This was a revelation to some medical and nursing staff, who in several cases in the first week were astonished by the complexity of the family relationship issues to be resolved before a successful discharge could be achieved. This process led to a much better acceptance of the social worker's role and to a supportive response to the difficulties the social worker faced.

MAKING YOUR TEAM A PRACTICE COMMUNITY

Achieving a practice community means focusing on shared learning among members of a multiprofessional team that also seeks to be inclusive of the interests and involvement of clients and their families. In this section, we examine a number of different ways of engaging people in learning together as a way of developing teamwork.

Review

An important aspect of any social work is reviewing process, progress, and outcomes with client systems, and this can be made to form part of everyday knowledge-based teamwork. *Monitoring* means checking consistently that care and other plans are working appropriately; *evaluation* means examining whether they are achieving the best outcomes for clients, informal caregivers, and other systems. *Review* looks back in an organized way at the progress of the case, and further plans are often founded on it. These mechanisms are connected with organizational audit processes, discussed in the next section.

A crucial element of all these client-oriented processes is the active involvement of clients, informal caregivers, and other systems surrounding the client, so that they participate in planning. In end-of-life care, participation should focus on:

- Clients' priorities because approaching death may limit the time they have left to achieve what they want

- Informal caregivers' needs, because they carry an increasing burden of care as the client's condition deteriorates and also face pre-bereavement and bereavement experiences

Monitoring

Monitoring involves two aspects of care; one focused on client systems, the other on agency systems. The first aspect checks that people within client systems feel secure in their present situation. Changes may occur, but security means that users and caregivers are able to self-manage change. We saw in Chapter 2 that the trajectory of many end-of-life situations is a decline in the client system's capacity to manage, perhaps with occasional crises. In these situations, monitoring is supportive because it enables users and caregivers to feel confidence that there will be a response to crisis; practitioners can only achieve this security if people within the client system are actively aware of and involved in the monitoring.

Various services offer this kind of monitoring:

- Support within clients' own homes by professionals or para-professionals, to provide the confidence of regular checks to identify deterioration. Continuous knowledge of the client is important so that changes in condition can be identified.
- Regular visits from professionals or informal caregivers. Where there are multiple visits and therefore probably multiple problems, it is useful to plan these in a program, so that more regular monitoring is possible. Also, where some of the services are from a succession of caregivers from an agency (serial caregivers), and different personnel visit throughout the day to perform different tasks, it is useful to intersperse these with visits from staff who have a continuous relationship with users and caregivers. This enables someone who knows the user to identify problems and also to integrate serial caregivers' contributions carefully with the care plan, through offering guidance and supervision on an every-day basis.
- Respite or periodic care in a care home, hospital, or hospice to enable problematic symptoms to be dealt with and to relieve caregivers' stress. This can restore or increase quality of life as it is deteriorating.
- Day center or drop-in provision, so that a regular check on clients' physical and psychological condition can be made. More practical elements of clients' lives can also be helped on a day basis. For example, several patients at St. Christopher's Hospice asked to bathe in the hospice in order to avoid specialized equipment

cluttering up a small bathroom at home and also because, while the patients were able to take a bath on their own and so did not require a visiting caregiver to help them, they felt more secure if a nurse could be called. Therefore, the hospice developed a bathing suite to permit this service to be offered more routinely.

- Radio and telephone call systems that enable frail people to call for assistance if they have a sudden crisis.

For people with severe or long-term difficulties, several of these monitoring devices can be used in combination.

The second aspect of monitoring, to meet the agency's requirements, may be part of managed care or care-management processes or other requirements set by funders. The personal relationship established with clients and informal caregivers in early contacts with them can build trust for practitioners and respect for their agencies' competence in responding to situations that arise. This in turn enables agencies to establish a reliable and responsive individual connection with the client system.

Because many people at end of life experience deterioration, rapid variation, and complex interactions of symptoms and social circumstances, monitoring is important for continuous reassessment. Rapid changes in physical condition can be frightening to clients and informal caregivers, and the knowledge that practitioners are constantly alert to changes enhances clients' and caregivers' feelings of security and strengthens their resilience when difficulties arise. Where people in long-term conditions or frailty trajectories have long periods where their condition is fairly stable, care services can become complacent and routine. It is important to recognize and respect the anxiety caused when there is a sudden deterioration or change.

Bell (2005) connects such professional practices with research, showing how the two involve similar processes of investigation. She proposes four elements of any review process:

- Context, including values that are relevant and power relations among the people involved
- Setting, including the family home, care home, day center, and community in which care takes place
- Situated activity, including the interpersonal relationships and behavior (e.g., degree of distress), that occur and the factors that affect them (e.g., isolation or unhelpful relationships with peers)
- Self, including the biography of the people involved and the trajectory of the problems they are dealing with and the impact on them

Monitoring should be an active, forward-looking process in which the complex interacting factors involved in the situation should be fully reconsidered.

Critical-Incident, Ethical, and After-Event Reviews

A useful way of developing teamwork and shared learning is to have a regular multiprofessional team process for reporting on and learning from important experiences in the team. *Critical-incident reviews* look at specific events that seem to be important in the work with a particular client or family, while *after-event reviews* look at the decisions and actions taken about a particular event that caused difficulty.

Critical-incident analysis was developed by Flanagan (1954) as a research technique. He defined an incident as critical if it made a "significant" contribution, either positively or negatively, to the general aim of the activity observed (Flanagan, 1954, p. 338). The analysis provides raw data on which a review of the case may take place (Flanagan, 1954, p. 355).

Fook and Askeland (2006) outline the review process as follows:

- Describe the critical incident, making and restructuring the meaning of it by analyzing and understanding the situation. Reveal deep-seated assumptions that are taken for granted.
- Explore the individual experience in light of historical, social, political, economic, cultural, and religious contexts.
- Create emancipatory knowledge resulting in professional growth and development.
- Create a collective professional knowledge base to be followed by transformative change. (Fook & Askeland, 2006)

A number of end-of-life and palliative care services also have ethical and after-event reviews as part of their staff development process. Some health-care organizations have set up ethical review panels or committees; major hospitals often employ medical ethicists to provide consultation. These consistently consider changes in ethical requirements of the different professions involved. Social workers need to ensure that their own ethical and standards requirements are logged and included in the process, since this ensures recognition by the organization of their responsibilities, it also helps to educate colleagues in the particular challenges of their role. Ethics committees also review difficult cases that have arisen and make recommendations for developments in service policies and practice. Again, it is important to ensure that social work contributions are made so that psychosocial issues are included. Ethics committees may also establish panels to give advice and consultation, usually provided by a small group of people from different professions, to practitioners in difficult cases at the time that decisions are being made. Social workers should ensure that social work consultants are available for such processes, again so that psychosocial issues are raised and considered alongside health-care issues.

After-event reviews are a form of debriefing following an adverse event in the care of a client or patient, which might include:

- Episodes of physical violence or aggression between patients, relatives, and staff
- Attempted or successful suicides
- Unusual behaviors, especially where these might involve a reputational risk to the agency

An important aspect of after-event reviews is caring for the stress and concern raised for members of staff involved, as well as planning for any changes that will reduce the risk of the event recurring.

Case example: Harriet

Harriet, an aged patient with dementia, newly admitted to a hospice, was found to have wandered away from the building. The nurse in charge of the ward notified the police, who instituted a search, eventually using heat-seeking equipment mounted on a helicopter, at some expense to the local police force. The patient was found sleeping in the bushes in a park near the hospice grounds by a local person walking his dog. An after-event review was held the following week, chaired by a senior manager in the hospice. The story of the events was told from different points of view, and an important concern of the early part of the meeting was reassuring the admitting physician that it had been appropriate to admit the patient, and the nurse that, after her initial search around the hospice, it was entirely appropriate to call the police. The meeting moved on to discussing whether particular security arrangements needed to be made for patients with dementia who had a history of wandering. This led to the recognition that the change of location to the hospice might well lead to wandering (where this was not preexisting behavior), because the patient would be in unfamiliar surroundings. Therefore, new procedures were instituted so that patients with dementia alongside other illnesses would have this identified at an earlier stage of the admission process, and appropriate security arrangements set up. This enabled the hospice chief executive to meet with relatives of the patient and with the police and maintain the hospice's reputation for good care by showing the care that had been taken in this case and the new procedures that had been established as a result of the experience.

Educational and Professional Development in Teamwork

As well as team development that arises from planning and reviewing the everyday work of teams, a variety of educational structures can also help to develop multiprofessional work:

- Presentations of cases by professional teams or patient teams, to report on achievements and allow discussion of learning that emerges from experience.
- Journal clubs. A number of structures are possible. Particular professions can discuss the content of important research or professional journals and report back to the multiprofessional team. Professions can also present articles from their own journals for discussion more widely.
- Resource searches. Team members take responsibility for researching community and professional services available to clients and patients and reporting back to colleagues, establishing an information bank.
- Policy and law reports. Team members can take responsibility for reporting back on new policy or legal developments or official guidance, each team member taking a chapter and reporting back until everyone has taken a turn in reporting and the whole of an innovation has been covered.
- Setting up a team blog in which people take turns to make an entry reporting on something of interest to the team each day.
- A reading group to look at popular literature or informational books for patients, clients, and children. A review by the hospice librarian of novels and other literature dealing with bereavement and end-of-life issues is a very popular annual event for the bereavement service volunteers at St. Christopher's Hospice; her published blog (http://bereavementupdate.blogspot.com/) shows the kind of material covered.
- Carrying out audits of practice, by identifying an area of work that is not well understood by the team or employer, deciding objectives and testing whether those objectives are met over a period of time.

AGENCY SETTINGS, DISCIPLINES, AND PROFESSIONS

So far in this chapter, we have examined partnership within end-of-life and palliative care teams in general, where everyone has a responsibility to contribute to teamwork and team-building. However, social workers also have to concern themselves with specific aspects of relationships with other professions, disciplines, and settings. A profession is an occupational group of people recognized as possessing the knowledge, skills, and values associated with a particular social identity and role. Disciplines are branches of knowledge associated with education and research that produce systematic, well-organized behavior, and in health and social care are associated with professions, which focus on different areas of a shared field of knowledge. Agency settings are workplaces within organizations that provide services to the public, where professional disciplines are implemented and occupational tasks are carried out.

Settings for Psychosocial Care

End-of-life care takes place in a range of settings:

- Hospitals, where active treatment for a medical condition is being provided, but death nevertheless occurs
- Emergency health-care facilities such as hospital emergency rooms, where death may arise as a result of accident, traumatic injury, self-harm, and suicide
- Hospices, where care is provided for people known to be moving toward the end of their lives
- Care homes and nursing homes, where a high proportion of older people, are likely to reach the end of their lives
- People's own homes or the homes of relatives, friends, or landlords.
- Other institutions, such as prisons or psychiatric or other specialized hospitals, where people reach the end of their lives while being housed for some social purpose

We have extended here Hodgson's (2005) analysis of the organizational structures in such settings through which social workers often play a role, which require multiprofessional practice:

- Admission decision making: social workers often contribute the perspective of psychosocial needs.
- Discharge planning: social workers often help patients and family members to contribute their differing perspectives and have an

important role in bringing together internal and external staff as part of their role in working across the boundaries of agencies and health-care and social care systems.

- In-patient, day-patient, and home-care multiprofessional team meetings: social workers contribute a focus on family and community needs and psychosocial perspectives.
- Family meetings/conferences: social workers often take a major role in planning and chairing these and deciding whom to involve, bringing together appropriate professionals and family members (see Chapter 3 for a detailed case example).

Within these settings and structures, social workers are often characterized as providing psychosocial care, a term that connects psychological and social aspects of service, and reflects the international definition of social work. One way of understanding psychosocial care is to examine who is thought to be appropriate to provide it. Table 7.1 compares three studies, a U.K. policy analysis, a U.K. research study, and a U.S. policy analysis. The U.K. analysis identifies the main professions with a specialized role in psychosocial care. The U.S. study reflects the assumption that at a certain level, all people involved with patients need to be able to recognize and respond to psychosocial need; it therefore includes physicians

TABLE 7.1 Occupational roles in psychosocial end-of-life care: Three studies

Dix & Glickman, 1997 (U.K.)	Price et al., 2006 (U.K.)	Adler & Page, 2008 (U.S.)
Social workers	Social workers Dual-qualified practitioners, most often social workers with an additional counseling qualification	Social workers
Clinical psychologists	Clinical psychologists	Licensed mental health providers such as psychologists and counselors
Counselors	Counselors	
		Physicians
Psychiatrists	Psychiatrists	
	Psychotherapists	
	Creative therapists	
		Registered nurses
	Registered mental nurse	
Chaplains or spiritual care advisers	Spiritual advisers	Pastoral counselors
Family therapists		
	Complementary therapists	

and nurses as part of the workforce concerned with psychosocial care, who thus need appropriate education and preparation for this aspect of their roles. It may also be useful for social workers involved with non-specialized colleagues to consider how they can update colleagues with psychosocial information. The three studies include social workers, counselors, and psychologists together with chaplains or spiritual care staff as potential providers of psychosocial care. Finally, the U.K. survey by Price and colleagues (Price, Hotopf, Higginson, Monroe, & Henderson, 2006) identifies a wider range of staff with some psychosocial responsibilities who made contributions to care in some hospices.

Professions Contributing to Psychosocial Care

How is a social worker to relate to this variety of colleagues all potentially contributing to psychosocial care? The U.K. NICE guidance (2004) on supportive and palliative care for cancer patients suggests in two places, referring to psychological support and spiritual support, a model of practice that assumes levels of competence and skill. In psychological support for example, there are four levels. At level 1, covering all staff in health and social care, there should be competence to recognize and refer psychological and spiritual problems. Level 2 covers people with some additional preparation and training, whose role is to screen for distress and engage in simple problem solving. Level 3 refers to trained and accredited professionals such as those recognized in the studies in table 7.1. Finally, level 4 refers to people with additional therapeutic qualifications in psychology and counseling. A similar three-level model is proposed for spiritual care.

The value of such a model is that it recognizes that staff involved in the daily care of patients in in-patient and home care settings will need to be able to respond appropriately to problems presented to them, calling on specialized expertise as required. This is recognized in the chapter on social support, which identifies practical and financial assistance and information and social assessments for care services as particular roles of social workers, but suggests that a wide range of professions may make contributions to psychosocial care. The problem with such a model is that it fails to recognize the difficulty of referring patients for a specialized service, particularly where, as with social work or psychiatry, there may be stigma attached to "not being able to cope."

Without careful engagement by social workers in multiprofessional teams, therefore, their skills may not be valued or accepted. In particular, the focus on individualized problem-solving implied by participation in a medicalized service may fail to provide for the social elements of the social work role, which might be less well understood. Social workers therefore need to make a special effort to engage in team activities and to make themselves available for consultation to colleagues whose role has a health care focus. Presence at team meetings and hospital rounds, and participation in reviews and education activities are crucial ways of presenting the psychosocial perspective. Even if social workers find this personally uncongenial, contributing a social science perspective actively in a journal club and making sure they actively mention social assessment and community issues as part of their professional assessments is an important way of reminding colleagues whose work has another focus that their role is different.

Similarly, social workers need to distinguish the social work from other similar roles. A starting point is that social work and counseling professions generally use the same sets of interpersonal skills. We suggested in Chapters 4 and 5 following Gelderd and Gelderd's (2005) analysis that this included skills concerned with facilitating effective communication and interpersonal interaction, and then skills concerned with intervention in the issues that the client presents. There is, therefore, a considerable shared heritage of understanding and skill.

The difference between social work and other professions with similar skill sets is in how the skills are applied. For example, psychotherapy and clinical psychology usually focus on specific assessments and interventions for mental capacity and identifiable psychological distress, often using specific techniques in a structured form, such as cognitive-behavioral or solution-focused therapies. Counseling often focuses on the individual patient or relative, rather than the system within which the individual lives, so that people may be helped to understand and deal with their emotions or thinking in relation to a problem. In addition to this, social workers engage in environmental work to help the system respect, adjust to, and assist the client, and develop and implement plans for social support systems and services in the community. Most psychotherapy and counseling does not attempt this to anything like the same degree. On the other hand, it is important to help colleagues understand that arranging services and dealing with boundary and system issues in clients' lives involves counseling and psychological skills, and that this is integral to social work if it is to assist people appropriately and ethically, as we have shown in the case examples in this volume. Otherwise, we would be sorting out practical difficulties, organizing services, and making plans for people without gaining their genuine participation and consent. Also, social workers use their counseling skills as part of these demonstrations of how to sort out problems, to help clients and families develop the future capacity to manage their affairs more independently and take control of their lives more effectively, since we have argued that this is one of the most important objectives for people approaching the end of life.

Social Work and Health-Care Professions

We have seen in previous chapters that end-of-life care is often medicalized. Since most end-of-life care takes place in health-care organizations, or connects with health care, social workers need to consider their relationships with health-care professions and the health-care system. A high proportion of social work in the United States is provided in health-care settings, although this is less true of other countries, where social workers are mostly employed in welfare state services often provided through local government or social security administrations.

As with counseling and psychotherapeutic practice, there are shared and distinct values between social work and health-care professions. Many colleagues can build on their own professional skills to respond to patients and clients' needs, with support and consultation from social workers and counselors, to deal with a difficulty with a family or client. Providing consultation for a colleague to carry out the direct work can be the best option for a client where the health-care practitioner already has a relationship with the family and can respond from a position of trust, while a social worker would have to create a new relationship to make a contribution.

Case example: Wanda and Derek

The practitioner's account follows. The home-care nurse asked me to accompany her because she could not get Wanda and Derek to discuss clearly how they were managing Derek's symptoms of lung cancer. On visiting, we found the situation as she described it, with Wanda and Derek talking over each other, talking about different things at the same time, and when they disagreed, which was often, talking louder to shout each other down. I firmly suggested the rules that only one person should talk at a time and that they should take it in turns to say things. After some time enforcing this by interrupting behavior that deviated from these rules so that some discussion was able to proceed, I introduced a further rule that neither person should make a criticism without a suggestion about something that should be done about it. Again, this needed enforcing for a while, but it allowed some positive discussion to take place. Leaving the home, the nurse said to me that she would not have felt able to be so assertive between husband and wife or set rules of behavior.

This was a situation in which confidence in being able to manage dissent and experience in dealing with difficult communication problems helped to facilitate the discussion to make some progress. If the couple had resisted this form of management, I would have been ready to negotiate with them about the rules, explaining how following the rules would help them to deal with the issues they were in dispute about in an orderly way, but this proved unnecessary. After this example set the pattern of behavior with professionals, the nurse felt able to be more assertive in managing communication between Derek and Wanda because she had seen it work and had thought "I can do that, too." And she found herself more able to do this with other families as well.

Communication and Patient Records

Records, particularly multiprofessional health-care records, are an important form of communication between professionals. Social workers have a responsibility to their clients to communicate effectively by documenting the essence of their assessments, interventions, and understanding of the patient's situation to their multidisciplinary colleagues. Confidentiality is usually held within the team and this explained to patients, so that they are aware that something told to one person may be shared with others. Much of the social worker's interaction with a patient and family is invisible unless it is brought to the attention of the team through records, and this means avoiding excessive length and jargon, which may stop colleagues who have only a limited interest in psychosocial issues from incorporating them into their thinking. On the other hand, a succinct and vivid explanation of the range of social factors and a brief summary about what the practitioner is doing, may help the patient by getting other colleagues to recognize the psychological and social issues affecting their medical progress.

Other Specialist Social Workers

In everyday teamwork, all members of a multiprofessional team bear responsibility for ensuring that intercommunication takes place; it is important that doctors, nurses, physical therapists, and others remember to make connections with their colleagues. Social workers have a particular role in ensuring that appropriate connections are made with non-specialized care services and with patients, service users and their families, and social networks (Hodgson, 2005). Often the work schedules of professionals make it difficult to contact them; home care nurses, for example, are often away from their desk for much of the day visiting patients and can only be contacted in the mornings or late afternoons.

In-patient nurses or doctors may also be out of contact for much of the day. Therefore, social workers or administrative staff often have the job of contacting outside agencies on their behalf. It is important to think through with multiprofessional colleagues, whether in contacting external services it is better for doctor to speak to doctor and nurse to nurse, rather than a social worker or administrator making external contacts.

End-of-life care social workers therefore also have to consider their relationship with specialized social workers in multiprofessional teams in other specialties dealing with care of patients who may be referred for end-of-life care. Meier and Beresford (2008) suggest that there may be difficulties in a hospital setting in getting social workers attached to specialized teams to accept a separate role for an end-of-life or palliative care social worker. There are two models for dealing with this issue: having a separate end-of-life practitioner or explicitly allowing for time and training within the role of other specialized social workers for them to take up an end-of-life or palliative care role. The main issue is likely to be creating an appropriate partnership for deciding which aspects of the situation a social worker concerned with end-of-life care would deal with or for the transfer of the entire family. Sharing the work is likely to be more appropriate where, say, an oncology or renal team is involved, but end-of-life care issues are dealt with by a palliative care team. It may not be only professional attitudes that affect other social workers' decisions. For example, Becker's (2004) American survey of oncology social workers found that they approved of hospice philosophies and services but met resistance from families to referral to hospices.

Excluded Colleagues

However, internally, some people are often excluded from decision making, particularly in core and periphery teams. Often those who are excluded are the least powerful and often in social groups that are excluded or discriminated against in other situations too, such as females, people from minority ethnic groups, and people from low-status, blue-collar, or routine jobs. Some, such as drivers, porters, cleaning staff, and administrative staff are almost unseen. However, they often have important and extended contacts with patients. For example, a practitioner with the role of introducing volunteer drivers to their job, points out to them that day-patients with perhaps an hour-long journey coming into the hospice and returning home at the end of the day, spend the longest continuous one-on-one time with drivers of any member of the hospice team. Consequently, he trains them to report to professional staff about any difficulties disclosed to them on the journey. Cleaners may have long periods of time with patients and be able to help them informally, particularly because blue-collar patients may have more in common socially and in life experience with a cleaner than with a social worker or doctor.

Staff Support

Staff support is crucial in end-of-life social work for three reasons. First, employers have a legal and moral responsibility to ensure the well-being of the people they employ, so services should have a concern for staff well-being. Second, staff well-being at work has an impact on quality of service for patients and clients. Third, death and bereavement are major social transitions that bring social and psychological strains and opportunities. Social and psychological strains may be transferred to the workplace and the staff within it. One reason why staff support is important in end-of-life care is the "accumulated loss phenomenon" (Adams, Hershatter, & Moritz, 1991). That is, staff may experience one loss through death after another over an extended period of time. Since repeated loss in bereaved people increases the risk of mental ill-health, so risk to palliative care staff will be high, simply because of the work of their service. However, a range of recent studies reviewed in Payne (2008b) suggests that this may be compensated for by good working conditions. Such experienced commentators as Parkes (1986) and Worden (2003; 178) suggest that in a well-run supportive agency, experience will strengthen rather than weaken people's capacity to deal with loss.

Stress and Support

Human beings will vary in what they find supportive, and so their psychological perceptions and reactions are important. Support implies helpful ways of sustaining or restoring an individuals' sense of wholeness and their capacity to manage life events. Staff support takes place in an employment relationship and in a special social situation: the workplace. Therefore an important aspect of staff support will be the way in which people see work in their lives, the particular work that they do and how they conceive of workplace relationships. For example, an active trade unionist employed in a blue-collar role will see staff support differently than a fairly apolitical senior medical practitioner. Three factors contribute to the way people cope with stress at work:

- The individual's personality and coping mechanisms
- Life and work conditions and the stressors within them that may be challenging
- Organizational factors in the workplace that may be stressful or helpful (Buchanan & Huczynski, 2004)

Burnout and compassion fatigue are two important ideas that have developed from the concept of stress. They refer to the effects of long-term stress. *Burnout* derives from the work of Maslach (1982) and his colleagues. The Maslach Burnout Inventory (MBI), introduced in the 1980s (Maslach & Jackson, 1981) has been validated in various versions among widely varying Western populations (for example, Schutte, Oppinen, Kalimo, & Schaufeli; 2000) and is often used in palliative care studies as a rating scale. MBI builds upon the concept of burnout: ". . . a syndrome of emotional exhaustion, depersonalization and reduced personal accomplishment that can occur among individuals who do 'people work' of some kind" (Maslach & Jackson, 1981, p. 1). *Compassion fatigue* is a feeling of helplessness, confusion, and isolation said to result from knowing about and closeness to repeated difficult illness experiences and deaths, not, as in burnout, personally experiencing them. Compassion fatigue is "a state of exhaustion and dysfunction, biologically, physiologically, and emotionally, as a result of prolonged exposure to compassion stress" (Figley, 1995, p. 1).

A systematic literature review of workplace stress in nursing indicates the type of stress experienced by health-care professionals, with which palliative care experience may be compared. Covering the period 1985 to 2003, McVicar (2003) concluded that studies found that workload, leadership style, professional conflict, and the emotional cost of caring were the main sources of distress. Lack of reward and shift-work had more recently become important as contributing factors. Not all staff involved in end-of-life care work in specialized palliative care settings. A qualitative interview study of residential care and nursing homes for the U.K. Department of Health (Katz, Sidell, & Komaromy, 2001) found that mainly young female staff had little experience of death. They were thought to need emotional and practical support in dealing with the needs of dying people. However, organizational and budgetary pressures meant that few care homes had the flexibility to provide for intensive caring or time off for staff who were under stress because of feelings of grief. Most support was ad hoc and consisted of sympathetic listening. Similar outcomes emerged from an American study (Ersek & Wilson, 2003).

Three broad approaches to dealing with staff stress in organizations are:

- Organizational adjustments, such as management, organizational, or personnel changes, which seek to prevent, reduce, or remove the effect of stressors in organizations.
- Development actions, such as training in personal skills and coping mechanisms.

- Individual emotion-focused actions, which aim to improve individuals' resilience and coping mechanisms (Buchanan & Huczybski, 2004; Williams & Cooper, 2002).

In a useful and critical review of literature on supervision and support strategies responding to burnout in community-based AIDS/HIV nurse specialists, Hayter (2000) suggests that:

- Supervision is adapted to emphasize restorative tasks, which enable professionals to deal with feelings that arise from working with people in distress; and formative tasks, an educative approach teaching new methods and insights.
- Teaching coping skills in relation to stress and providing mechanisms to express concerns and anxieties related to practice have been found effective.
- Informal and less-structured support from colleagues has been found effective.

Supervision

Supervision is a major means of education, staff support, and management in most social work settings. Social work has historically organized supervision so that the manager of a service or group of staff members is also responsible for the professional supervision of staff, thus including management with professional and educational interventions. However, this is another difference with psychological and health care supervision, where there is a tendency to separate management responsibility from professional supervision. The advantage of the social work model in end-of-life care is that the manager can be responsible for workplace and organizational adjustments to recognize stress arising from the emotional consequences of working continually with death and bereavement. This goes alongside ensuring that appropriate professional boundaries are maintained and personal reactions to a particular death situation do not influence the practitioner's work adversely.

In end-of-life care, it is important, where managers are also responsible for professional supervision, for them to be able to provide support regarding the emotional consequences of dealing with death and dying, or to facilitate peer support within the team. This includes being able to discuss the impact of a particular work experience on the individual practitioner, or the practitioner's personal experience on a work situation. This means that a distanced managerial style of supervision is not appropriate. Maintaining interpersonal trust and a relatively equal dialogue between manager and practitioner in supervision is a crucial aspect of social work supervision.

CONCLUSION

This chapter has focused on the multiprofessional character of end-of-life practice. To ensure that practice is holistic, agencies, professions, and disciplines covering a wide range of specialties must be brought together so that specialized expertise is applied to the end-of-life situation. Social workers have an important role to play in this because they often have a role in connecting resources from a wide range of agencies and people with clients and families. We have argued that this requires effective multiprofessional teamwork practice, and good staff and supervision support of individual practitioners.

FURTHER READING

Gysels, M., & Higginson, I. (2004). *Improving supportive and palliative care for adults with cancer, Research evidence*. London: National Institute for Clinical Excellence. This important systematic review of the literature identifies the evidence on the role of social work and of the value of multiprofessional teamwork in palliative care.

Opie, A. (2003). *Thinking teams/thinking clients: Knowledge-based teamwork*. New York: Columbia University Press. A very imaginative research study that shows how effective knowledge-based teamwork may be in a range of settings.

Payne, M. (2000). *Teamwork in multiprofessional care*. Chicago: Lyceum Books. A general introduction to multiprofessional teamwork, which emphasizes the importance of practitioners working to bring resources from their own networks into teams, as well as improving intrateam relationships.

Speck, P. (ed.) (2006). *Teamwork in palliative care*. Oxford, England: Oxford University Press, A recent edited book on teamwork in palliative care.

West, M. A. (2004). *Effective teamwork: practical lessons from organizational research*. (2nd ed.) Oxford, England: BPS Blackwell. A good practical account of the psychological evidence on teamwork.

JOURNAL

• *Journal of Interprofessional Care*, Taylor & Francis, London.

Chapter 8

ETHICAL AND VALUE ISSUES FOR END-OF-LIFE SOCIAL WORK

CHAPTER AIMS

The main aim of this chapter is to identify value and ethical issues that arise in end-of-life social work, particularly from social work's focus on the system and family surrounding the dying person.

After working through this chapter, readers will be able to:

- Understand ethical principles in end-of-life care;
- Identify social work's particular role in responding to ethical issues in end-of-life services;
- Identify and implement social work roles and responses in helping clients and their families with assisted dying and suicide;
- Consider ethical issues in incorporating social work within end-of-life care; and
- Help clients with advance care planning and advance directives.

SOCIAL WORK VALUES AT THE END OF LIFE

Throughout this book, we have emphasized that dying, death, and bereavement are social events in people's lives that have personal importance to individuals and to the social network around them. Importance implies value. Therefore, these processes engage with people's values, and social workers must work on value issues when working at the end of life. As in other areas of practice discussed in this book, social work's systems and family focus and social science background makes a particular contribution to ethics and raises specific problems for social workers.

The medical values issues raised in palliative care focus on issues around medical treatment. The social work role in dealing with these issues is primarily of ensuring that they are raised appropriately and dealt with in an inclusive way that involves families and social networks of patients. Since medicine and nursing is individualistic, rather than socially focused in its work and decision making, only patients themselves have rights to make decisions and have access to information.

However, we have discussed how family involvement, and avoiding exclusion of family members such as children and people with intellectual disabilities, may have long-term implications for the bereavement and future resilience of the family.

APPROACHES TO ETHICAL DECISION MAKING

Writers on social work ethics (Banks, 2006; Beckett & Maynard, 2005; Reamer, 1999) distinguish a number of different approaches to ethical decision making, that is, deciding between possible alternative actions according to what is a right rather than, for example, what is convenient or most practicable. Among the most important for social work are:

- Rights-based ethics. People are assumed to have rights that come from being a human being, from the particular social role or position that they occupy, or from the rights of a citizen. Famous examples of such statements of rights are the American constitution and the Universal Declaration of Human Rights. Professional codes of ethics are usually rights-based.
- Consequence-based ethics. People are assumed to work out what is right according to the consequences of actions they might take. Utilitarianism is an example of consequence-based ethics: it proposes that we should act in ways that will produce the most benefit for the greatest number of people.
- Virtue-based ethics. People can work out what to do by seeing if how they are proposing to act fits with socially accepted virtues such as courage, honesty, integrity, and kindness. This approach connects ethical decisions with social and cultural expectations, and may be particularly important when working with people from different ethnicities and cultures.
- Ethics of care. People can choose to act in the most caring way. Caring enhances connections between people and connectedness in society. This approach is therefore particularly relevant for the social work role of improving the way the societies that we work in function.

We suggest that a mix of these approaches is useful in practice, not least because many clients and their families also switch between them. For example, they may say that they value a practitioner's caring approach, an ethics of care view, because it helps all members of the family cope with the dying process of one of them, a utilitarian consequence-based view. They are, of course connected, since making people feel cared for often has positive results for them psychologically.

SOCIAL WORK ETHICAL PRACTICE IN
HEALTH-CARE SETTINGS

While many ethical issues in end-of-life care are primarily medical, social workers may be asked to help explain and interpret medical and nursing decisions to patients and therefore need to understand and take a position, or know and accept their agency's position, on these issues. Political and public debate about euthanasia and assisted dying is also relevant to social workers if they play a role in end-of-life care. Social workers need to contribute a social work perspective, mainly about the implications for family members and the client's social network of decisions.

The central health-care issues, according to Twycross (1999, p. 9) are the dual responsibility of physicians to preserve life by treating illness and to relieve suffering. At the end of life, the balance between these responsibilities shifts to a heavier focus on relieving suffering. Both patients and caregivers may also need help in managing the transition between curative and palliative care.

Ethical rights in health care lead to important duties of practitioners:

- Beneficence, the duty to do good to people
- Nonmaleficence, the duty not to do harm
- Autonomy, the duty to facilitate patients to make free choices about the kind and amount of health care that they receive
- Justice, the duty to facilitate equal access to services and care (Beauchamp & Childress, 2001)

Family members and members of the local community more generally will have greater confidence in end-of-life care services if they perceive and understand that principles such as these are being followed as physicians and others take these difficult decisions. They will usually have explained them, but relatives and others involved will often need to go through them repeatedly to review their own participation and free themselves from guilt or anger about the decisions made.

RELATIVES, INFORMAL CAREGIVERS,
AND PEOPLE AT THE END OF LIFE

In medicine, it is clear that patients are entitled to autonomy and to control of the decision making about their treatment. The medical patient is entitled to accept or refuse treatment, and physicians and nurses must receive informed consent from patients to provide treatment; informed means that patients must understand the potential benefits and risks of the proposed treatment and their consent must be individually obtained from them. Generally, physicians must provide treatment that is appropriate in their professional judgment; they cannot be forced to provide unsuitable treatment that, for example, may actually damage the patient's health. However, where there is room for discretion, physicians may choose to follow their patients' wishes, even though they are not hopeful of a good outcome.

If the patient is unable to give consent, because he or she is comatose or unable to communicate, for example, the physician or nurse acts in the best interests of the patient. Routine procedures that are well-known to everyone and not particularly dangerous, such as collecting blood for tests, are subject to tacit or implied consent, unless the patient protests.

In these consent-giving regimes, relatives and caregivers are not entitled to know information or express an opinion about the patient's condition or treatment. Such an individualistic approach to treatment is also commonplace with psychotherapists and counselors.

However, social work's role to focus on the family and caregiver is inconsistent with this way of dealing with consent. This may require social workers to interpret and explain health-care procedures and to advocate for the participation of relatives and caregivers at least in explanation and discussion, if not in decision making. If this is not possible, they may have to help relatives and family members understand the reasons for the way the service is making the decisions. Another role of social work is to understand and pursue the interests of all the relatives and family members involved in the situations. However, this has to be done without contravening the right of patients to make their own decision.

Pause and reflect—case study: Mr. Mendoza's family

Mr. Mendoza, age sixty-two, was admitted to a hospice for terminal care; the physician arranging the admission expected that he would die within a few days. He had a partner and two children living with him; the children were eight and ten years old. As the genogram was drawn, it became apparent that he had several children by three previous partners; he wanted to have the children and one of the previous wives informed of his admission and for them to visit him. Moreover, his mother and sisters lived in Portugal and when they were informed of the admission by the present partner, they also decided to visit, being accommodated in the hospice apartment for visiting families. The present partner did not agree to the previous wife visiting, and would not disclose the address from Mr. Mendoza's papers at home. He was tired and felt unable to have an argument about it. Mr. Mendoza, his mother, and sisters were committed Catholics, while the present partner and the children were not practicing Christians. The social worker was asked to mediate about family contacts; the spiritual care adviser was asked to explore the arrangements for the funeral. Mr. Mendoza's mother wanted a Catholic funeral with a very wide attendance; the partner sought a less formal cremation. Mr. Mendoza's mother knew the previous wife's address and contacted her; she then came to visit and there was an argument in the ward, approaching a physical fight. What would you do?

Some suggestions

This case presents one of the difficulties of palliative care where, at the end of life, the practitioners caring for the patient do not have extended contact with the family and have not built a relationship with them. In an end-of-life situation, on the other hand, practitioners might have had more extensive contact with the family. It is also typical of commonplace frailty trajectories, where the possibility of advance care planning has not been picked up with the family, and no preparation was made for dealing with some of the issues. Randall and Downie (2006) suggest that practitioners cannot pursue the interests of relatives in ways that are contrary to the patients' health care interests. Moreover, they argue that patients should not be deprived of care in order to devote time to the relatives and that a palliative care service should not set out to offer the best quality of life to relatives, but should give priority to patients. This is what everyone would want, but it does not negate the importance of helping the relatives too.

However, most of the issues here are not really about the health care interests of Mr. Mendoza. One of the ways in which the nurses and physicians have dealt with their responsibility to give priority to the patient is by referring the issues over the relatives to the social worker and spiritual care adviser. The arguments and difficulties should not interfere with the care of the patients and others in the vicinity. Randall and Downie avoid dealing with the full responsibilities of palliative care by simply rejecting this as a proper role of professionals in palliative care; it is an example of the limitations of medicalization since it applies mainly to medical professionals rather than acknowledging the rather different professional duties of social workers.

The best approach, therefore, is to separate the different interests, including different members of the different families by providing enough staff to see them separately to listen to their issues. Although to the health care practitioner, the patient's rights are the most important, a social work perspective imposes a duty to meet as many of the needs of the relatives as possible; their mental health, particularly during the bereavement, is also important. In this particular case, the social worker and spiritual adviser saw the three different families separately, and negotiated a visiting timetable to separate the visitors. A Catholic memorial service was organized, while another memorial service was held for other members of the family who preferred a more informal event, and a cremation was arranged.

ADVANCE CARE PLANNING

Since patients' consent is always required for health-care treatment, health-care services have developed mechanisms for obtaining that consent where the patients' conditions may deteriorate to the point that they cannot express their wishes. This is common in many neurological illnesses, such as ALS, where the patient is mentally alert but unable to communicate. People with such conditions in particular, and others in general, may want to participate in advance care planning with their physician, sometimes involving their lawyer. Patients often prepare an "advance directive" (previously called a "living will") expressing the preference that unnecessary medical interventions should be avoided when the patient arrives at a terminal condition.

The physician's duty to act in the best interests of the patient, according to the expected medical standards, remains, and a generally drafted document is unhelpful to physicians if it does not specify the circumstances in which they might act or not act. Advance care planning is easier if there is a recognized progression of a condition like ALS and it is possible to list circumstances that typically arise, and specify the patient's preferences in each potential situation. This is a complex process, but many patients want to do this, although many are happy to leave it to the physician. It requires quite a lot of detailed discussion and work by the physician, however, and a patient who is able to understand the potential complexity of the decisions that the physician will make. The directive can have no force unless it is clear that the patient was both competent and sufficiently well-informed to make the decisions.

Much of the debate has been about decisions on medical treatment. In U.S. law, the Patient Self-Determination Act 1990, makes provision for advance directives (Csikai & Chaitin, 2006, p. 73). In U.K. law, physicians may accept the requests made by patients in a valid advance care planning document, an advance directive. Where patients do not have the mental capacity to make the decision themselves, physicians must act in what they consider to be patients' "best interests," which may include psychosocial factors (Samanta & Samanta, 2006). The U.K. Mental Capacity Act 2005 provides for early discussion with people when they are well and with patients as they are becoming ill about a range of care decisions at the end of life. This distinguishes between:

- The general process of planning care in advance of need. This suggests that practitioners should always take the opportunity to discuss future wishes with clients when carrying out an assessment or review.
- Making a statement of wishes and feelings.
- Formulating an advance direction which requires medical and possibly legal discussion, so that all necessary aspects of the decision are considered.

Where a patient does not have the capacity to make decisions, an independent mental capacity advocate, often a social worker, is appointed to represent the patient's interests, using information and evidence from the patient's past life and decisions. Useful information about points to cover is provided in the Mental Capacity Act guidance (DCA, 2007).

A particular issue is cardiopulmonary resuscitation (CPR), particularly the use of defibrillators, machines that stimulate the heartbeat. These are increasingly commonly available, and people are sometimes trained to use them in first-aid courses. Patients are also accustomed to seeing dramatic representations in films and television programs of the revival of dying people in emergency situations. However, many end-of-life organizations do not make these resources available, because they are ineffective and may be harmful when used with people with advanced illness. Many such organizations have a policy about this, and offer patients and caregivers a leaflet and opportunity to discuss the policy with a physician.

Patients and their families are interested in wider care decisions than medical treatment. In Barnes and colleagues' (Barnes, Jones, Tookman, & King, 2007) focus group study of using an advance care planning questionnaire, some patients and caregivers felt ready to engage with this process, while others did not. Those who did, felt that the focus should be on wider end-of-life issues rather than just decisions to refuse treatments. Therefore, practitioners taking up this issue need to be able to respond to cues that the patient is not ready, and be able to discuss wider psychosocial issues than physical treatment. This could be an important role for social workers, and it is useful to identify care preferences, such as preferred care homes, preferred care staff, and meals (e.g., the availability of halal meat) or other processes that are important to clients.

The basic principle of advance care planning is that people should be able to discuss with care providers of any discipline, and with family and friends if they wish:

- Their concerns about future care
- Important values and goals for their care
- Their understanding of their illness, condition, and prognosis
- Particular preferences for types of care or treatment available presently and in the future

This discussion should be documented, regularly reviewed, and communicated to the people who will provide their care.

All practitioners, including social workers, therefore, may be involved in careful discussions with people moving toward the end of life about their wishes. Henry and Seymour (2007) argue that everyone involved in direct care should be aware of and understand the risks and benefits of advance care planning, and trained and qualified health and social work staff should be able to facilitate discussions and a statement of wishes. It is necessary for a physician to be involved in the discussion of an advance decision about treatment, because this involves reviewing the risks and benefits of particular treatments. Senior legal and medical consultation is required where there are complex legal and ethical questions.

EUTHANASIA, ASSISTED DYING, AND SUICIDE

There is considerable public and professional debate about these issues, in which terms that should mean different things are sometimes confused. *Euthanasia* is taking positive action to end someone's life at his or her spontaneous request (Ryan, 2006, p. 161) and for the benefit of that person. *Assisted dying* is helping people to take their own life. Physician-assisted dying occurs when a physician helps someone take his or her own life, for example, by prescribing or administering drugs that will lead to death. *Suicide* is taking one's own life. Euthanasia and assisted dying are illegal and defined as murder in most legal jurisdictions. A small number of countries or states permit assisted dying in particular circumstances or with safeguards; at the time of writing these include the Netherlands, Switzerland, and the U.S. state of Oregon, all with different legal and procedural requirements. Suicide is or has been illegal in some jurisdictions. All these acts are regarded as undesirable in most belief systems or religious denominations since taking one's own life is regarded as interfering in matters that should be God's decision. Some religions see suffering and illness as a test of character and religious commitment. Most arguments in favor of legalizing euthanasia, assisted dying, and suicide focus on people's right to autonomy in decisions regarding their own body and life, or reducing the distress that comes from painful or unpleasant symptoms.

Debate about these issues has become more active in recent years for a number of reasons:

- A small number of patients have degenerative diseases, such as ALS, that lead to almost complete physical incapacity while the mind is still active. Medical science has become increasingly successful in maintaining very disabled people alive. Some patients have argued for the right to be helped to take their own life if they are physically incapable of doing so, and there are more such people around with the success of medical science in treating serious illness and managing very debilitating symptoms.
- The number of older people is growing in most Western societies because of successful medical treatment and social and public health policies to reduce unnecessary mortality. This has sometimes led to a poor quality of life with people suffering increasing physical and mental frailty and high care costs. Some people and their families would prefer death to a lingering, frail, expensive old age. This is especially so if nursing home or other residential care is required, incurring heavy financial costs. This means that people have to give up their family home to live in a communal setting, which is an important psychological loss of independence and may also lead to the loss of social networks; they may feel they are just waiting to die. Such care is expensive and most states across the world require a contribution toward the cost that is higher than insurance or personal income, and therefore diminishes the capital available to the family. For example, the patient or family may have to sell property including the patient's home. Family members may, therefore, resist long-term care. There is also a risk that they may want to encourage or press a frail and vulnerable person to take his or her own life, or agree to any assisted dying option that is available. Even if relatives do not feel like this, their older relative may be aware of the issue and want to preserve the family's capital.
- Dangerous drugs are controlled in most jurisdictions, so it is difficult to obtain drugs to achieve suicide or assisted dying.
- It is difficult to kill people in a nonviolent way, and attempts at suicide or death assisted by friends or family members are uncertain and distressing. Medical intervention would be more likely to be successful and dignified.

In situations like these, people have argued for a right to autonomy to make the decision to take their own life. Studies of terminally ill people's attitudes suggest that a desire for death has been found, but it is often transient and may be linked to depression (Brown, Henteleff, Barakat, & Rowe, 1986; 1995; Emamuel, Fairclough, & Emanuel 2000). It is not necessarily linked in people's minds to assisted dying and euthanasia. Pacheco and colleagues' (Pacheco et al., 2003) study of thirty people with incurable cancers found that they might welcome death when it came but rejected hastening it, building their resilience with emotional, social, and spiritual support. Therefore, in discussing this with patients and caregivers an important place to start is to find out whether their attitudes are maintained over time, moving on to whether enough help may be offered to support a good quality of life. Practitioners should also explain how help will be provided in the last few hours and days of life, so that patients feel more in control of the process and can understand what will happen.

As well as religious and moral objections to euthanasia, assisted dying, and suicide, there are a number of practical and organizational difficulties:

- There is a gradation of situations, and it is hard to distinguish between situations where most people might agree that patients should have the autonomy to be helped to take their own lives and apparently similar situations that are less severe. Where would we draw the line? Who would decide and how? Once we agree to one apparently very clear case, would we be starting on a "slippery slope" where we would argue over slight differences in circumstances? Would this lead to bureaucratic and slow decision making?
- If we accept patients' autonomy to decide on their own death, we must also accept a physician's autonomy to decide not to take life, and the autonomy of friends, relatives, and family members not to do so. This makes access to euthanasia or assisted dying unequal or random, or applies pressure to physicians and family members to participate in acts that may be morally or socially abhorrent to them.
- If some medical teams are able to opt out of assisted dying, those who are prepared to help will come under pressure to help in cases that have been rejected on moral or practical grounds elsewhere; they will become known as teams where assistance with dying is available. While their members might be prepared to help in particular instances, with patients that they have known for a long time and are committed to, teams might become labeled as "killers," and campaigners may target them with abuse; some abortion clinics have experienced this.

- Most medical, nursing, counseling, and social work treatment relies on trust between patient, clients, and practitioners. If clients knew that the teams involved might be able to make a decision to assist them in dying, or commonly did so, they might be less likely to trust the practitioner and communicate openly about other treatment or help.
- Euthanasia and assisted dying expects patients and families to be honest and spontaneous, and for the decision to be a genuine expression of their wishes. However, patients and families may fear the financial losses to the family of a long period of care or have other reasons that might put the patient under pressure to agree to assisted dying. This might be specially the case where there are family conflicts, such as in Mr. Mendoza's case, discussed above, or where patients are indecisive or there is a history of domination by other family members.
- People may change their minds. In calm contemplation, talking about advance care planning, they might think it is sensible to plan for assisted dying. When it comes time to implement the decision, however, they may want to refuse it but may not have the mental or physical capacity to express their change of mind. Also, they may feel that they must stick with it, when they now realize that they do not want to.
- Good end-of-life and palliative care will usually reduce the impact of symptoms of illness, so that people can be comfortable and carry on with their life during the dying process. This makes euthanasia and assisted dying unnecessary in most cases, but people's fears about how they might suffer may not be realistic, and they may not trust their physicians, family, or social workers to explain things honestly.
- There is a risk that the diagnosis or prognosis on which the patient decides to seek assisted dying is wrong. Illnesses may go into remission or not be as serious as at first thought, but there is no going back after death has been procured.
- A particular issue arises over the diagnosis and treatment of anxiety and depression. At some stages of the illness, the emotional distress that patients experience may be unpleasant, but this may often be managed by medication or psychological treatments.
- Finally, people may be mistaken in their understanding of what might happen at death. For example, a patient experiencing breathlessness may fear choking or gasping for breath during the dying process. However, as we saw in Chapter 2, many symptoms have less impact near death, and with good care most people die peacefully.

Social workers cannot escape concern for these issues simply because they do not prescribe or administer drugs. For example, if they are part of a team in which a physician takes the decision to assist in the death, or the patient decides on his or her own, they may be asked to comfort the patient or family members, assist them in making the decision, or in making practical arrangements to travel to a legal jurisdiction where assisted dying is permitted. It may also affect all their work. If there is doubt about whether the request for assisted dying or euthanasia is spontaneous, social workers might be asked to investigate family relationships; or social work and counseling records made in the past without thought that the possibility of assisted dying might arise, might be used to establish the history of interactions about the issue. In turn, this might be further reason for clients in general not to trust social workers with information.

THE ETHICS OF PSYCHOLOGICAL AND SOCIAL INTERVENTIONS

Consent to Psychosocial Interventions

Questions have been raised by Randall and Downie (1999, ch. 10) about the justification for psychological and social intervention as part of specialized palliative care, and by implication more broadly in end-of-life care. They also reject the value of counseling and the idea that there is expertise in "emotional" care (p. 287). The issues are about consent and derive from the perceived inefficacy of psychological interventions in helping with emotional care. Nothing is specifically said about social interventions, for example to arrange services or mediate in family conflicts.

In their later book (Randall & Downie, 2006, ch. 7), they go further and say:

> The requirement for the development of a close personal relationship between patient and professional should not be part of the philosophy of palliative care, nor should the development of the client/counselor relationship be advocated. The goal of controlling the patient's psychological, social and spiritual problems, or of assessing and treating them, should be abandoned. It should be replaced by the idea of alleviating those problems within the context of the traditional, professional/patient relationship, using ordinary human interaction, sensitive explanations and advice based on professional knowledge and experience, and friendly professional interest. (Randall & Downie, 2006, p. 179)

They (Randall & Downie, 1999, ch. 10) argue that patients seek medical care for an illness, and may then accept health-care services for palliative care. However, it is not clear that they have also given consent for psychological and social services. Although, as we have seen, end-of-life and palliative care services generally operate on a holistic model and include emotional, psychological, social, and spiritual aspects of care, these nonmedical interventions are less well-understood and may be unexpected for patients. They may appreciate them, or they may see it as the health-care system interfering in their private business; they might particularly take this latter view if they are from an ethnic or faith minority.

Moreover, as we have seen, end-of-life and palliative care practitioners maintain a professional philosophy of openness about what may be, to some people, particularly people in some minority ethnic groups, private matters. People already vulnerable because of their illness and a prognosis of impending death may feel oppressed by the assumptions of palliative care or end-of-life professionals. They may feel pressed into greater openness than they would normally accept and persuaded into emotional openness, and consideration of, say, spiritual matters, as part of the health-care interventions than they might usually keep private. Sweeping these interventions into an overall health-care service is quite different from giving consent for a psychological intervention if you go to a counseling service or social work agency. Another factor is that the evidence base for psychological and social work interventions is generally less strong than the evidence for medical and nursing interventions. A final issue may be that people of different ethnicities, faiths, or cultural backgrounds may vary in the extent to which they will accept psychological help from a professional or anyone outside their family or spiritual network.

The problem with this position is that it utterly rejects the value of separate social and psychological services and professions within health-care provision at all. Yet for more than a hundred years, these have been accepted as a valid part of public provision across the world, and are integral to government policy on provision of services to patients in health care. It assumes physicians and nurses, as the people providing the health care, should alleviate distress as a natural part of their work and that their friendly interest and commitment is all that is required.

There are practical and policy issues here about the role of professions other than specifically health-care professions in health-care services; this is not the place for an extensive discussion about that debate. However, genuine issues are being raised: coming to have your cancer cured or your progressive disability nursed should not automatically mean that you get people digging into your psychological, spiritual, and social problems. Where those problems exist within or alongside the distress caused by the illness or disability, it is also unreasonable to expect all physicians and all nurses in every situation to stand ready to deal with them in all their complexity, alongside the complexity of everything else that they have to deal with. Similarly, it is unreasonable for a health-care service to maintain its ethical purity by expecting patients to trail off to a separate service in another place. Moreover, in most end-of-life situations, medical care is not the main issue; social services professionals will have been involved in providing social care services often for many years and have a continuing helpful relationship with the patient. The logic of Randall and Downie's position would accept this, since their objections seem to be mainly concerned with detailed excavation of emotional issues in patients' lives, without genuine consent, particularly when it takes up the patient's time when this is not a priority at the end of life. Of course, to some extent patients can decide this themselves, but the point is well made that the service should not be set up in such a way that intrusive involvement in personal matters is taken for granted. Randall and Downie's formulation rather preciously reserves the position of palliative care physicians. This ignores the reality of their patients' family lives, which are sometimes chaotic and deprived and the entirely legitimate role in society of social work and the social services. There is a reasonable need for people to focus on these issues where they need to be dealt with, rather than expecting nurses and physicians with other responsibilities to deal with them by taking a "friendly interest." Massive family, financial, and other social problems, and the care of children and dependents are often far more important to patients at the end of life than their own medical and nursing care.

Pause and reflect—thinking about consent to social work

You are working in a health-care service where medical and nursing colleagues routinely refer patients to you, telling them that you will be able to help them deal with their depression or concerns about family reactions to the illness. You are often introduced as a member of the team helping them. Consider what approach you would take to dealing with the issues raised in the preceding paragraph.

Some suggestions

In Chapters 3 to 5, we emphasized the importance of being clear about who you are and explaining your role. The problem with doing this is that many people are not familiar with the role of a social worker or counselor, and may not understand the value of psychological or spiritual help from a professional. We often compromise and explain that we help people with consequences of their illness for themselves or their family.

Dealing with these consent issues requires:

- An explicit recognition of the boundary between the health-care service and our own role. It may be useful to make clear that we are not a physician or nurse but concentrate on personal and psychological matters that come up for patients and their families.

- Explaining methods. For example, we might say that we will ask patients to talk about the personal and family issues that are bothering them, and we will ask questions to help explore and understand these better, and work out ways of dealing with them.
- Explaining our expectations. For example, we could say that after hearing the client's story, we will suggest ways in which we might be helpful, which the patient may choose from, and come to a clear agreement about what we will or will not do.
- Explaining specific therapeutic techniques such as cognitive-behavioral or solution-focused therapy when we offer them. We can introduce a technique as a specific way of helping that has been shown to be effective with problems like those the client is facing.
- Emphasizing the client's autonomy in deciding to address a particular issue. We can make it clear, for example, that patients may prefer to keep some topics to deal within their family or with a spiritual adviser, and that we are open to reserve some topics to be dealt with later.
- Avoiding pressing clients to deal with issues that they are uncomfortable about, even though we think they are important. However, professional duty may require interventions to prevent risk to the patient or to others.

Empowerment: Building Control and Removing Hindrances

An important positive ethical consideration in end-of-life care is finding appropriate practice that permits dying or bereaved people to build control of their situation and the direction of the work with them. Unlike many social work clients, who have themselves identified "problems" in managing their affairs, or those referred by someone else or some agency that has suggested they need help, people at the end of life are independent adults going through an important and natural life process mainly in a health-care setting. We do not want to substitute inappropriate medicalization with inappropriate psychologization. Therefore, ethical practice should not focus on end-of-life care as "problem-solving" to deal with negative aspects of life, but as removing hindrances and barriers to taking an appropriate part in a natural life process. For this reason, we have emphasized the importance of social work practice that:

- Helps people build and maintain control of their life situation
- Allows participants in the practice to express their own stories in their own way

The idea, drawn from Egan (1992) and Hodgson (2005) of finding the "best fit" between the social situation and perceptions and objectives held by the people involved may be helpful (see Chapter 5).

Confidentiality and Openness in End-of-Life Care

Professional codes of ethics often take a rights-based approach to confidentiality, ruling that clients' privacy should always be respected. We suggest that in all social work the position is more complex, and this is particularly so in end-of-life care. In general, the existence of a rule often serves to draw attention to a difficult area of practice, where the practitioner should beware, and will often need to balance the practice advocated by the rule with many complexities (Payne, 2006, ch. 4). In end-of-life care, we have advocated an openness with clients, caregivers, and families that sometimes needs to be balanced with the privacy of clients.

There are both practical and moral aims in maintaining confidentiality. The practical aim is that an assurance of confidentiality in personal information encourages clients to trust practitioners with information that helps the treatment and that they might not otherwise provide. The moral aim is to protect people's privacy from intrusion. Generally, these principles support each other, but there are often complexities, which we explore in the following case example.

Pause and reflect—case example: Mrs. Robinson

The practitioner's account is as follows: Mrs. Robinson applied to have access to health care records on her father, who had died at a hospice. She had found the whole process of admission and care very confusing and felt that she wanted reminding about the sequence of events. Reading the file, I found many minute-by-minute details of her father's symptoms and treatment, written mainly by nurses. In U.K. law, Mrs. Robinson was legally entitled to see the whole record.

What would you do?

Some suggestions

The practitioner again: I talked to Mrs. Robinson and explained that there was a lot of personal detail about her father's body, his illness, and symptoms. I suggested that although she could see the record, it might be unfair for her father to have every minor symptom laid out for his daughter. I suggested instead that I should prepare an account of the sequence of events for her to keep, and she could have an interview with a nurse who cared for her father, who would talk her through what happened, without her needing to see the record. Mrs. Robinson was happy with this, and the example suggests how much effort and time is needed to get the balance of openness and confidentiality right.

CONCLUSION

All social work practitioners will be involved with colleagues from other professions in ethical conflicts and difficulties from time to time.

Because end-of-life care is a multiprofessional area, it is important that they understand the issues that their colleagues face in making important medical and nursing decisions. But, these are not just medical decisions, they are life and care decisions that affect how people live their lives and how they will be cared for, much more broadly.

We have argued, therefore, that social workers have a particular responsibility in end-of-life care to pick up the importance of these issues in the lives of clients, their caregivers, and their families and help them to explore the social and personal consequences of the options that people are thinking through. They may also need to interpret social and family pressures to health-care professionals, so that they may be properly taken into account.

FURTHER READING

Csikai, E. L., & Chaitin, E. (2006). *Ethics in end-of-life decisions in social work practice*. Chicago: Lyceum Books. This book covers the up-to-date legal and professional ethics in many of the end-of-life situations that social workers get involved in, combined with an understanding of the social work role. It has a useful chapter about advance planning, drawing on the U.S. law and practice.

DCA. (2007). *Mental Capacity Act 2005: Code of practice*. London: TSO.

Henry, C., & Seymour, J. (2007). *Advance care planning: A guide for health and social care staff*. London: Department of Health. These two official documents refer to the U.K. law, but have sensible practical information that could help practitioners anywhere in the world with advance care planning. Both are available on the Internet.

Randall, F., & Downie, R. S. (1999). *Palliative care ethics: A companion for all specialties* (2nd ed.). Oxford, England: Oxford University Press. A comprehensive general overview of ethical issues in palliative care, written by a palliative care medical consultant (senior physician) and a philosopher, which focuses on health-care ethics and medical decision making, although it also covers decisions about the management of the patient, such as the place of care, which are likely to affect social workers particularly in end-of-life care. The second edition has a—largely unrepentant—reply to their critics.

Randall, F., & Downie, R. S. (2006). *The philosophy of palliative care: Critique and reconstruction*. Oxford, England: Oxford University Press. A discussion of difficult issues in the philosophy of palliative care, including discussion of conflicts of interest with relatives and quality of life. This book has a useful chapter about advance care planning.

Social work readers might find Randall and Downie's views on psychological and social care uncongenial. However, they are worth reading so that practitioners can consider the extent to which their services engage people in "counseling" without achieving genuine consent, and therefore might negate the practice assumptions on which counseling are based.

Chapter 9

GROUP AND
MACRO INTERVENTIONS

CHAPTER AIMS

The main aim of this chapter is to demonstrate the potential value of group and macro interventions in end-of-life social work.

After working through this chapter, readers will be able to:

- Consider the contribution of group and macro interventions to end-of-life social work;
- Review a range of group-work approaches with caregivers and people with advanced illnesses;
- Contribute to macro social work interventions in developing responsiveness to dying and bereaved people in our communities and societies, service design, and reducing service inequalities; and
- Contribute to public education activities that enhance community resilience and capacity to respond to end-of-life issues.

GROUP AND MACRO SOCIAL WORK IN END-OF-LIFE CARE

So far, in this book we have mainly reviewed individual social work practice in end-of-life care. However, since social work has a role in connecting end-of-life care with wider social systems, including care systems and the social structures that surround death, dying, and bereavement in general, group and macro interventions are also a necessary part of end-of-life social work.

Group work is valuable because patients, families, and caregivers need peer support to manage emotional and cognitive reactions to illness and the end of life. Moreover, educational approaches to information-giving in financial and practical help use group techniques so that participants may stimulate each other's thinking. Spiritual care often involves group participation such as meditation and rituals of various kinds. Where people at the end of life are already in group settings, such as care homes, hospital wards, or day care, activity-based group work may be useful.

Macro social work is needed because societies need to learn how to deal more effectively and humanely with death and bereavement. Communities and social networks would benefit from a stronger capacity to respond to issues about death and bereavement. Previous chapters have shown that:

- Death may be socially hidden, dying people conceal their plight, and bereaved people cannot show their grief.
- Many individuals at the end of life feel socially isolated because people "don't know what to say" and avoid someone who is ill or frail.
- People often do not know how to prepare and speak to children or people with intellectual disabilities.

In addition, nonspecialized agencies such as the police, emergency services, schools, and workplaces must deal with people facing death from illness, accident, crime, and disaster.

Practitioners in palliative and end-of-life care have a reservoir of skill and knowledge that should be transferred to communities to strengthen their resilience to respond to death and dying. Social workers who only occasionally deal with end-of-life situations can also strengthen their capacity to help where the end of life affects people who are clients for other reasons.

GROUP WORK WITH PATIENTS, BEREAVED PEOPLE, CHILDREN, AND CAREGIVERS

Firth (2005) suggests that a wide range of group work is practiced in palliative care, including:

- Self-help groups, where patients support each other calling on the trust that develops from sharing similar experiences
- Children's groups
- Groups for bereaved adults
- Groups for cancer patients
- Client or service-user groups, to enable them to participate in service planning and feedback on their own experiences
- Caregiver groups

Within such groups a range of work is possible and would benefit people more widely in end-of-life care. We would identify interventions designed to:

- Assist people to deal with emotional and cognitive issues
- Offer information and practical assistance

- Enable people to take part in activities that achieve fulfilling experiences for them
- Enable people to have spiritual guidance and reflection

Caregiver Groups

Group support can make a significant contribution to the range of interventions with diverse and complex needs among family members and caregivers.

The literature suggests that one of the difficulties encountered when running such groups is recruitment. Because "family caregivers tend to put the needs of the ill person ahead of their own" (Rabow et al., 2004, p. 485) they often find it difficult initially to find the space and energy to come to a group. Therefore, when planning a group for caregivers, several considerations need careful decision making:

- Will the group be run as an open or closed group? Closed groups are where the membership is set at the beginning and nobody is allowed to join later. Open groups allow new members to join at any time, with the consequence that the group must adjust to new members.
- Will it run for a fixed number of sessions or be open-ended? For caregivers, a fixed program offers certainty in the commitment they will make, since they give priority to caring responsibilities.
- Frequency of meetings. Frequent meetings assist continuity, but caregivers may not have the time for regular meetings.
- Who will facilitate it? Organizers might consider a balance of male and female leaders, paid and volunteer personnel, levels of experience in facilitating groups and involving different professions, particularly if information-giving is to be part of the group activity, so that nursing, medical, and other information might be available. This also raises the question of whether there might be other specialized staff involved as well as the facilitators.
- How will referrals be made, how much information will be required, and from whom? Sometimes it is an advantage to require potential group members to commit themselves, for example by making an application and providing information about their aims in attending the group.

Other considerations include transportation for the caregivers and care for patients or children to enable primary caregivers to attend the group meetings. Attention is also required to find a suitable venue, for example, a hospice or hospital, community organization or church, or offices of a social or housing agency convenient for caregivers. What will be a convenient time of day?

We have been involved in planning and running several such groups, open and closed, time-limited and open-ended, and we discuss here some of the issues that arise. Offering an open group that meets once a week for an hour and a half can work well. When caregivers first join a group they often find it difficult to leave the person they are caring for, but once they have established a routine that allows them to attend the group, this difficulty diminishes. On the other hand, we share the experience of Harding et al. (2004, p. 398) evaluating a short-term, closed group for caregivers who "found carers to be highly ambivalent both to their own needs and to accessing supportive interventions." A closed group with a clear endpoint therefore may provide a useful alternative structure, which helps caregivers accept a place at the outset. The research shows that a ninty-minute time span, with a structured information program for a six-week period is very acceptable to many carers. We have found that after such a group ends, there are often reunions or further informal meetings organized through links made at the group.

Recurring Issues

The predominant focus of sessions in less-structured groups has, in our experience, emphasized emotional issues, although practical concerns are also an important dimension. In structured groups, the information is absorbed and valued and so practical issues have their place, but the emotional implications and current concerns also need to be raised and addressed.

Recurring themes of the emotional experiences shared within groups include:

- Discussion about depression and how to combat it
- Communication difficulties with the person who is ill and how to resolve them
- Communication issues with other family members
- Dealing with uncertainty
- Adjustment to being a caregiver
- Emotions connected with the dying process, such as guilt, regret, and anger
- Exhaustion and coping with other people's distress

Practical issues include:

- Providing information on a range of topics such as financial and legal matters
- Welfare benefits
- Adaptations for the home together with advice on showering and bathing

The real strengths of a group are the combined resources within the group itself for offering suggestions to counter difficulties and the support provided by members to each other. The direct sharing of experiences between caregivers is a potent means of empowering people to help each other.

Evaluation of Caregiver Groups

A practitioner's account of one evaluation of the benefits people derived from attending unstructured caregivers' groups is as follows: One attendee described how they felt before attending the group: "You feel terribly isolated. Even after the first meeting, having been and shared the experience, it does make you feel: 'I'm not the only one.' And then as more people join the group you think: 'I'm not only not the only one, but there are actually people who are worse off than I am, who have been a carer for longer and possibly have a lot more to put up with in the disability of their husband and so on."

Attendees were asked for the three most important things gained by being in the group. A typical answer was: "The first is that you're not isolated, you're not on your own—there are other people in the same situation. The second is you can say anything you like, without being judged or criticized. You can have a good laugh—you can also have a cry. Thirdly, of course, you've always got someone such as [facilitator] for giving advice and tips on things, how to do something or what to do about something."

Caregiver Groups and Bereavement Issues

Another issue to address when facilitating a caregivers' group is to find out how the group wants to deal with bereavement issues when a caregiver becomes bereaved. A practitioner's comments are as follows: When we have raised this with groups, the responses have been thoughtful. In closed groups lasting for a fixed number of sessions, caregivers did not usually return once the person they were caring for had died. However, in open groups that were ongoing, caregivers opted for a different approach and wanted to be able to continue to attend for several sessions during their bereavement. We did not find problems with either model, but what is important is for the group facilitators to create a climate in which there can be open and honest communication about the issues raised.

Groups for People with Advanced Illness

"A support group is an optimal environment to gain reflection and perception on the internalized stigma of being ill, dying, care giving, or being bereaved" (del Rio, 2004, p. 511). Groups for people facing their own end-of-life issues can provide a safe and confidential environment to explore issues around living with dying and can provide the opportunity to share strategies for coping with difficult situations, such as giving and receiving bad news. The group's shared experience can be used to explore quality-of-life issues. Again, decisions need to be made about whether a group should be open or closed, and open-ended or not. Difficulties with attendance because of advancing illness may indicate running a closed group for a fixed number of sessions, but an open-ended group allows people to cease attending when they no longer wish to do so (del Rio, 2004, p. 519).

Case example: Structured & unstructured patient groups

A practitioner's account is as follows (first of a structured group). We found that a patient group can work well if it runs for four sessions, with each session having a theme and direction. The first session includes introductions, aims, and expectations of the group, establishing an agreed upon set of ground rules and brief storytelling. The theme of the second session might be adjustments, which can include adjusting to the diagnosis, facing news of recurring disease, changes in lifestyle, changes in the patient's role within the family, changes in body image, relationships, and feelings. The third session might deal with communication issues. This session might cover difficulties achieving open and honest communication with family members. The last session can focus on quality-of-life issues versus treatments, the importance of having adequate knowledge to make informed decisions and retain control. The session needs to focus on endings, moving on, pleasure and sadness and can include the gifts made to those left behind.

An account of experience with unstructured work follows: A group of young mothers found it particularly difficult to communicate honestly with elderly parents as well as with their children and partners. Often patient groups share similar experiences of other family members tending to protect the ill person and not feeling able to share sadness and distress. If patients are experiencing insensitive communication with health care professionals, this may be shared, and strategies of how to deal with unhelpful communication can be developed. Group work with patients involves some risk-taking on the part of the leaders but generates rich material and demonstrates the enormous capacity of members to support and value each other.

The risks of group work with people facing emotional turmoil sometimes come from our own fears about the effects on members at a more advanced stage of illness or who die during the course of the group meetings. In practice, we have found that these differences within a group enable people to deal with difficult fears and feelings that need to be addressed. One group member's comment was: "I found the others in the group quite inspirational and it brought home to me to value every moment of my life! Sharing our feelings and difficulties was very beneficial."

ACTIVITY GROUPS

A range of activity groups can also be organized in day settings, in care homes by visiting or resident staff, or on wards and in community settings or in-patient units, where a joint project can draw both visitors and people at the end of life (Hartley & Payne, 2008). Activities might include:

- Arts and crafts work, including pottery, painting, and making cards and small gifts, such as silk scarves or hangings, rugs, or embroidery
- Artistic work with digital images, such as those produced with cameras and computers
- Play and poetry reading
- Creative writing including stories, plays, comic strips, and poetry
- Making clothes or hats
- Simple dancing and keep-fit exercises
- Reminiscing about people's lives, the local community, and important public events that people share some experience of
- Classes on local political and controversial issues, or foreign affairs, using television programs or newspapers as discussion points
- Music making, collectively or individually
- Games, including computer games, some of which can be played with several participants
- Cooking

Activities provide distraction from the illness and end-of-life situation as well as enable people to share in physical or intellectual pursuits, achieve something as an outcome, such as a craft or art object, and also have the opportunity for informal peer support. It can feel less daunting, but no less powerful, for people at the end of life or for caregivers to join in activities together as a way of stimulating discussion.

Many of these activities can be shared at the bedside, even with someone who is quite ill, by family members including children. The shared activitity makes visiting a very ill person easier to manage and creates a casual context that may facilitate a discussion of feelings.

SOCIAL WORK MACRO INTERVENTIONS

Social work macro interventions include:

- Incorporating the need for appropriate end-of-life care into public debate and advocating for appropriate service designs
- Supporting family and community resilience in responding to end-of-life issues
- Achieving opportunities for public expression of experience of the end of life and bereavement.

Policy Development and Community Resilience

We saw in Chapter 2 that improving quality of life near the end of life had become a focus on policy development in the United States (Lynn, 2000). In an important discussion of the WHO healthy cities program, Kellehear (2005) argues that current approaches to end-of-life care fail to develop public health responses to death in society. End-of-life care has become equated with medicalized palliative care. As a health care provision, palliative care has, in turn, focused too much on clinical interventions, including clinical psychological interventions. Kellehear argues that social work can contribute to a redirection of effort to develop a health-promoting practice in palliative care; and end-of-life care can support communities to respond effectively to death and dying in their midst and also to make changes in patterns of death.

Among Kellehear's (2005) policy proposals are:

- Fostering community education that connects health care and compassion in society
- Fostering and supporting practical compassion in workplaces, schools, and facilities for caring for older people
- Fostering understanding of effective responses to death and loss
- Fostering a positive view of the special needs of aging, dying, and bereaved people
- Supporting positive views of the experience of aging, dying, and bereavement

- Fostering commitment to effective social responses to cultural difference and social inequalities in services for older people, and people who are dying or bereaved

Kellehear's work is concerned with a broad social advocacy for the needs of people approaching the end of life. This is because societies where many people are aging will have large groups of people, many of whom may be clustered together in particular communities, who need local facilities that are adapted to increasing frailty and social networks that accept people living with long-term illness and frailty and who are aware of their closeness to the end of life. People need the interpersonal skills and relationships to be open to talk about death, dying, and bereavement in the way we have advocated in this book.

End-of-life care services have the knowledge, skills, experience, and respect to make a contribution to this development. Social work practitioners with macro intervention skills can provide leadership in developing such "compassionate" values in local communities, among professions, and in advocating for service and policy development. Gilbert (2003) argues that this is because their work means that they are in touch with and receptive to people's experiences as they go through dying and bereavement processes. Therefore, they can use research, study, and other promotional resources to help convey the experience of clients and their families. They are also able to model appropriate reactions in death, dying, and bereavement situations to others. Managers and politicians may be perceived as having sectional or organizational interests in advocating for improved services, or as being too involved in financial or other social responsibilities to model compassionate values. Medical and nursing team members may easily be seen as focusing on health priorities and service development to respond to illness, or giving people caring advice rather than the broader social conception of the importance of dying and bereavement.

Service Design: Linking End-of-Life Care with Other Care Provision

Public and policy debate is needed to decide how end-of-life care should interconnect with other health and social care services. Public views in many countries support good end-of-life care, but the public has little opportunity to influence what it might consist of. The U.K. end-of-life strategy (DH, 2008) promotes being open about end-of-life choices and strategies.

Macro social work should contribute to helping communities and services think about the policy implications of the developing need for end-of-life care. Social workers have the experience of managing boundary relationships between end-of-life services and other health and social care provision and can contribute to ensure that a psychosocial perspective on what is appropriate care is included in debate.

Building on Quinn's (2005) analysis, we suggest that some options for local strategies might include:

- Developing specialized palliative care services as a hub connecting with generalized facilities. The aim would be to develop mutual support among colleagues working in isolated settings such as care homes or the community and share in maintaining and developing skills in all aspects of end-of-life care.
- Maintaining a separation between specialized and generalized services in end-of-life care but building referral systems between them.
- Integrating end-of-life care as part of the roles of a wide range of practitioners in health and social care, transferring expertise in end-of-life care so that it is spread wide.
- Extending palliative care to offer a wider range of less complex and intense interventions, since the resources are not available to provide palliative care in its present form to all who might need it.
- A community strategy of promoting local and service-user-controlled bereavement and general support services, supported by education and service development resources from specialized palliative care services. This also recognizes that specialized palliative care may be stigmatized because it is seen as dealing mainly with people suffering from very severe illnesses.

As the populations in Western societies age, increasing numbers of older people need care for longer periods of time than in previous decades. This is offered mainly in their existing homes through home care services, but increasingly older people are becoming part of assisted living communities, supported housing schemes, extra-care housing, and similar provision. While residents have a high degree of independence, care is available in difficult periods or as disabilities increase. People may move into residential care homes with a higher degree of communal living, shared lounges and meals, and even shared rooms; where they often have a higher degree of staff intervention and less privacy. Nursing homes, in the U.K. legal parlance "care homes with nursing," provide similar communal facilities with registered nurses available to provide care.

Han and colleagues' (Han, Tiggle, & Remsburg, 2008) survey comparing home care hospice patients with those in care homes in the

United States found that care home residents are unlike home hospice patients, being older, with dementia or another noncancer diagnosis, and funded by Medicaid, the state insurance scheme for poorer people. On the other hand, they were more likely to receive help with nutrition, medication management, and services from a physician than home care patients. Seale and Kelly (1997) compared the views of the surviving spouse of patients who had died in a hospice and local hospitals, finding that during the 1990s symptom control had improved in hospitals, but they were experienced as "busy," and psychosocial care was better in the hospice.

Care outside hospitals and hospices is often provided mainly by paraprofessional caregivers, through occasional visits, or by alarm systems so that help may be summoned in an emergency. Inevitably, as populations live to greater ages following the trends outlined in Chapter 2, a higher proportion will need such care. Even where community nurses or caregivers are available, they may not have experience of the complexity of symptoms from multiple illnesses or disabilities that people may experience close to the end of life. However, many older people live in assisted living communities, supported housing, or care homes and an increasing proportion of them reach the end of life in such settings. Unfortunately, close to the end of life, care staff may feel unable to manage their care, or proprietors and regulators of older people's facilities prefer not to have people dying on the premises, feeling that this may upset other residents. This may mean that they are taken to the hospital, sometimes as an emergency, and this is both costly and moves them away from their home and into a busy environment focused on active cure rather than empathetic care.

Therefore, it is increasingly important to support the confidence and skills of staff without experience of the more complex nursing tasks (Froggatt, 2001; Katz & Peace, 2003). Much of this support lies in nursing tasks, but social work skills are also required (Lacey, 2005), since staff in supported housing and care homes may not get enough support in psychological and social care. Payne and colleagues' (Payne et al., 2004) study of small local community hospitals operating particularly in rural areas in the United Kingdom found, for example, that while many have some expertise in palliative care and contacts with twenty-four-hour palliative care support, few had specific palliative care beds and policies and guidelines for nonspecialist staff on patient assessment or symptom control. An important strategy for developing end-of-life care, therefore, is building skills and support in general facilities of this kind, possibly including access to social workers and others able to provide appropriate psychosocial care.

Professional developments need to mirror the policy choices being made to integrate end-of-life care into the wider system of health and social care, in the United States (Fields & Cassel, 1997) and many other countries. U.K. developments include three models of care, which have been introduced in a number of settings and are also being used to improve standards of care in care and nursing homes (NCPC, 2007):

- Preferred priorities of care (originally preferred place of care; Pemberton, Storey, & Howard, 2003) is a system of advance care planning prior to entry into supported housing or care homes, or prior to a move to a more intensive form of care. It enables people to chart their preferences for care and produces a document for them to take with them to communicate their wishes.
- The Gold Standards Framework is an advance care planning process that aims to identify people at the end of life, assess their needs, and plan care appropriately. It started in primary care (family doctor) settings. There are seven key tasks, which include coding to identify needs, advance care planning, assessment tools, educational resources to support staff, and a practice protocol for the dying stage, which leads onto the Liverpool Care Pathway.
- The Liverpool Care Pathway, pioneered at the Marie Curie Centre in Liverpool, England (Ellershaw & Ward, 2003; Ellershaw & Wilkinson, 2003), provides a care protocol for the last few days of life. This ensures that psychological, spiritual, and social needs are taken care of, and nursing and medical practice meet standards typical of hospice care.

Macro Social Work Intervention in Service Issues: Combating Inequalities

Various studies and commentaries suggest that, as with many health and social care services, there are inequalities in the provision of palliative care; this is likely also to be true of end-of-life care. In the United States, poor and ethnic minority populations are disproportionately affected by terminal illness, are more likely to be undertreated for pain, and pharmacies in poor areas are less likely to carry opioids for pain relief treatment (Morrison, Wallenstein, Natale, Senzel, & Huang, 2000). Patients from minority groups are less likely to receive good care in the early stages of a serious illness, and this probably makes them less receptive to accepting palliative care at later stages; they may also have different support strategies that lead to differences in their approach or referral to services (Francoeur et al, 2007; Bourjolly, 2001; Karim, 2000). Kessler et al (2005) in a U.K. study, found that patients from the lower socio-economic class suffered social inequality in access to palliative care services, because of passivity in seeking services by informal caregivers. However, patients in middle and lower socio-economic classes received more consistent support from informal caregivers than patients in higher classes. Similarly, there is a body of evidence in the United States that minorities are less likely than white social groups to access palliative care services (Rosenfeld et al 2007).

An important role for social work may be, through its awareness and responsibility for providing a social focus in health care services, to develop and contribute cultural competence and anti-oppressive practice, and policy concern for more equal provision. Francoeur and colleagues (Francoeur, Payne, Raveis, & Shim, 2007) studied 146 African American and Latino patients in inner-city New York, and found that the less-well-insured patients were more likely to be hopeful if they had a religious affiliation and thus more likely to seek treatment than nonaffiliated uninsured or underinsured patients. This led the authors to suggest that working through religious organizations might assist in supporting patients to come forward for palliative care support at an early stage of their illness. Hall and colleagues (Hall, Stone, & Fiset, 1998) commenting on Canadian experience suggest that palliative services need to identify shared and distinct aspects of cultural frameworks in different ethnic groups' thinking about death, dying, and bereavement. A recent small New York study (Rosenfeld et al., 2007) found that race did not seem to be a factor in whether a patient with a poor prognosis received home hospice care. However, poor communication from physicians and other local services about end-of-life decision making and poor availability of hospice care meant that most patients had very little end-of-life help.

We saw in Chapter 5 that artistic activities are an important part of palliative care work, both as personal arts psychotherapy and because they provide fulfilling experiences as people live until the moment that they die. The quality of work produced often challenges the excluding attitude that the creative arts are owned only by the gifted few; supported and encouraged, many people can produce work that communicates something of their life experience. Because dying and bereaved people share significant experiences, artistic expression of their experience can help others. It can be motivating to members of the public to see the achievements possible at the end of life, and also acts as a memorial to the dying person, which is often valued by the person's family.

Public Communication and Involvement

Public communication activities allow people involved in dying and bereavement to convey their experiences. There is an extensive catalog of people who have written about their experiences of dying and bereavement, for example, C. S. Lewis (1961), Victor and Rosemary Zorza (1980), Simone de Beauvoir (1966) and Joan Didion (2005) are examples of influential writers who have raised issues of end-of-life care and bereavement over the past half-century. Sometimes such writing has been in an academic context. Examples are:

- The description by the eminent American palliative care physician Ira Byock of his father's death, showing how openness and family involvement were crucial to dying well (1997).
- The account by Richard Titmuss (1974), the eminent social policy academic, describing his cancer treatment in the U.K. National Health Service. His free treatment alongside working people explained his personal commitment to free medical help for all.
- Peter Houghton's (2001) account of the period when he was expecting to die. He was the subject of an experiment, eventually becoming the world's longest survivor with an artificial heart (Maugh, 2007; Richmond, 2007). His story therefore reflects the experience of knowing that he was going to die and being saved from that risk. One of the reasons he was chosen for the experience was that he was physically fit, and as a psychologist and counselor, it was thought that he would be better able to cope with the stress of his reliance on an artificial life-support system than other potential patients. He carried his artificial heart in a shoulder bag, and once, when it was stolen, causing the disconnection alarm to go off, the thief dropped the bag and Houghton calmly plugged himself back in. He has also written about his spiritual reactions to his experiences (Houghton, 2002).

In addition to published work, there is potential for the artistic products created by patients and carers within health care, hospice, and older persons' facilities to connect the experience of end-of-life care with the local community to be used as part of exhibitions, and as elements in producing promotional material for end-of-life agencies. Music, art, and craftwork are important parts of our everyday lives, sources of leisure and entertainment for many people, and also a part of a community heritage (Hartley, 2008). Many people are interested in the arts; they are involved in creative writing, collective performance of music, or painting. Adult education classes often stimulate and develop skills, and the arts are also an important part of school curricula. Hartley (2008) argues that this is because art has the potential to move and inspire us, grab our attention, and change who we are and the way that we relate to the world and those around us.

Any end-of-life care service has opportunities through open house events, annual meetings, reporting and accountability mechanisms, and fund-raising initiatives to contribute to the development of public understanding in this way. Examples of public education activities from St. Christopher's Hospice would be easily developed by end-of-life services anywhere, adapted to local needs, and include:

- A schools project. A local school class, usually of nine- to ten-years-old, visits the hospice and meets a group of patients in the day unit to ask questions about their life and the fact that they are dying. Art work is shared between patients and children over several weeks, and culminates in a display of patients' and children's work, involving parents and children. In this way, children's resilience to death and bereavement issues in their lives is strengthened; this rubs off on parents as well. Patients feel they are making a positive social contribution (Sands, 2008).
- Care homes education. An evening meeting in a local community center provides information about creative arts work, group work, and support available in local care homes for people at the end of life. While this is mainly a fund-raising device, information about options for care for older people and funding for different types of care is very popular with middle-aged audiences whose parents and relatives are reaching the stage of needing care and increases community knowledge about options, costs, and available resources.
- Open house for professionals. A periodic open house is held; while this is public, it mainly attracts nonspecialist professionals who might connect with the hospice, often local physicians, community nurses, and clergy. This enables staff to build links with new personnel in the area and for them to feel comfortable in approaching the hospice where end-of-life issues affect their work. There is a program of short talks as well as visits to different parts of the service.

Volunteer Involvement and Training

Volunteer engagement can also be developed to be a form of public education, since volunteers working in an end-of-life service convey their experiences much more widely to friends and others in their social network. There are about 96,000 hospice volunteers in the United States (HFA, 2008), providing support for patients, family members, and bereaved people, and fundraising, administrative, and other logistical support. The picture is similar in other countries, where many palliative care services are part of not-for-profit organizations. Both simple and complex volunteer roles are possible. The most complex roles are often volunteer work in spiritual care and bereavement care, and this means that a contribution of social work skills and attitudes is often a significant part of end-of-life volunteer training. Training for volunteers increases the strength and range of skills available in any community to provide increased support for people facing death and bereavement.

CONCLUSION

This chapter expresses our commitment to moving policy and practice in end-of-life care forward, so that everyone who needs it has the opportunity to benefit from appropriate services. As populations in Western societies age, local communities and individuals' social networks can develop greater awareness, knowledge, and skills to support people approaching the end of life. In this book, we have argued that openness to death and competence in responding to bereavement need to be widely spread in every community. The hope for the future for people at the end of life, their families, their caregivers, and our communities and societies is that we can all contribute to creating a society that cares that its citizens die and grieve well. Social workers in end-of-life care have special experience and skills to offer as part of the social contribution of end-of-life care services that will enable our societies to be places where everyone dies well and their loved ones have the chance to grieve and renew their lives.

FURTHER READING

Kellehear, A. (2005). *Compassionate cities: Public health and end-of-life Care*. New York: Routledge. The most recent and comprehensive of Kellehear's research on the need for macro practice and public health developments to facilitate societies that can respond better to end-of-life needs.

Hartley, N., & Payne M. (Ed.) (2008). *Creative arts in palliative care*. Philadelphia: Jessica Kingsley. This book discusses using the arts in a range of settings publicizing end-of-life care services and enabling people at the end of life to celebrate their lives with artistic and cultural achievements. It contains a great deal of practical advice and ideas that practitioners may adapt.

Katz, J. S., & Peace, S. (Ed.) (2003). *End of life in care homes: A palliative care approach*. Oxford, England: Oxford University Press. A useful volume on extending end-of-life care skills in care homes. A useful American publication on the same topic is:

Bern-Klug, M., & Ellis, K. (2004). End of life care in nursing homes. In J. Berzoff, & P. Silverman, (Ed.) *Living with dying: A handbook for end-of-life practitioners* (pp. 628–41). New York: Columbia University Press.

WEBSITES

Volunteer websites relevant to palliative care include:

Volunteering Australia (includes information about a regular conference on palliative care volunteering): http://www.volunteeringaustralia.org/html/s12_content/default.asp?tnid=10

Hospice Volunteer Association, a U.S. coordinating organization for hospice volunteer organizers: http://www.hospicevolunteerassociation.org/Default.aspx

Volunteer Canada: http://www.volunteer.ca/index-eng.php

Volunteering England, the largest coordinating body for volunteering in the U.K.: http://www.volunteering.org.uk

Association of Voluntary Service Managers (Help the Hospices, U.K.) http://www.helpthehospices.org.uk/NPA/avsm/index.asp

An interesting site about arts work in palliative care, including examples of artistic work by patients and families:

Rosetta Life: http://www.rosettalife.org

BIBLIOGRAPHY

Abendroth, A., & Flannery, J. (2006). Predicting the risk of compassion fatigue. *Journal of Hospice and Palliative Nursing, 8*(6), 346–356.

Adams, J., Hershatter, M. J., & Moritz, A. (1991). Accumulated loss phenomenon among hospice caregivers. *American Journal of Hospice and Palliative Care, 8*(3), 29–37.

Adler, N. E., & Page, A. E. K. (Eds.). (2008). *Cancer care for the whole patient: Meeting psychosocial health needs.* Washington DC: National Academies Press.

Aiken, L. R. (1994). *Dying, death and bereavement* (3rd ed.). Boston: Allyn and Bacon.

Ariès, P. (1974). *Western attitudes towards death: From the Middle Ages to the present.* Baltimore: Johns Hopkins University Press.

Attig, T. (1995). Respecting the spirituality of the dying and the bereaved. In I. B. Corless, B. B., Germino, & M. A. Pittman (Eds.), *A challenge for living and dying: Dying, death and bereavement* (pp. 117–130). Boston: Jones and Bartlett.

Auger, J. A. (2000). *Social perspective on death and dying.* Halifax, Canada: Fernwood.

Aulino, F., & Foley, K. (2001). The project on death in America. *Journal of the Royal Society of Medicine, 94,* 492–495.

Bailey, L. W., & Yates, J. (Eds.). (1996). *The near death experience: A reader.* New York: Routledge.

Banks, S. (2006). *Ethics and values in social work* (3rd ed.). Basingstoke, England: Palgrave Macmillan.

Barnes, K., Jones, L., Tookman, A., & King, M. (2007). Acceptability of an advance care planning interview schedule: A focus group study. *Palliative Medicine, 21,* 23–28.

Beauchamp, T. L., & Childress, J. F. (2001). *Principles of biomedical ethics* (5th ed.). Oxford, England: Oxford University Press.

Bechelet, L., Heal, R., Leam C., & Payne, M. (2008). Empowering carers to reconstruct their finances. *Practice, 20*(4), 223–234.

Becker, J. E. (2004). Oncology social workers' attitudes toward hospice care and referral behaviour. *Health and Social Work, 29*(1), 36–46.

Beckett, C., & Maynard, A. (2005). *Values and ethics in social work: An introduction.* London: Sage.

Beder, J. (2006). *Hospital social work: The interface of medicine and caring.* New York: Routledge.

Bell, L. (2005). Review. In R. Adams, L. Dominelli, & M. Payne (Eds.), *Social work futures: Crossing boundaries, transforming practice* (pp. 83–96). Basingstoke, England: Palgrave Macmillan.

Beresford, P., Adshead, L., & Croft, S. (2007). *Social work, palliative care and service users: Making life possible.* Philadelphia: Jessica Kingsley.

Bern-Klug, M. (2004). The ambiguous dying syndrome. *Health and Social Work, 29*(1), 55–65.

Bern-Klug, M., & Ellis, K. (2004). End of life care in nursing homes. In J. Berzoff & P. Silverman (Eds.), *Living with dying: A handbook for end-of-life practitioners* (pp. 628–641). New York: Columbia University Press.

Bern-Klug, M., Forbes, S., & Gessert, C. (2001). The need to revise assumptions about the end of life: Implications for social work practice. *Health and Social Work, 26*(1), 38–48.

Berzoff, J., & Silverman, R. (Eds.). (2004). *Living with dying: A handbook for end-of-life healthcare practitioners.* New York: Columbia University Press.

Blackman, N. (2003). *Loss and learning disability.* London: Worth.

Blackman, N., & Todd, S. (2005). *Caring for people with learning disabilities who are dying.* London: Worth.

Blank, R. H. (2001). Technology and death policy: Redefining death. *Mortality, 6*(2), 191–202.

Booth, K., Maguire, P., Butterworth, T., & Hillier, V. F. (1996). Perceived professional support and the use of blocking behaviours by hospice nurses. *Journal of Advanced Nursing, 6*(5), 220–227.

Borrill, C. S., Carletta, J., Carter, C. S., Dawson, J. F., Garrod, S., Rees, A., Richards, A., Shapiro, D., & West, M. A. (2001). *The effectiveness of health care teams in the National Health Service.* Birmingham, England: University of Aston. Retrieved October 29, 2008, from http://homepages.inf.ed.ac.uk/jeanc/DOH-final-report.pdf

Bourjolly, J. N., & Hirschman, K.B. (2001). Similarities in coping strategies but difference in sources of support among African American women and white women coping with breast cancer. *Journal of Psychosocial Oncology, 19*(1), 17–38.

Bowlby, J. (1969). *Attachment and loss: Volume 1: Attachment.* New York: Basic Books.

Bowlby, J. (1973). *Attachment and loss: Volume 2: Separation.* New York: Basic Books.

Bowlby, J. (1980). *Attachment and loss: Volume 3: Sadness and depression.* New York: Basic Books.

Boyle, D. (1998). The cultural context of dying from cancer. *International Journal of Palliative Nursing, 2*, 70–83.

Brown, J. (2003). User, carer and professional experiences of care in motor neurone disease. *Primary Health Care Research and Development, 4*, 207–217.

Brown, J. H., Henteleff, P., Barakat, S., & Rowe, C. J. (1986). Is it normal for terminally ill patients to desire death? *American Journal of Psychiatry, 143*, 208–11.

Brown, L., & Brown, M. (1996). *When dinosaurs die: A guide to understanding death.* New York: Little, Brown and Company.

Brown, M. (2003). Overview of the health needs of people with learning disabilities in Scotland. In SHS Trust (Ed.), *Palliative care and people with learning disabilities* (pp. 16–17). Edinburgh, Scotland: SHS Trust.

Bruce, E. J., & Schultz, C. L. (2001). *Nonfinite loss and grief: A psychoeducational approach*. Baltimore: Brookes.

Buchanan, D., & Huczynski, A. (2004). *Organizational behaviour: An introductory text* (5th ed.). Harlow, England: Prentice-Hall.

Buckman, R. (1994). *Lost for words: How to talk to someone with cancer*. London: CancerBACUP.

Buckman, R. (2000). Communication in Palliative Care. In D. Dickenson, M. Johnson, & J. S. Katz (Eds.), *Death, dying and bereavement* (pp. 146–173). London: Sage.

Byock, I. (1997). *Dying well: Peace and possibilities at the end of life*. New York: Riverhead.

Caplan, G. (1965). *Principles of preventive psychiatry*. London: Tavistock.

Carkhuff, R. R., & Berenson, B. C. (1977). *Beyond counseling and therapy* (2nd ed.). New York: Holt, Rinehart and Winston.

Chochinov, H. M., Wilson, K. G., Enns, M., Mowchun, N., Lander, S., Levitt, S., et al. (1995). Desire for death in the terminally ill. *American Journal of Psychiatry, 152*, 1185–1195.

Christ, G. C. (2000). *Healing children's grief: Surviving a parent's death from cancer*. New York: Oxford University Press.

Clacket, M., & Higgins, A. (2008). The grief experience of same-sex couples within an Irish context: tacit acknowledgement. *International Journal of Palliative Nursing, 14*(6), 297–302.

Clark, D. (Ed.). (2005). *Cicely Saunders—founder of the hospice movement: Selected letters 1959–1999*. Oxford, England: Oxford University Press.

Clausen, H., Kendall, M., Murray, S., Worth, A., Boyd, K., & Benton, F. (2005). Would palliative care patients benefit from social workers retaining the traditional 'casework' role rather than working as care managers? A prospective serial interview study. *British Journal of Social Work, 35*, 277–285.

Coffey, E., (2004). The symptom is stillness: Living with and dying from ALS. In J. Berzoff & P. Silverman (Eds.), *Living with dying: A handbook for end-of-life practitioners* (pp. 43–56). New York: Columbia University Press.

Corr, C. (1999). Enhancing the concept of disenfranchised grief. *Omega, 38*(1), 1–20.

Corr, C. A., Nabe, C. M., & Corr, D. M. (2006). *Death and dying: Life and living* (6th ed.). Belmont, CA: Wadsworth.

Cosh, R. (1995). Spiritual care of the dying. In I. B. Corless, B. B., Germino, & M. A. Pittman (Eds.), *A challenge for living and dying: Dying, death and bereavement* (pp. 131–143). Boston: Jones and Bartlett.

Council of Europe (1999). *Recommendation 1418: Protection of the human rights and dignity of the terminally ill and the dying*. Retrieved October 29, 2008, from http://assembly.coe.int/Main.asp?link=/Documents/AdoptedText/ta99/EREC1418.htm

Craig, G. C. (Ed.). *No water—no life: Hydration in the dying*. Alsager, England: Fairway Folio.

Crossley, D. (2000). *Muddles, puddles and sunshine: Your activity book to help when someone has died*. Cheltenham, England: Winston's Wish.

Csikai, E., & Chaitin, E. (2006). *Ethics in end-of-life decisions in social work practice.* Chicago: Lyceum Books.

Currer, C. (2001). *Responding to grief: Dying, bereavement and social care.* Basingstoke, England: Palgrave.

Currer, C. (2007). *Loss and social work.* Exeter, England: Learning Matters.

Davies, D. J. (2002). *Death, ritual and belief: The rhetoric of funerary rites* (2nd ed.). London: Continuum.

DCA. (2007). *Mental Capacity Act 2005: Code of practice.* London: TSO.

de Beauvoir, S. (1966 [1964]). *A very easy death* [Une mort très douce]. London: Deutsch/Weidenfeld and Nicholson.

Dean, R. A. (1997). Humor and laughter in palliative care. *Journal of Palliative Care, 13*(1), 34–39.

Dein, S., & Thomas, K. (2002). To tell or not to tell. *European Journal of Palliative Care, 9*(5), 209–212.

Del Rio, N. (2004). A framework for multicultural end-of-life care: Enhancing social work practice. In J. Berzoff & P. Silverman (Eds.), *Living with dying: A handbook for end-of-life practitioners* (pp. 437–461). New York: Columbia University Press.

DeMaria, R., Weeks, G., & Hof, L. (1999). *Focused genograms: Intergenerational assessment of individuals, couples and families.* Philadelphia, PA: Brunner/Mazel.

DESA. (2005). *World population prospects: The 2004 revision: Highlights.* New York: United Nations Department of Economic and Social Affairs, Population Division.

DH. (2000). *The NHS cancer plan: A plan for investment, a plan for reform.* London: Department of Health.

DH. (2008). *End of life care strategy: Promoting high quality care for all adults at the end of life.* London: Department of Health.

Didion, J. (2005). *The year of magical thinking.* New York: Knopf.

Dix, O., & Glickman, M. (1997). *Feeling better: Psychosocial care in specialist palliative care.* London: National Council for Hospice and Specialist Palliative Care Services.

Doka, K. (1989). *Disenfranchised grief: Recognizing hidden sorrow.* New York: Lexington.

Doka, K. (2002). *Disenfranchised grief: New directions, challenges and strategies for practice.* Champaign, IL: Research Press.

Donaghey, V. (2002). It's not all bad news. In V. Donaghey, J. Bernal, I. Tuffrey-Wijne, & S. Hollins (Eds.), *Getting on with cancer.* London: Gaskell.

Downman, T. (2008). Hope and hopelessness: Theory and reality. *Journal of the Royal Society of Medicine, 101,* 428–430.

Drew, A., & Fawcett, T. N. (2002). Responding to the information needs of patients with cancer. *Professional Nurse, 17*(7), 443–446.

du Boulay, S., & Rankin, M. (2007). *Cicely Saunders: The founder of the modern hospice movement* (2nd ed.). London: SPCK.

Dunn, K., & Forman, L. (2002). Facing death with confidence. *European Journal of Palliative Care, 9*(3), 123–5.

Dyregrov, A. (2008). *Grief in children: A handbook for adults* (2nd ed.). Philadelphia: Jessica Kingsley.

Dyregrov, A. (2008). *Grief in young children: A handbook for adults.* Philadelphia: Jessica Kingsley.

Dyrgrov, K., & Dyregrov, A. (2008). *Effective grief and bereavement support: The role of family, friends, colleagues, schools and support professionals.* Philadelphia: Jessica Kingsley.

Eadie, B. (1992). *Embraced by the light.* Placerville, CA: Gold Leaf.

Edgley, C. (2003). Dying as deviance: An update on the relationship between terminal patients and medical settings. In C. D. Bryant (Ed.), *Handbook of death and dying, Vol. 1: The presence of death* (pp. 448–456). Thousand Oaks, CA: Sage.

Egan, G. (1992). *The skilled helper: A systematic approach to effective helping* (5th ed.). Pacific Grove, CA: Brooks/Cole.

Elison, J., & McGonigle, C. (2003). *Liberating losses: When death brings relief.* Cambridge, MA: Da Capo.

Ellershaw, J., & Ward, C. (2003). Care of the dying patient: The last hours or days of life. *British Medical Journal, 326*(7379), 30–34.

Ellershaw, J., & Wilkinson, S. (Eds.). (2003). *Care of the dying and pathway to excellence.* Oxford, England: Oxford University Press.

Emanuel, E. J., Fairclough, D. L., & Emanuel, L. L. (2000). Attitudes and desires related to euthanasia and physician-assisted suicide among terminally-ill patients and their caregivers. *Journal of the American Medical Association, 284,* 2460–2468.

Eng, D. (2006). Management guidelines for motor neurone disease [ALS] patients on non-invasive ventilation at home. *Palliative Medicine, 20,* 69–79.

Erikson, E. (1965). *Childhood and society* (2nd ed.). London: Hogarth Press.

Ersek, M., & Wilson, S. A. (2003). The challenges and opportunities in providing end-of-life care in nursing homes. *Journal of Palliative Medicine, 6*(1) 7–9.

Farber, S., Egnew, T., & Farber, A. (2004). What is a respectful death? In J. Berzoff & P. Silverman (Eds.), *Living with dying: A handbook for end-of-life practitioners* (pp. 102–127). New York: Columbia University Press.

Fenimore, A. (1991). *Beyond the darkness: My near-death journey to the edge of hell and back.* New York: Simon and Schuster.

Fields, M. J., & Cassel C. K. (Eds.). (1997). *Approaching death: Improving care at the end of life.* Washington DC: National Academies Press.

Figley, C. R. (1995). Compassion fatigue as a secondary traumatic stress disorder: An overview. In C. R. Figley (Ed.), *Compassion fatigue* (pp. 1–20). New York: Brunner/Maazel.

Fine, R. L. (2004). The imperative for hospital-based palliative care. *Baylor University Medical Center Proceedings, 17*(3), 259–264.

Firth, P. (2005). Groupwork in palliative care. In P. Firth, G. Luff, & D. Oliviere (Eds.), *Loss, change and bereavement in palliative care* (pp. 167–184). Maidenhead: Open University Press.

Firth, S. (1996). The good death: Attitudes of British Hindus. In G. Howarth & P. C. Jupp (Eds.), *Contemporary issues in the sociology of death, dying and disposal.* Basingstoke, England: Macmillan.

Fisher, J., & Barnett, M. (2002). Communication with the dying and their loved ones. In R. Charlton (Ed.), *Primary palliative care: Dying, death and bereavement in the community* (pp. 31–47). Oxford, England: Radcliffe.

Flanagan, J. C. (1954). The critical incident technique. *Psychological Bulletin, 51*(4), 327–358.

Flew, A. (1964). Introduction. In A. Flew (Ed.), *Body, mind and death* (pp. 1–28). New York: Macmillan

Fook, J., & Askeland, G. A. (2006). The "critical" in critical reflection. In S. White, J. Fook, & F. Gardner (Eds.), *Critical reflection in health and social care.* Maidenhead, England: Open University Press.

Forrest, G., Plumb, C., Ziebland, S., & Stein, A. (2006). Breast cancer in the family—children's perceptions of their mother's cancer and its initial treatment: Qualitative study. *British Medical Journal, 332*, 988–1001.

Forte, A. L., Hill, M., Pazder, R., & Feudtner, C. (2004). Bereavement care interventions: A systematic review. *BMC Palliative Care, 3*(3). (Retrieved October 29, 2008, from http://www.biomedcentral.com/1472-684X/3/3

Fox, M. (2003). *Religion, spirituality and the near-death experience.* London: Routledge.

Francoeur, R. B., Payne, R., Raveis, V., & Shim, H. (2007). Palliative care in the inner city: Patient religious affiliation, underinsurance, and symptom attitude. *Cancer, 109* (2nd supplement), 425–434.

Froggatt, K. A. (2001). Palliative care and nursing homes: Where next? *Palliative Medicine, 15*, 42–48.

Furst, C. J., & Doyle, D. (2004). The terminal phase. In D. Doyle, G. Hanks, N. Cherny, & K. Calman (Eds.), *Oxford textbook of palliative medicine* (pp. 1119–1133). Oxford University Press.

Gelderd, K., & Gelderd, D. (2005). *Practical counselling skills: An integrative approach.* Basingstoke, England: Palgrave Macmillan.

Gilbert, P. (2003). *The value of everything: Social work and its importance in the field of mental health.* Lyme Regis, England: Russell House.

Gillis, C. N. (Ed.). (2001). *Seeing the difference: Conversations on death and dying.* Berkeley, CA: Darren B. Townsend Center for the Humanities, University of California.

Glackin, M., & Higgins, A. (2008). The grief experience of same-sex couples within an Irish context: Tacit acknowledgment. *International Journal of Palliative Nursing, 14*(6), 297–302.

Glaser, B. G., & Strauss, A. L. (1965). *Awareness of dying.* New York: Aldine.

Glaser, B. G., & Strauss, A. L. (1968). *Time for dying.* Chicago: Aldine.

Glick, I. O., Parkes, C. M., & Weiss, R. (1974). *The first year of bereavement.* New York: Wiley.

Gorer, G. (1967). *Death, grief and mourning.* Garden City, NY: Doubleday.

Grant, E., Murray, S. A., Kendall, M., Boyd, K., Tilley, S., & Ryan, D. (2004). Spiritual issues and needs: Perspectives from patients with advanced cancer and non-malignant disease: A qualitative study. *Supportive and Palliative Care, 2*, 371–378.

Gysels, M., & Higginson, I. (2004). *Improving supportive and palliative care for adults with cancer: Research evidence.* London: National Institute for Clinical Excellence.

Haight, B. K., & Bahr, R. T. (1984). The therapeutic role of life review in the elderly. *Academic Psychology Bulletin, 6*(3), 289–299.

Hall, P., Stone, G., & Fiset, V. J. (1998). Palliative care: How can we meet the needs of our multicultural communities? *Journal of Palliative Care, 14*(2), 46–49.

Han, B., Tiggle, R. B., & Remsburg, R. E. (2008). Characteristics of patients receiving care at home versus in nursing homes: Results from the National Home and Hospice Care Survey and the National Nursing Home Survey. *American Journal of Hospice and Palliative Medicine, 24*(6), 479–486.

Harding, R., Higginson, I., Leam, C., Donaldson, N., Pearce, A., George, R., Robinson, V., & Taylor L. (2004). Evaluation of a short-term group intervention for informal carers of patients attending a home palliative care service. *Journal of Pain and Symptom Management, 27*(5), 396–408.

Harding, R., & Leam, C. (2005). Clinical notes for informal carers in palliative care: Recommendations from a random patient file audit. *Palliative Medicine, 19*, 639–642.

Hartley, N. (2008). Exhibiting, promoting and funding the arts in healthcare settings. In N. Hartley & M. Payne (Eds.), *Creative arts in palliative care* (pp. 52–65), Philadelphia: Jessica Kingsley.

Hartley, N., & Payne, M. (Eds.). (2008). *Creative arts in palliative care*. Philadelphia: Jessica Kingsley.

Hayter, M. (2000). Utilizing the Maslach Burnout Inventory to measure burnout in HIV/AIDS specialist community nurses: The implications for clinical supervision and support. *Primary Health Care Research and Development, 1*, 243–253.

Hearn, F. (2005). Excluded and vulnerable groups of service users. In P. Firth, G. Luff, & D. Oliviere (Eds.), *Loss, change and bereavement in palliative care* (pp. 133–149). Maidenhead, England: Open University Press.

Henry, C., & Seymour, J. (2007). *Advance care planning: A guide for health and social care staff*. London: Department of Health.

HFA. (2008). *Volunteering and hospice*. Miami, FL: Hospice Association of America. Retrieved May 3, 2008, from http://www.hospicefoundation.org/news room/articles/volunteering.asp

Hilliard, R. E. (2005). Music therapy in hospice and palliative care: A review of the empirical data. *Evidence-based Complementary and Alternative Medicine, 2*(2), 173–178.

Hocking, C., Briott, T., & Paddy, A. (2006). Caring for people with motor neurone disease. *International Journal of Therapy and Rehabilitation, 13*(8), 351–355.

Hodgson, J. (2005). Working together—a multidisciplinary concern. In J. Parker (Ed.), *Aspects of social work and palliative care* (pp. 51–66). London: Quay.

Hollins, S., & Sireling, L. (2004a). *When Mum died* (3rd ed.). London: Gaskell.

Hollins, S., & Sireling, L. (2004b). *When Dad died* (3rd ed.). London: Gaskell.

Houghton, P. (2001). *On death, dying and not dying*. Philadelphia: Jessica Kingsley.

Houghton, P. (2002). *The world within me: A personal journey to spiritual understanding*. Philadelphia: Jessica Kingsley.

Howarth, G. (2007). *Death and dying: A sociological introduction*. Cambridge, England: Polity.

Howarth, G., & Jupp, P. C. (Eds.). (1996). *Contemporary issues in the sociology of death, dying and disposal.* Basingstoke, England: Macmillan.

Howarth, G., & Leaman, O. (Eds.). (2001). *Encyclopedia of death and dying.* New York: Routledge.

Ingleton, C., Payne, S., Nolan, M., & Carey, I. (2003). Respite in palliative care: A review and discussion of the literature. *Palliative Medicine, 17,* 567–575.

James, N. (1993). Divisions of emotional labour: Disclosure and cancer. In M. Robb, S. Barrett, C. Komaromy, & A. Rogers (Eds.), *Communication, relationships and care: A reader* (2004). London: Routledge.

Jeffreys, J. S. (2005). *Helping grieving people when tears are not enough: A handbook for care providers.* New York: Brunner-Routledge.

Jenkins, C., & Merry, J. (2005). *Relative grief.* Philadephia: Jessica Kingsley.

Jo, S., Brazil, K., Lohfeld, L., & Willison, K. (2007). Caregiving at the end of life: Perspectives from spousal caregivers and care recipients. *Palliative and Supportive Care, 5,* 11–17.

Johnston Taylor, E., Baird, S., Malone, D., & McCorkle, R. (1993). Factors associated with anger in cancer patients and their caregivers. *Cancer Practice,* July/August 1993, *1*(2), 101–109.

Jones, A., Tuffrey-Wijne, I., Butler, G., & Hollins, S. (2006). Meeting the cancer information needs of people with learning disabilities: Experiences of paid carers. *British Journal of Learning Disabilities, 35,* 12–18.

Jones, E. (2001). *Bibliotherapy for bereaved children: Healing reading.* London: Jessica Kingsley.

Jünger, S., Pestner, M., Eisner, F., Krumm, N., & Radbruch, L. (2007). Criteria for successful multiprofessional cooperation in palliative care teams. *Palliative Medicine, 21,* 347–354.

Karim, K., Bailey, M., & Tunna, K. (2000). Nonwhite ethnicity and the provision of specialist palliative care services: Factors affecting doctors' referral patterns. *Palliative Medicine, 14,* 471–478.

Karlsen, S., & Addington-Hall, J. (1998). How do cancer patients who die at home differ from those who die elsewhere? *Palliative Medicine, 12,* 279–286.

Katz, J. S., & Peace, S. (Eds.). (2003). *End of life in care homes: A palliative care approach.* Oxford, England: Oxford University Press.

Katz, J. S., Sidell, M., & Komaromy, C. (2001). Dying in long-term care facilities: Support needs of other residents, relatives and staff. *American Journal of Hospice and Palliative Care, 18*(5), 321–326.

Kellehear, A. (1990). *Dying of cancer: The final year of life.* Chur, Switzerland: Harwood.

Kellehear, A. (1996). *Experiences near death: Beyond medicine and religion.* New York: Oxford University Press.

Kellehear, A. (1999). *Health-promoting palliative care.* Melbourne, Australia: Oxford University Press.

Kellehear, A. (2005). *Compassionate cities: Public health and end-of-life care.* New York: Routledge.

Kellehear, A. (2006). *A social history of dying.* Cambridge, England: Cambridge University Press.

Kessler, D., Peter, T. J., Lea, L., & Parr, S. (2005). Social class and access to specialist palliative care services. *Palliative Medicine, 19,* 105–110.

Kissane, D., Bloch, S., & McKenzie, D. (1997). Family coping and bereavement outcomes. *Palliative Medicine, 11*(3), 191–201.

Klass, D. (1996). Grief in an Eastern culture: Japanese ancestor worship. In D. Klass, P. Silverman, & S. Nickman (Eds.), *Continuing bonds: New understanding of grief* (pp. 59–70). Washington DC: Taylor and Francis.

Kovacs, P., & Bronstein, L. (1999). Preparation for oncology settings: What hospice social workers say they need. *Health and Social Work, 25*(1), 3–8.

Kramer, B. J., Parourek, L., & Hovland-Scafe, C. (2003). Analysis of end-of-life content in social work textbooks. *Journal of Social Work Education, 39*(2), 299–320.

Kristjanson, L. J., Cousins, K., Smith, J., & Lewin, G. (2005). Evaluation of the Bereavement Risk Index (BRI): A community hospice protocol. *International Journal of Palliative Nursing, 11*(12), 610–618.

Kristjanson, L. J., Sloan, J. A., Dudgeon, D., & Adaskin, E. (1996). Family members' perception of palliative cancer care: Predictors of family functioning and family members' health. *Journal of Palliative Care, 12*(4), 10–20.

Kübler-Ross, E. (1969). *On death and dying.* New York: Macmillan.

Kupferman, J. (1992). *When the crying's done: A journey through widowhood.* London: Robson.

Lacey, D. (2005). Predictors of social service staff involvement in selected palliative care tasks in nursing homes: An exploratory model. *American Journal of Hospice and Palliative Care, 22*(4), 269–276.

Lappe, J. M. (1987). Reminiscing: The life review therapy. *Journal of Gerontological Nursing, 13*(4), 12–16.

Larkin, P. J., Dierckx de Casterlé, B., & Schotsmans, P. (2007). Towards a conceptual evaluation of transience in relation to palliative care. *Journal of Advanced Nursing, 59*(1), 86–96.

Lau, F., Cloutier-Fisher, D., Kuziemsky, C., Black, F., Downing, M., Borycki, E., & Ho, F. (2007). A systematic review of prognostic tools for estimating survival time in palliative care. *Journal of Palliative Care, 23*(2), 93–112.

Lendrum, S., & Syme, G. (2004). *Gift of tears: A practical approach to loss and bereavement counselling and psychotherapy* (2nd ed.). London: Routledge.

Lester, J. (2005). Life review with the terminally ill—narrative therapies. In P. Firth, G. Luff, & D. Oliviere (Eds.), *Loss, change and bereavement in palliative care* (pp. 66–79). Maidenhead, England: Open University Press.

Lewis, C. S. (writing as N. W. Clerk). (1961). *A grief observed.* London: Faber.

Lindemann, E. (1944). Symptomatology and management of acute grief. In H. J. Parad (Ed.), *Crisis intervention: Selected readings* (pp. 7–21). New York: Family Service Association of America.

Lloyd, M. (2002). A framework for working with loss. In N. Thompson (Ed.), *Loss and grief: A guide for human services practitioners* (pp. 208–220). Basingstoke, England: Palgrave.

Luptak, M. (2004). Social work and end-of-life care for older people: A historical perspective. *Health and Social Work, 29*(1), 7–15.

Lynn, J. (2000). Learning to care for people with chronic illness facing the end of life. *Journal of the American Medical Association, 284*, 2508–2511.

Lynn, J., & Adamson, D. M. (2003). *Living well at the end of life: Adapting health care to serious chronic illness in old age*. Washington DC: Rand Health.

Machin, L., & Spall, B. (2004). Mapping grief: A study in practice using a quantitative and qualitative approach to exploring and addressing the range of responses to loss. *Counselling and Psychotherapy Research, 4*(1), 9–17.

Marie Curie Holme Tower. (2001). *Helping children when someone close dies*. London: Marie Curie Cancer Care.

Marshall, S. (2007). Bereavement counselling—is it viable? *Therapy Today, 18*(5), 4–6.

Martin, T., & Doka, K. (2000). *Men don't cry . . . women do*. Philadelphia: Taylor and Francis.

Maslach, C. (1982). *Burnout: The cost of caring*. Englewood Cliffs, NJ: Prentice-Hall.

Maslach, C., & Jackson, S.E. (1981). The measurement of experienced burnout. *Journal of Occupational Behaviour, 2*, 99–113.

Materstvedt, J. (2007). Must we accept death? A philosopher's view. *European Journal of Palliative Care, 14*(2), 70–72.

Matthew, A., Cowley, S., Billes, J., & Thistlewood, G. (2003). The development of palliative care in national government policy in England, 1986–2000. *Palliative Medicine, 17*, 270–282.

Maugh, T. I. (2007, December 7). Peter Houghton, 68; survived the longest on artificial heart, hiked the Alps. *Boston Globe*. Retrieved February 10, 2008, from http://www.boston.com/bostonglobe/obituaries/articles/2007/12/07/peter_houghton_68_survived_the_longest_on_artificial_heart_hiked_the_alps/

McVicar, A. (2003). Workplace stress in nursing: A literature review. *Journal of Advanced Nursing, 44*(6), 633–642.

Meier, D. E., & Beresford, L. (2008). Social workers advocate for a seat at the palliative care table. *Journal of Palliative Medicine, 11*(1), 10–14.

Miller C., Freeman M., & Ross, N. (2001). *Interprofessional practice in health and social care: Challenging the shared learning agenda*. London: Arnold.

Monaghan, P. (2002). The unsettled question of brain death. *Chronicle of Higher Education*, February, 22, 2002, 14–16.

Monroe, B. (2004). Social work in palliative medicine. In D. Doyle, G. Hanks, N. Cherny, & K. Calman (Eds.), *Oxford textbook of palliative medicine* (3rd ed.) (pp. 1007–1017). Oxford, England: Oxford University Press.

Monroe, B., & Sheldon, F. (2004). Psychosocial dimensions of care. In N. Sykes, P. Edmonds, & J. Wiles (Eds.), *Management of advanced disease* (pp. 405–437). London: Arnold.

Moorey, S., & Greer, S. (2002). *Cognitive behaviour therapy for people with cancer*. Oxford, England: Oxford University Press.

Morgan, D. (1995). *Family connections*. Cambridge, England: Polity.

Morrison, R. S., Wallenstein, S., Natale, D. K., Senzel, R. S., & Huang, L. L. (2000). "We don't carry that"—failure of pharmacies in predominantly nonwhite neighborhoods to stock opioid analgesics. *New England Journal of Medicine, 342*, 1023–1026.

Morse, M. (1996). Parting visions: A new scientific paradigm. In L. W. Bailey & J. Yates (Eds.), *The near death experience: A reader* (pp. 299–318). New York: Routledge.

Moss, B. (2002). Spirituality: A personal view. In N. Thompson (Ed.), *Loss and grief: A guide for human service practitioners* (pp. 34–44). Basingstoke, England: Palgrave.

Mullan, J. T., Pearlin, L. I., & Skaff, M. M. (1995). The bereavement process: Loss, grief and recovery. In I. B. Corless, B. B. Germino, & M. A. Pittman (Eds.), *A challenge of living and dying: Dying, death and bereavement* (pp. 221–240). Boston: Jones and Bartlett.

Murray, S. A., Kendall, M., Boyd, K., & Sheikh, A. (2005). Illness trajectories and palliative care. *British Medical Journal, 330,* 1007–1011.

Mystakidou, K., Parpa, E., Msilika, E., Athanasouli, P., Pathaki, M., Galanos, A., Pagoropoulou, A., & Vlahos, L. (2007). Preparatory grief, psychological distress and hopelessness in advanced cancer patients. *European Journal of Cancer Care, 17,* 145–151.

NASW. (1994). *Client self-determination in end-of-life decisions.* Washington DC: National Association of Social Workers.

NASW. (2003). *Standards for social work practice in palliative and end of life care.* Washington DC: National Association of Social Workers.

National Institute for Clinical Excellence (NICE). (2004). *Improving supportive and palliative care for adults with cancer: The manual.* London: National Institute for Clinical Excellence.

NCPC. (2006). *Introductory guide to end of life care in care homes.* London: National Council on Palliative Care.

NCPC. (2007). *Building on firm foundations: Improving end of life care in care homes: Examples of innovative practice.* London: National Council for Palliative Care.

Neimeyer, R. (2001). The language of loss: Grief therapy as a process of meaning reconstruction. In R. Neimeyer (Ed.), *Meaning reconstruction and the experience of loss* (pp. 261–292). Washington DC: American Psychological Association.

Neimeyer, R. A., & Anderson, A. (2002). Meaning reconstruction theory. In N. Thompson (Ed.), *Loss and Grief* (pp. 45–64). New York: Routledge.

Neimeyer, R. (2005). Grief, loss and the quest for meaning: Narrative contributions to bereavement care. *Bereavement Care, 24*(2), 27–30.

Neto, I., & Trindade, N. (2007). Family meetings as a means of support for patients. *European Journal of Palliative Care, 14*(3), 105–108

Neuberger, J. (2004). *Caring for dying people of different faiths* (3rd ed.). Abingdon, England: Radcliffe.

NFCA. (2008). *Caregiving statistics.* Kensington, MD: National Family Caregivers Association. Retrieved April 29, 2008, from http://www.nfcacares.org/who_are_family_caregivers/care_giving_statstics.cfm

Ng, L., Schumacher, A., & Goh, C. (2000). Autonomy for whom? A perspective from the Orient. *Palliative Medicine, 14,* 163–164.

O'Keeffe, M., Hills, A., Doyle, M., McCreadie, C., Scholes, S., Constantine, R., Tinker, A., Manthorpe, J., & Erens, B. (2007). *UK study of abuse and neglect of older people: Prevalence survey report.* London: National Centre for Social Research.

O'Kelly, J. (2002). Music therapy in palliative care: Current perspectives. *International Journal of Palliative Nursing, 8*(3), 130–136.

Oliviere, D., Hargreaves, R., & Monroe, B. (1997). Assessment. In D. Oliviere, R, Hargreaves, & B. Monroe (Eds.), *Good practice in palliative care: A psychosocial perspective* (pp. 25–48). Phliadelphia: Ashgate.

Opie, A. (2003). *Thinking teams/thinking clients: Knowledge-based teamwork.* New York: Columbia University Press.

OSI. (2004). *Transforming the culture of dying: The project on death in America, October 1994 to December 2003.* New York: Open Society Institute.

Pacheco, J., Hershberger, P. J., Markert, R. J., & Kumar, G. (2003). A longitudinal study of attitudes toward physician-asssisted suicide and euthanasia among patients with non-curable malignancy. *American Journal of Hospice and Palliative Medicine, 20*(2), 99–104.

Padesky, C. A. (1993). *Socratic quesioning: Changing minds or guiding discovery.* Address to the European Congress of Behavioral and Cognitive Therapies, September 24, 1993. Retrieved April 29, 2008, from http://www.padesky.com/clinicalcorner/pdf/socquest.pdf

Parad, H. J., & Parad, L. G. (1990). *Crisis intervention: Book 2: The practitioner's sourcebook for brief therapy.* Milwaukee, WI: Family Service America.

Parkes, C. M. (1986). Orienteering the caregiver's grief. *Journal of Palliative Care, 1*(1), 7.

Parkes, C. M. (1993). Bereavement. In D. Doyle, G. Hanks, & N. MacDonald (Eds.), *Oxford Textbook of Palliative Medicine* (pp. 663–678). Oxford, England: Oxford University Press.

Parkes, C. M. (2001). *Bereavement: Studies of grief in adult life* (3rd ed.). London: Routledge.

Parkes, C. M., Relf, M., & Couldrick, A. (1996). *Counselling in terminal care and bereavement.* London: British Psychological Society.

Parkes, C. M., & Stevenson-Hinde, J. (1982). *The place of attachment in human behaviour.* London: Routledge and Kegan Paul.

Parkes, C. M., & Weiss, R. S. (1983). *Recovery from bereavement.* New York: Basic Books.

Parkes, C. M., & Weiss, R. (1995). *Recovery from bereavement* (2nd ed.). New York: Aronson.

Parry, J. K. (2001). *Social work theory and practice with the terminally ill* (2nd ed.). Binghampton, NY: Haworth.

Pattison, E. M. (1977). *The experience of dying.* Englewood Cliffs, NJ: Prentice-Hall.

Payne, M. (2000). *Teamwork in multiprofessional care.* Chicago: Lyceum Books.

Payne, M. (2004). Social class, poverty and social exclusion. In D. Oliviere & B. Monroe (Eds.), *Death, dying, and social differences* (pp. 7–23). Oxford, England: Oxford University Press.

Payne, M. (2005). Adult protection cases in a hospice: An audit. *Journal of Adult Protection, 7*(2), 4–12.

Payne, M. (2006a). Teambuilding: How, why and where? In P. Speck (Ed.), *Teamwork in palliative care: Fulfilling or frustrating?* Oxford, England: Oxford University Press.

Payne, M. (2006b). Identity politics in multiprofessional teams: Palliative care social work. *Journal of Social Work, 6*(2), 137–150.

Payne, M. (2006c). *What is professional social work?* (2nd ed.). Chicago: Lyceum Books.

Payne, M. (2008a). *Social care practice in context*. Basingstoke, England: Palgrave Macmillan.

Payne, M. (2008b). Staff support. In M. Lloyd Williams (Ed.), *Psychosocial Issues in Palliative Care* (2nd ed.) (pp. 231–251). Oxford, England: Oxford University Press.

Payne, M. (2008c). Safeguarding adults at end of life: Audit and case analysis in a palliative care setting. *Journal of Social Work in End-of-Life and Palliative Care, 3*(4), 31–46.

Payne, S., Horn, S., & Relf, M. (1999). *Loss and bereavement.* Buckingham, England: Open University Press.

Payne, S., Kerr, C., Hawker, S., Seamark, D., Davis, C., Roberts, H., Jarrett, N., Roderick, P., & Smith, H. (2004). Community hospitals: An under-recognized resource for palliative care. *Journal of the Royal Society of Medicine, 97*, 428–431.

Pemberton, C., Storey, L., & Howard, A. (2003). The preferred place of care document: An opportunity for communication. *International Journal of Palliative Nursing, 9*(10), 439–441.

Pickrel, J. (1989). "Tell me your story": Using life review in counselling the terminally ill. *Death Studies, 13*, 127–135.

Pillemer, K., & Finkelhor, D. (1988). The prevalence of elder abuse: A random sample survey. *Gerontologist, 28*, 51–57.

Pincus, L. (1976). *Death in the family*. London: Faber and Faber.

Powazki, R. D., & Walsh, D. (1999). Acute care palliative medicine: Psychosocial assessment of patients and primary caregivers. *Palliative Medicine, 13*, 367–374.

President's Commission for the Study of Ethical Problems in Medicine and Biomedical and Behavioral Resarch. (1981). *Defining death: Medical, legal and ethical issues in the determination of death*. Washington DC: U.S. Government Printing Office.

Price, A., Hotopf, M., Higginson, I. J., Monroe, B., & Henderson, M. (2006). Psychological services in hospices in the UK and Republic of Ireland. *Journal of the Royal Society of Medicine, 99*, 637–639.

Quinn, A. (2005). The context of loss, change, and bereavement in palliative care. In P. Firth, G. Luff, & D. Oliviere (Eds.), Loss, change, and bereavement in palliative care (pp. 1–17). Basingstoke: Macmillan.

Rabow, M., Hauser, J., & Adams, J. (2004). Supporting family caregivers at the end of life. *Journal of the American Medical Association, 291*(4), 483–491.

Read, S. (2007). *Bereavement counselling for people with learning disabilities: A handbook*. London: Quay.

Reamer., F. G. (1999). *Social work values and ethics* (2nd ed.). New York: Columbia University Press.

Rees, D. (1997). *Death and bereavement: The psychological, religious and cultural interfaces*. London: Whurr.

Reese, D. J., & Raymer, M. (2004). Relationships between social work involvement and hospice outcomes: Results of the national hospice social work survey. *Social Work, 49*(3), 415–422.

Reese, D. J., & Sontag, M. A. (2001). Successful interprofessional collaboration on the hospice team. *Health and Social Work, 26*(3), 167–175.

Reith, M. (2001). *Talking to children when someone close is very ill*. London: Marie Curie Cancer Care.

Reith, M. (2007). Care of families during and after the death of a loved one. *End of Life Care, 1*(2), 22–26.

Reith, M., & Lucas, C. (2008). Questioning the evidence for service assumptions: Audit of transfers from a hospice to nursing home care. *Journal of Social Work, 8*(1), 233–245.

Relf, M., Machin, L., & Archer, N. (2008). *Guidance for bereavement needs assessment in palliative care*. London: Help the Hospices.

Renzenbrink, I. (2004). Relentless self-care. In J. Berzoff & P. Silverman (Eds.), *Living with dying: A handbook for end-of-life practitioners* (pp. 848–867). New York: Columbia University Press.

Richmond, C. (2007, December 18). Peter Houghton. *The Guardian*. Retrieved February 10, 2008, from http://www.guardian.co.uk/obituaries/story/0,,2229000,00.html

Robinson, A. (2004). A personal exploration of the power of poetry in palliative care, loss and bereavement. *International Journal of Palliative Nursing, 10*(1), 32–39.

Robinson, V. (2006). What is palliative care? In J. Cooper (Ed.), *Stepping into palliative care: Relationships and responses* (pp. 18–27). Oxford, England: Radcliffe.

Rogers, C. R. (1961). *On becoming a person: A therapist's view of psychotherapy*. London: Constable.

Rosenblatt, P. (1993). Cross-cultural variation in the experience, expression, and understanding of grief. In D. Irish, K. Lundquist, & V. Nelsen (Eds.), *Ethnic variations in dying, death, and grief: Diversity in universality* (pp. 13–20). Washington DC: Taylor and Francis.

Rosenfeld, P., Dennis, J., Hanen, S., Henriquez, E., Schwartz, T. M., Correoso, L., Murtauh, C. M., & Fleishman, A. (2007). Are there racial differences in attitudes toward hospice care? A study of hospice-eligible patients at the visiting nurse service of New York. *American Journal of Hospice and Palliative Medicine, 24*(5), 408–416.

Ryan, M. (2006). Ethical dilemmas. In J. Cooper (Ed.), *Stepping into palliative care, 1: Relationships and responses* (pp. 158–170). Oxford, England: Radcliffe

Sage, N., Sowden, M., Chorlton, E., & Edeleanu, A. (2008). *CBT for chronic illness and palliative care*. Chichester, England: Wiley-Blackwell.

Sahyoun, N. R., Lentzner, H., Hoyert, D., & Robinson, K. N. (2005). Trends in causes of death among the elderly. In G. E. Dickinson & M. Leming (Eds.), *Dying, death and bereavement 05/06* (pp. 51–57). Dubuque, IA: McGraw-Hill/Dushkin.

Samanta, A., & Samanta, J., (2006). Advance directives: Best interest and clinical judgement: Shifting sands at the end of life. *Clinical Medicine, 6*(3), 274–278.

Sands, M. (2008). Beginning to work as a community artist in palliative care. In N. Hartley & M. Payne (Eds.), *Creative arts in palliative care* (pp. 152–161). Philadelphia: Jessica Kingsley.

Saunders, C. (2004). Introduction. In N. Sykes, P. Edmonds, & J. Wiles (Eds.), *Management of advanced disease* (4th ed.). London: Arnold.

Saunders, C. (Ed. D. Clark) (2006). *Cicely Saunders: Selected writings: 1958– 2004*. Oxford, England: Oxford University Press.

Saunders, C., Seymour, J., Clarke, A., Gott, M., & Welton, M. (2006). Development of a peer education programme for advance end-of-life care planning. *International Journal of Palliative Nursing, 12*(5), 214–223.

Seale, C., & Kelly, M. (1997). A comparison of hospice and hospital care for people who die: Views of the surviving spouse. *Palliative Medicine, 11*, 93–100.

Seale, C. F. (1998). *Constructing death: The sociology of dying and bereavement*. New York: Cambridge University Press.

Sessana, L., Finnell, D., & Jezewski, M. A. (2007). Spirituality in nursing and health-related literature: A concept analysis. *Journal of Holistic Nursing, 25*(4), 252–262.

Seymour, J., Clark, D., & Marples, R. (2002). Palliative care and policy in England: A review of health improvement plans for 1999–2003. *Palliative Medicine, 16*, 5–11.

Schutte, N., Oppinen, S., Kalimo, R., & Schaufeli, W. (2000). The factorial validity of the Maslach Burnout Inventory—General Survey (MBI-GS) across occupational groups and nations. *Journal of Occupational and Organizational Psychology, 73*, 53–66.

Sheldon, F. (1997). *Psychosocial palliative care: Good practice in the care of the dying and bereaved*. Cheltenham, England: Thornes.

Silverman, J. (1999). *Help me say goodbye: Activities for helping kids cope when a special person dies*. Minneapolis, MN: Fairview.

Silverman, P. R. (1980). *Mutual help: Organization and development*. Beverly Hills, CA: Sage.

Silverman, P. (2000). *Never too young to know: Death in children's lives*. New York: Oxford University Press.

Singer, O. A., Martin, D. K., & Kelner, M. (1999). Quality end-of-life care: Patients' perspectives. *Journal of the American Medical Association, 281*, 163–168.

Singer, P. (1994). *Rethinking life and death: The collapse of our traditional ethics*. Oxford, England: Oxford University Press.

Smaje, C., & Field, D. (1997). Absent minorities? Ethnicity and the use of palliative care services. In D. Field, J. Hockey, & N. Small (Eds.), *Death, gender and ethnicity*. London: Routledge.

Small, N. (2001a). Theories of grief: A critical review. In J. Hockey, J. Katz, & N. Small (Eds.), *Grief, mourning and death ritual* (pp. 19–48). Buckingham, England: Open University Press.

Small, N. (2001b). Social work and palliative care. *British Journal of Social Work, 31*(6), 961–971.

Smith, C. (1982). *Social work with the dying and bereaved*. Basingstoke, England: Macmillan.

Smith, S. (1999). *The forgotten mourners: Guidelines for working with bereaved children* (2nd ed.). London: Jessica Kingsley.

Stokes, J. (2004). *Then, now and always: Supporting children as they journey through grief: A guide for practitioners.* Cheltenham, England: Winston's Wish.

Stokes, J., & Crossley, D. (2001). *As big as it gets: Supporting a child when someone in their family is seriously ill.* Cheltenham, England: Winston's Wish.

Stokes, J., & Oxley, P. (2006). *Out of the blue: Making memories last when someone has died.* Gloucestershire, England: Hawthorn.

Stroebe, M., & Schut, H. (1999). The dual process model of coping with bereavement: Rationale and description. *Death Studies, 23*(3), 197–224.

Stroebe, M., Schut, H., & Stroebe, W. (2007). Health outcomes of bereavement. *Lancet, 370,* 1960–1973.

Sutton, A., & Liechty, D. (2004). Clinical practice with groups in end-of-life care. In J. Berzoff & P. Silverman (Eds.), *Living with dying: A handbook for end-of-life practitioners* (pp. 508–533). New York: Columbia University Press.

Thomas, P. (2000). *I miss you: A first look at death.* London: Hodder Wayland.

Thompson, S., & Thompson, N. (2004). Working with dying and bereaved older people. In J. Berzoff & P. Silverman (Eds.), *Living with dying: A handbook for end-of-life practitioners* (pp. 348–359). New York: Columbia University Press.

Thomson, G. F. (2003). Discrimination in health care. *Annals of Internal Medicine, 126*(11), 910–912.

Titmuss, R. M. (1974). *Social policy: An introduction* (Eds. B. Abel Smith & K. Titmuss) London: Allen and Unwin.

Triparthy, D. (2001). Time: Counting the moment/making moments count. In C. N. Gillis (Ed.), *Seeing the difference: Conversations on death and dying* (pp. 55–58). Berkeley, CA: Dorren B. Townsend Center for the Humanities, University of California.

Tuffrey-Wijne, I. (2002). The palliative care needs of people with intellectual disabilities: A case study. *International Journal of Palliative Nursing, 8,* 222–232.

Tuffrey-Wijne, I., & Davies, J. (2007). This is my story: I've got cancer. "The Veronica Project": An ethnographic study of the experiences of people with learning disabilities who have cancer. *British Journal of Learning Disabilities, 35,* 7–11.

Tuffrey-Wijne, I., Hollins, S., & Curfs, L. (2005). End-of-life and palliative care for people with intellectual disabilities who have cancer or other life-limiting illness: A review of the literature and available resources. *Journal of Applied Research into Intellectual Disabilities, 20,* 331–344.

Twycross, R. (1999). *Introducing palliative care.* Oxford, England: Radcliffe.

Varley, S. (1984). *Badger's parting gifts.* London, England: Andersen.

Walsh, F., & McGoldrick, M. (1998). A family systems perspective on loss, recovery and resilience. In P. Sutcliffe, G. Tufnell, & U. Cornish (Eds.), *Working with the dying and bereaved: Systemic approaches to therapeutic work* (pp. 1–26). Basingstoke, England: Palgrave.

Walter, T. (1992). Modern death: Taboo or not taboo? *Sociology, 25*(2), 293–310.

Webb, M. (1997). *The good death: The new American search to reshape the end of life.* New York: Bantam.

Wee, B., Hillier, R., Coles, C., Mountford, D., Sheldon, F., & Turner, P. (2001). Palliative care: A suitable setting for undergraduate interprofessional education. *Palliative Medicine, 15*, 487–492.

Wenger, E. (1998). *Communities of practice: Learning, meaning, and identity.* Cambridge, England: Cambridge University Press.

Werth, J., Blevins, D., Toussaint, K., & Durham, M. (2002). The influence of cultural diversity on end-of-life care and decisions. *American Behavioral Scientist, 46*(2), 204–219.

West, M. A. (2004). *Effective teamwork: Practical lessons from organizational research* (2nd ed.). Oxford, England: BPS Blackwell.

WHO. (1990). *Cancer pain relief and palliative care: Report of a WHO expert committee* (Technical Report 804). Geneva, Switzerland: World Health Organization.

WHO. (2007). *WHO definition of palliative care.* Geneva, Switzerland: World Health Organization. Retrieved August 25, 2007, from http://www.who.int/cancer/palliative/definition/en/

Williams, S., & Cooper, C. (2002). *Managing workplace stress: A best practice blueprint.* Chichester, England: Wiley.

Worden, J. W. (1996). *Children and grief: When a parent dies.* New York: Guilford.

Worden, J. W. (2003). *Grief counselling and grief therapy: A handbook for the mental health practitioner* (3rd ed.). East Sussex, England: Brunner-Routledge.

Zilberfein, F., & Hurwitz, E. (2004). Clinical social work practice at the end of life. In J. Berzoff & P. Silverman (Eds.), *Living with dying: A handbook for end-of-life practitioners* (pp. 297–317). New York: Columbia University Press.

Zorza, V., & Zorza, R. (1980). *A way to die: Living to the end.* London: Deutsch.

LIST OF RELEVANT WEBSITES

A short list of websites, many of which of course have links to other websites and allow users to register for e-mail updates. The first list is of organizations of social workers or those relevant to end-of-life social work; the second list is of end-of-life, hospice, and palliative care websites. With one exception (a regional organization for South America in Spanish) only English-language websites are listed.

END-OF-LIFE CARE SOCIAL WORK ORGANIZATIONS AND WEBSITES

Association of Palliative Care Social Workers (U.K.): http://www.helpthe hospices.org.uk/NPA/socialworkers/index.asp

Canadian Hospice Palliative Care Association, Social Worker/Counsellors Interest Group: http://www.chpca.net/interest_groups/social_workers-counsellors .htm

National Association of Social Workers (U.S.): Web page on end-of-life care: http://www.socialworkers.org/research/naswResearch/EndofLifeCare/default.asp

National Association of Social Workers (U.S.): NASW Standards for Social Work Practice in Palliative and End of Life Care: http://www.socialworkers.org/ practice/bereavement/standards/default.asp

National Association of Social Workers (U.S.): Web-based courses on cancer caregiving, the social worker's role and end-of-life care, (members only): http://www.naswwebed.org/

Social Work in Hospice and Palliative Care Network (U.S.): http://www .swhpn.org/

END-OF-LIFE AND PALLIATIVE CARE ORGANIZATION WEBSITES

American Academy of Hospice and Palliative Medicine: http://www.aahpm .org/

Asia-Pacific Hospice Palliative Care Network: http://www.aphn.org/

Association for Palliative Medicine of Great Britain and Ireland: http://www .palliative-medicine.org/

Australia and New Zealand Society of Palliative Medicine: http://www. anzspm.org.au/index.html

Canadian Hospice Care Association: http://www.chpca.net/home.htm

European Association of Palliative Care: http://www.eapcnet.org/
Help the Hospices (U.K.): http://www.helpthehospices.org.uk/
Hospice Africa: http://www.hospiceafrica.org/
Hospice Education Institute (U.S.): http://www.hospiceworld.org/
Hospice Information (U.K. and international): http://www.hospice
information.info/
Hospice Net (U.S.): http://www.hospicenet.org/
Hospice New Zealand: http://www.hospice.org.nz/
International Association for Palliative Care: http://www.hospicecare.com/
International Observatory on End-of-life Care: http://www.eolc-observatory
.net/
Irish Association for Palliative Care: http://www.iapc.ie/
Irish Hospice Foundation: http://www.hospice-foundation.ie/
Latin American Palliative Care Association (in Spanish): http://www.cuidado
spaliativos.org/
National Consensus Project for Quality Palliative Care (U.S.): http://www
.nationalconsensusproject.org/
National Council for Palliative Care (U.K.): http://www.ncpc.org.uk/
National Health Service (U.K.): End of Life Care Programme website:
http://www.endoflifecare.nhs.uk/eolc
National Hospice and Palliative Care Organisation (U.S.): http://www.nhpco
.org/templates/1/homepage.cfm
Palliative Care Australia: http://www.palliativecare.org.au/
Palliative Care Research Society (U.K.): http://www.pcrs.org.uk/
Palliative Dementia Care Resources (U.S.): http://www.pdcronline.org/index
.php
Scottish Partnership for Palliative Care: http://www.palliativecarescotland
.org.uk/
World Health Organization (WHO): Palliative Care Website: http://www.who
.int/cancer/palliative/en/

INDEX